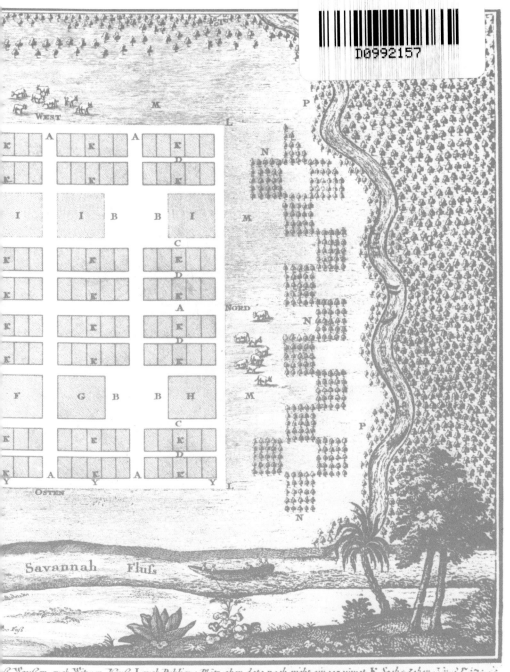

WEST

OSTEN

NORD

Savannah Fluſs

achrichten, 13te Continuation, Erster Theil (Halle and Augsburg, 1747).
ollection, University of Georgia Library.

Detailed Reports on the
Salzburger Emigrants
Who Settled in America . . .
Edited by Samuel Urlsperger

BARLETT BUILDINGS IN LONDON, HOME OF THE SOCIETY
FOR PROMOTING CHRISTIAN KNOWLEDGE AT THE TIME IT
WAS SUPPORTING THE GEORGIA SALZBURGERS
(Kindly furnished by the SPCK)

Detailed Reports on the Salzburger Emigrants Who Settled in America . . . Edited by Samuel Urlsperger

VOLUME ELEVEN, 1747

Translated by
EVA PULGRAM
Edited by
GEORGE FENWICK JONES

VOLUME TWELVE, 1748

Translated by
IRMGARD NEUMANN
Edited by
GEORGE FENWICK JONES

THE UNIVERSITY OF GEORGIA PRESS
ATHENS AND LONDON

The paper in this book meets the guidelines for permanence
and durability of the Committee on Production Guidelines for
Book Longevity of the Council on Library Resources.

Printed in the United States of America

93 92 91 90 89   5 4 3 2 1

Library of Congress Cataloging in Publication Data

(Revised for vols. 11–12)

Urlsperger, Samuel, 1685–1772.
   Detailed reports on the Salzburger emigrants who settled in America.

   (Wormsloe Foundation. Publications, no. 9–   )
   Vol. 6 translated and edited by George Fenwick Jones and Renate Wilson.
   Vols. 7, 9 translated and edited by George Fenwick Jones and Don Savelle.
   Vol. 8 translated by Maria Magdalena Hoffmann-Loerzer, Renate Wilson,
and George Fenwick Jones.
   Vol. 11 translated by Eva Pulgram, edited by George Fenwick Jones.
   Vol. 12 translated by Irmgard Neumann, edited by George Fenwick Jones.
   Translation of Ausführliche Nachricht von den saltzburgischen
Emigranten, die sich in America niedergelassen haben.
   Vols. 1–5 issued in series: Publications (Wormsloe Foundation)
   Includes bibliographical references and indexes.
   Contents: v. 1. 1733–1734.—etc.—v. 11. 1747.—v. 12. 1748.
   1. Salzburgers—Georgia—History—18th century—Sources. 2. German
Americans—Georgia—History—18th century—Sources. 3. Lutherans—
Georgia—History—18th century—Sources. 4. Ebenezer (Ga.)—History—
Sources. 5. Georgia—History—Colonial period. ca. 1600–1775—Sources.
6. Stockbridge Indians—Missions—History—18th century—Sources.
7. Indians of North America—Georgia—Missions—History—18th
century—Sources. I. Jones, George Fenwick, 1916–   . II. Wilson,
Renate, 1930–   . III. Savelle, Don. IV. Title. V. Series: Publications
(Wormsloe Foundation); v. 9, etc.
F295.S1U813   975.8′00436   67-27137
ISBN 0-8203-1096-4 (alk. paper : v. 11–12)

British Library Cataloging in Publication Data available
Volumes 1–5 were published as part of the Wormsloe Foundation
Publications series.

Detailed Reports on the

Salzburger Emigrants

Who Settled in America . . .

Edited by Samuel Urlsperger

VOLUME ELEVEN, 1747

 *Contents*

⟨∼∙ Introduction ∙∼⟩

The following five paragraphs are taken from the introduction to the previous volume of this series and therefore need not be read by those who have already read them or who are otherwise familiar with the history of the Georgia Salzburgers. For those who come new to the field, the following resumé should suffice; those who wish more detail may consult the *Salzburger Saga*.[1] When the Lutherans were expelled from Salzburg in 1731, not all the exiles went to East Prussia and other Protestant lands in Europe: a small number, some two hundred, were taken to the colony of Georgia, then in its second year. Georgia, the last of Britain's thirteen North American colonies, was founded according to the grandiose schemes of a group of benevolent gentlemen in London, called the Trustees, who wished to provide homes for impoverished Englishmen and persecuted foreign Protestants, to protect the more northerly colonies from the Spaniards in Florida, and to provide raw materials for English industry.

The first Salzburger transport, or traveling party, consisted of recent exiles who had been recruited in and around Augsburg, a Swabian city just north of Salzburg. This group arrived in Georgia in 1734 and settled some twenty-five miles northwest of Savannah, where they founded a settlement which they named Ebenezer. By the time the second transport arrived a year later, the land that had been chosen had proved infertile and the stream on which it was built, Ebenezer Creek, had been found to be unnavigable. When a third transport arrived in 1736, composed mostly of Upper Austrian exiles, the survivors at Ebenezer joined them on the Red Bluff on the Savannah River, bringing the name of the earlier settlement with them. The orig-

---

[1]George F. Jones, *Salzburger Saga*. Athens, Ga.: U. of Ga. Press, 1983.

inal site, which became the Trustees' cowpen or cattle ranch, was henceforth called Old Ebenezer.

A fourth and last transport, consisting of Salzburger exiles who had been sojourning in Augsburg and other Swabian cities, arrived in 1741. The Salzburgers were joined by Swiss and Palatine settlers from Purysburg, a Swiss settlement a short way down the Savannah River on the Carolina side, and also by some Palatine servants donated by the Trustees. Finding insufficient fertile land on the Red Bluff, many Salzburgers moved their plantations to an area along Abercorn Creek where the lowland was flooded and enriched each winter by the Savannah River. This explains the terms "the town" and "the plantations." After some gristmills and sawmills were built on Abercorn Creek, it was usually called the Mill River (*Mühl-Fluss.*)

Despite appalling sickness and mortality and the hardships incident to settlement in a wilderness, the Salzburgers were the most successful community in Georgia. This relative success was largely due to the skill, devotion, and diligence of their spiritual leader, Johann Martin Boltzius, the author of most of these reports. This young divine had been trained at the University of Halle in eastern Germany and had taught in that city at the Francke Foundation, a charitable institution that was to have great influence on the development of Ebenezer. Although Boltzius was at heart a minister, his secular responsibilities in Georgia moulded him into a skilful administrator, economist, and diplomat. A few of the reports were written by Boltzius' admiring younger colleague, Christian Israel Gronau, who officiated whenever Boltzius was away in Savannah or elsewhere.

Boltzius' journals were edited contemporaneously by Samuel Urlsperger, the Senior of the Lutheran clergy in Augsburg. Comparison of the original manuscripts surviving in Halle with Urlsperger's published edition shows that he took considerable liberty in deleting unpleasant reports and suppressing proper names, which he replaces with N. or N.N. The original documents for 1747 no longer exist, so there is no way to know how much Urlsperger changed or deleted; but there is reason to believe that Boltzius made an entry for every day, as he had been instructed to, and that Urlsperger made major deletions for both diplomatic and economic reasons. In some cases he simply consolidated the material for two or more days into one. Urlsperger's deletions are very illogical: he often deletes a name in one passage even though it appears in another and can be easily recognized.

Before reading the diary for the year 1747, the reader may wish to know why the diaries for 1744, 1745, and 1746 were omitted. After publishing the volume of *Ausführliche Nachrichten* for the year 1743, Urlsperger waited three years before resuming the series, even though the Ebenezer pastors had submitted their reports regularly, in keeping with their duty. For reasons known best to him, Urlsperger suppressed their publication.[2] To make matters worse, these reports were not stored with the others and were presumed lost.

During the years in question, Urlsperger must have found the news from Ebenezer discouraging or difficult to present to his readers. Among other things, the Salzburgers were complaining against the much-praised orphanage, on which so many appeals for donations had been based. Despite the high birth rate at Ebenezer, children were at a premium because of the high infant mortality; and children were in great demand. Most of the children born in Old Ebenezer had died at, or soon after, birth; and a decade later only three of the many still survived. The bereaved parents, in many cases still childless, were in desperate need of labor.

Children occasioned little expense in Ebenezer except for food, which was plentiful, for their parents were not burdened by pediatricians, orthodontists, day-care centers, or ballet lessons. Children were, in fact, useful already by the age of six, a suitable age for frightening birds from the seed beds and raccoons from the chicken coop. By the age of twelve both boys and girls could help with the harvest and do various chores around the homestead. Consequently, the Salzburgers, particularly those who had lost their children, saw no sense in keeping able-

---

[2]See letters of 20 Jan. and 6 Aug. 46 (AN3:46, 63). "AN" stands for the *Ausführliche Nachrichten*, Halle 1735 ff., Urlsperger's edition of the diaries from which the *Detailed Reports* are translated.

bodied children in an orphanage. We get a faint indication of
this in Boltzius' letter of 4 June 44 to Urlsperger, which mentions
that he has acquiesced to the demands of some Salzburgers to
lend them the services of the boys and girls in the orphanage.
This was, of course, in accord with Divine Will.[3] We see from the
entries for 30 July and 16 December 1747 that the widow Glaner
adopted an orphaned girl, having lost the orphan Paul Klocker;
and from the entry for 24 May 1748 we learn that a Salzburger
tried to recover his godchildren, who had been orphaned in
Charleston. Widows were also in demand. Most Ebenezer
widows remarried within a few months after the death of their
dear husbands, always, of course, at Divine urging. Even old or
weak widows could serve as knitters, nurses, or baby-sitters.

Because the diaries from 1744 through 46 were believed lost,
we have had to depend upon correspondence, both in German
and English, to throw light on the happenings of those years.
Unfortunately, most of the surviving German correspondence
was bowdlerized before being published, largely in extract, by
Urlsperger; and as a result much of it is very uninformative[4]
These letters consist mostly of greetings, blessings, requests for
intercession, thanks for benefactions with accounts of how they
were spent, etc. Thus we learn a little, but not much, about the
mills, churches, cattle, cattle disease, crops, silk culture, and timber business. Boltzius also gives some secondhand information
about the Indians, much of which was given him by Joseph Watson, an Englishman who had visited them.

We also learn of the arrival of Pastor Ulrich Driesler at Frederica and his visit to Ebenezer, also of the last sickness and death of
Boltzius' colleague Gronau and of the excellent work of the surveyor Joseph Avery on the mills and of his untimely death.
Boltzius likewise related the arrival of his new colleague,
Heinrich Lemke, and mentioned the death of Walter Quarme,
the captain of the *Judith*, which brought the pastors Lemke and

[3]AN3:9.
[4]Much of this correspondence is found in Vol. III of the *Ausführliche Nachrichten* (AN3: 1–72, 151–152, 179–181, 186–192).

Bartholomäus Zouberbühler, as well as a cargo of indentured "Palatines." He also tells us that Lemke married Gronau's widow.

Believing himself the object of calumny, Boltzius had to defend himself against accusations of censorship and dishonesty by the Malcontents, the disaffected party in Savannah who wished to undo the plans of the Trustees. Boltzius mentioned that the surgeon Ludwig Meyer had been made schoolmaster, but he failed to give the reason; perhaps Urlsperger deleted the fact that Schoolmaster Christoph Ortmann had been expelled for conspiring with the Malcontents.

Possibly in hopes of receiving more plows for his people, Boltzius stressed their importance and assured the benefactors that the piney lands, if properly plowed and manured, could be as productive as the fields in Germany for German crops, especially if one followed the farming methods of Jethro Tull. Although benefactors were kept anonymous, there are clues that the agricultural information was mainly for Chrétien von Münch, a wealthy benefactor and banker of Augsburg, who seems to have had commercial aspirations in Ebenezer. As a man of the cloth, Boltzius apologized for having given so much space to "external things" (äusserliche dinge).[5]

The most informative item in these letters is a long argument against the introduction of slavery, an excellent analysis that Boltzius first composed in English as an answer to the English evangelist, George Whitefield, who was promoting the introduction of slavery.[6] Boltzius well summarized the economic, moral, and social arguments against slavery; and it is interesting that he frequently used the term "poor white" (armer Weisser), which later evoked more scorn than sympathy. Boltzius argued that free labor could not compete against slave labor and that the slaveowners would dump crops on the market so cheap that the free farmers could not survive and would have to leave. He contended that the weather in Georgia was not too hot for Europeans and that white men would prosper once they were numerous enough and well established. While many of Boltzius'

---

[5]AN3:30.
[6]AN3:30–46.

arguments had already been made by Oglethorpe and the Trustees, he assembled and expressed them perhaps better than anyone else. Much of the matter in the German correspondence also appears elsewhere, especially in the *Colonial Records of the State of Georgia*;[7] yet there are some facts not found elsewhere, such as that the passengers aboard the *Judith*, including Georgia's first elected governor, John Adam Treutlen, were mostly Wurttembergers and that the disease that afflicted them was spotted fever.[8]

A careful search twenty years ago in Halle appeared to confirm the belief that the diaries for the years 1744 through 1746 had been lost. However, soon after the type for this volume of the *Detailed Reports* (for 1747) had been set, my Ph. D. student, Renate Wilson, found extracts from the missing years in the Library of Congress. Unfortunately, these faded negative photostats were made in 1933 and are now scarcely legible. Positive microfilms made from these have been converted into negative microfilms and then into positive photographs, but the result makes for very unreliable reading of many words. It has therefore been decided to delay publishing them until better copies can be made rather than to postpone publication of the remaining volumes of the *Detailed Reports*. It is hoped that a satisfactory translation can be appended to a later volume.

The present volume for the year 1747 shows the Salzburgers well established and busy consolidating their position. The major progress was in silk manufacture, in which they surpassed all other inhabitants of Georgia. With the increased number of horses and plows, "European" crops like wheat, barley, rye, and oats were flourishing, and the gristmills were being kept busy and in repair. Also, the timber business was being pushed by the Salzburgers' friend, James Habersham, a merchant who traded with the West Indies. The fourth and last transport of Salzburgers had been assimilated, and a few Swiss and Palatines had joined the community. As mentioned, because of the high infant mortality, the farmers were in desperate need of labor. The inci-

---

[7]ed. Allen D. Candler, Atlanta, 1904 ff.
[8]AN3:55,70.

dence of sickness remained very high, according to modern standards, and deaths out-numbered births by five to three in the entries that Urlsperger published.

ACKNOWLEDGMENTS

The following two volumes are gratefully dedicated to the Society for Promoting Christian Knowledge, which was so instrumental in bringing the Salzburgers to Georgia. This missionary endeavor was founded on March 8, 1698, by an Anglican priest, Thomas Bray, and four benevolent laymen "to promote Religion and Learning in the Plantations abroad and to propagate Christian Knowledge at home." Despite its limited purpose, the Society enthusiastically supported the Protestant exiles expelled by the Archbishop of Salzburg in 1731 and immediately began collecting money for them. Ever since the reign of Good Queen Anne, Englishmen had felt themselves to be the champions of Protestantism; and many contributed generously to their distressed co-religionists on the Continent.

At first the alms were collected for all Salzburger exiles, but gradually the funds were restricted to the use of those exiles who elected to emigrate to the new colony of Georgia, which was still in the planning stage. The Society paid for the passage of the exiles to London, where they were put under the auspices of the Lord Trustees. But far more important for the history of the Georgia Salzburgers was the Society's support of two ministers and a schoolmaster, an expenditure it loyally bore for more than a half century, until the rebellious colonists separated themselves from the crown and their right to support from the SPCK.

The three salaries, as well as various monetary donations elicited by the Society, served as a catalyst in Ebenezer's economy. The frugal pastors, as true eighteenth-century mercantilists, tried to spend their money only in the community, with the result that it passed through many hands there before finally being drained off for purchases in Savannah or Charleston.

The Society's contribution to Ebenezer was not only financial, but also diplomatic, because its members, some of them Trustees, wielded considerable influence on the court and par-

liament. During the first decade of Ebenezer's existence the secretary of the Society was Henry Newman (known in Ebenezer as
Heinrich Neumann), a Yankee from Massachusetts, who kept
careful records of the Society's involvement with the exiles.[9] It is
of interest that, at the very time it was supporting the Lutheran
ministers at Ebenezer, the Society was also contributing to
Danish missions in India, which were conducted by Pietist ministers from Halle.

When the British authorities finally evacuated Georgia in
1782, they took the loyalist pastor, Christoph Friedrich Triebner,
along with them as chaplain for the British troops; and after the
treaty of peace the Society continued its support until the royal
government assumed it. Once the colonies had gained their in-
dependence, the Society was no longer permitted to respond to
Ebenezer's pleas for help; and all communication ended. In
1983, precisely two centuries after the colonies severed relations
with the mother country, and thus with SPCK, this vital institution has again entered North America by establishing an SPCK
USA. Now Americans will no longer be recipients, but fellow
contributors to this worthy cause.

To the SPCK, which has underwritten their publication costs,
these two volumes are respectfully and gratefully dedicated.

GEORGE FENWICK JONES

---

[9]Published in *Henry Newman's Salzburger Letterbooks*, ed. George F. Jones.
Athens, Ga.: U. of Ga. Press, 1966.

I.N.I.A.[1]
Daily Reports
Of the Year 1747

JANUARY

Sunday, the 18th of January 1747. Thomas Bichler, our constable, left for Frederica a few weeks ago in order to obtain money from Major Horton[2] for our rangers, or town dragoons. Just today I received a letter from him, which he had written to me from Frederica on January 6th., in which he praises the Lord for his health, since more than twenty people had been buried there in the course of three weeks. The air in Frederica is otherwise quite healthy; however, most people who live there contract dangerous diseases as a punishment for their sinful ways and go to their deaths early as a result of their bestial conduct. Bichler himself used, among others, this expression: "I find myself incapable of reporting to Your Grace in what a deplorable state the souls here are. O, how boundless is the Goodness of the Lord in Ebenezer!"

Wednesday, the 21 of January. Kogler, our carpenter, reported to me yesterday that the waterlevel of the river has done down sufficiently to allow the first millrun to grind again. Recently we suffered flooding twice, but no serious damage was done to either the dam or the mills. The mill conduits to the first run and to the sawmill, however, were lifted up somewhat and will have to be fastened more securely from now on. I praise God for His protection and benevolent goodness, and I exhort others to do likewise. Because our merciful God continues to manifest and make visible His fatherly providence in our mills, I hope that He in good time will use the mills as a blessed means for increasing our income, by which our community's widows, orphans, and others in need as well can be provided for as well as for establishing good institutions for the glory of God and the service of our fellow men.

May our all-powerful, wise, and loving God and Father, in His boundless mercy, continue to reward richly our known and unknown benefactors for their intercession for us as well as for their charitable gifts with spiritual blessing and earthly bounty. For the continuation of His purpose in Ebenezer those charitable gifts were put into the hands of His faithful servants, our most esteemed Fathers in Augsburg, Halle, London, and in other places and who continue, most lovingly, in their mission. May our Lord, for the sake of Christ, hear our humble sighs and prayers on their behalf. When I read again through the list of contributions of monies consigned to Ebenezer in the year 1745 from Halle, I was overjoyed once more, quite humbly, and moved to praise the Lord; and I felt duty-bound to pray again for our most honored benefactors. In my tribulations so far my motto has been: "O Lord! What shall be my consolation? I trust in Thee. Until this moment I have not been disappointed in my trust in the Lord. O God! Strenghten our faith so that we may behold Thy glory!"

Friday, the 23rd of January. On the occasion of the funeral of a deceased small child we made good use of the second part of the *Scriptural Instruction for the Sick and the Dying,*[2a] which deals with the main reason and the main purpose of diseases brought on us by God. The Lord granted me a great deal of edification and blessing from this; I hope the same for those few people who were also present. For the past thirteen years, the time we have been in Ebenezer, we have been plagued by various kinds of adversity, especially sickness and poverty. At all times, both in my public sermons, as well as in my visits to the healthy and the sick, I have been intent on de-emphasizing the minor subsidiary causes for distress and emphasizing the main cause of all troubles in order that God's purpose may be fulfilled: adversity is rooted in original sin and worsened further by the peoples' sinning.

The Lord also graced some of us with the insight that sickness (even if they did not realize this when they were healthy and fully benefitted from God's mercy) leads not only to contrition, but also to humility and shamefaced confession, as well as to a hunger and thirst for God's Grace in Christ, to a true change of heart and a mending of one's ways. Some still praise God and thank him for sending them such sickness; they understand the meaning of this second contemplation: it is good that you are sick. The final purpose of sickness is that evil be turned into good and that what is good be better. Exactly this lesson I took to heart recently and shared with those listening to me by citing it in my introduction (Apocalypse 3: 19).

Saturday, the 24th of January. I hold our medical man, Mr. Thilo, in high esteem because of his skill in medical and in other matters.[3] I hope wholeheartedly that our trustees will provide for him and his wife to some extent since he can not subsist on his income from such a small and poor community. If God would grant me some income from our sawmill and flourmill, I could then contribute what is necessary for his support as well as for that of Mr. /Ludwig/ Meyer, who is well liked by the whole community by virtue of his skill, industry, and good conduct.[4] Meanwhile, we all have to be patient until the Lord provides us with His help, and not complain, but rather take the blame ourselves if we have to suffer deprivations and afflictions.

This week, in our evening prayer hour we were able to learn several things from Kings 8:29:30. For instance, we heard about king Solomon's good resolution to attend divine service regularly and of offering humble prayers there according to the Hebrew; also, of his high hopes for the Israelites (v. 30) who, in his estimation, would likewise come to public services eagerly and apply themselves to prayer humbly and devoutly. This is the reason the temple (*cum emphasi*)[5] is called a house of prayer. Since Solomon pleaded so extensively for the Israelites and for strangers and since everything set down in the Bible is to serve us as a lesson and as an example, have I taken this opportunity to impress upon my listeners their Christian duties, citing in support God's express admonition by Paul (Timothy 2:1–3). I also have enumerated the reasons which ought to move us to private and public intercession on behalf of our dear benefactors.

Sunday, the 25th of January. Yesterday the sick Mrs. Glaner received Holy Communion in complete humbleness and joyful faith. She is an honest disciple of our Lord Christ, who is well content with His guidance in all things. A serving woman, one of the last Germans,[6] who had fallen sick before Christmas, is in very pitiable condition. God has shown her His great mercy in leading her and her bastard child—whom she had brought with her from Germany—to our community. We not only took good care of her physical needs but also showed her the path of salvation and gave her ample opportunity to mend her ways and to let herself be saved from her great ignorance and superstition and from her rather evil habits. Because she had neglected it in her health, God granted her a long period of grace on her sickbed. She was instructed in the order of salvation.[7] We showed her how much benefit she derived from it, we prayed with her, and we also comforted her and promised her to let her partake of Holy Communion, which she had asked for at the beginning of her sickness, if only she would herself be sufficiently prepared to receive it. She seemed to take my remonstrations to heart and denounced herself as a great sinner. She claimed to have asked God day and night for insight and remorse for her sins. However, she never confessed those sins she felt in her heart; and, on the contrary, showed her worldly thoughts all too greatly.

Since Thursday she had no longer been in complete possession of her reason; yesterday she fell into a kind of delirium and, while screaming, singing, cursing, and laughing, very much like drunken guests at a wedding, talked of many serious transgressions she may have committed at dances in Germany as well as on her trip. Shortly before her sickness she had been overheard saying that, if everybody who danced and enjoyed a good time were to be dammed, only a very few would find salvation. We can not do much more for her but to implore God that he may treat this pitiful soul with His Goodness, which is as boundless as He Himself. She is a terrible example of evil. Mr. Thilo treats her sickness with great diligence. Here, as otherwise, we see how inexplicable are His judgments and how inscrutable are His ways.

Tuesday, the 27th of January. As much as I am saddened by this woman and her pitiful state of body and soul, God has provided me with much joy regarding a young German who had served for eight years in Augusta and Savannah and whom I engaged in my service as a fieldhand three months ago. He wants to be here with us and wishes to be prepared for Holy Commu-

nion. He had been very ignorant and full of prejudice against
salvation, pious conduct, and us here in Ebenezer, partly because of the gossip of Germans in Savannah. However, God has
removed those prejudices one by one and given him instead a
great love for His teaching as well as an eagerness for learning to
read. He now sincerely regrets his sins and is beginning, humbly
and fervently, to marvel at his own blindness and God's plentiful
patience and forbearance. He praises God for His kindness in
leading him to blessed solitude, and he does his work with the
word of God and prayer, just as is written in Colossians 3:22–23.
A friend of his who had served with him and who had completed his indenture at the same time came likewise to us for the
purpose of instruction. I have high expectations for him, too,
and I hope that our servant will influence him for the better.

Thursday, the 29th of January. God has brought sickness to
my house, too, and we implore Him to fulfill His purpose with
such punishment. In addition to the aforementioned serving
woman, who still lingers on in her pitiful condition and often
fills the house with her terrible screaming and singing, our devout childrens' nurse, who has been with us for several years and
who has always been sickly, is suffering again from her epileptic
seizures brought on by the great heat. She too, talks, prays, and
sings, but properly and pleasantly, without screaming so that
one can well see her heart's treasure of goodness. The Saviour is
foremost in her thoughts and she can not praise Him enough:
she also enumerates her own shortcomings emphatically, as well
as those she has noticed in others, and she admonishes her
friends to penitence in a truly evangelic way. During the continuing sickness of the serving woman and of this devout maid
just mentioned, we have taken into our house a pious widow,
Mrs. Kurtz, whose devout daughter is also in a weak and pitiful
condition due to a wasting fever and is receiving necessary care
in our house.[8] She is a sweet, obedient child who dearly loves
Jesus. Mr. Thilo does not have much hope for her recovery; she
however, is not afraid of dying. We had to take this good widow
into our house because we need her help with the patients and
the daily chores.

The sad condition of our serving woman has caused my dear

wife's relapse into a state of very dangerous and highly painful hysteria. She is suffering day and night and, as a consequence, she cannot properly take care of our four children and the aforementioned patients, nor can she run the household with her usual joy. The fieldhand I mentioned two days ago is very useful to us in our present circumstances although it is not easy for me to provide for so many people in these hard times. We have to purchase all food, except milk and butter. But God in Heaven knows what we need: to Him we commend our fate, in Him we trust, He will make all well. My domestic affairs do not at all impede my service; and God's goodness blesses what He gives to me for my daily needs and for my health. I am experiencing the *effatum* of Christ in all its richness (Matthew 4:4).[9]

Friday, the 30th of January. At noon yesterday five Englishmen, some from Old-Ebenezer and some from Fort Argyle on the Ogeechee River, arrived here and asked me to baptize a three month old boy. I could not refuse, especially since both parents, the child, and a man who had been asked to be a witness to the baptism had made the long journey from Fort Argyle in bad weather. A man and his wife from Old-Ebenezer had been chosen as the other two witnesses. I will notify the English preacher in Savannah of this baptism and will let him know the name of the child, the parents, and the witnesses so that he may enter all this in his baptismal records. I will also ask him whether he has any objections to my procedure so that in the future, if and when I am expected to act again on behalf of Englishmen, I can act accordingly. The previous preachers in Savannah, Mr. John Wesley and Christopher Orton, allowed only teachers ordained by an English bishop to perform such baptisms.[10] Therefore, in the past, I have refrained from overstepping the bounds of my own office and have gladly left them to their opinions and ways of running their office.

Today, at noon, as I held my usual weekly service at the plantations, our serving woman, of whom this diary has had to tell some sad things, died. She had been out of her mind for the past eight days; and, even when it seemed that she was capable of understanding mundane affairs, was it nevertheless impossible to instruct her in spiritual matters, and it became hopeless to get a single good word out of her. Lately nothing could be done for her spiritually but to commend her as a miserable object in soul and body to the boundless goodness of God in Christ. Our childrens' nurse has recovered from her sickness; I trust that God in His eternal mercy will not let that pitiful spectacle of the serving woman and the manifold disquiet and discomfort she caused, especially towards the end, harm anyone's health in my house. Rather, we hope that those sad things we heard and witnessed will better our souls.

Saturday, the 31 of January. A Frenchman from Purysburg[11] sent me upon my request a good number of white mulberry trees. In a note he inquired whether it was true that no one with blacks was allowed to come to our mills by boat and whether our rangers were empowered to intercept them. This is obvious slander by those envious of us in Purysburg and Savannah. It certainly never occurred to us to ever hinder anyone to come to our settlement or to our mills with their blacks or Negro slaves.[12] Mean people like to fabricate tales about us, especially such which portray us as being responsible for others' not being able to bring blacks in. The constable of our rangers, Bichler, has returned from Frederica, where he had to stay for almost two months in order to get the money for himself and his men, which he properly received. However, he brought nothing back for me in return for the lumber, a horse, and other things which Major Horton obtained from us.

I have to be patient therefore in my present tribulations until God gives me counsel. Today in my reading from the Scriptures I found strength from Samuel 2:5–10: David went and prospered, and the Lord God of Sabboth was with him. God wishes to teach me likewise through this experience that it is good to trust in the Lord and that one should not put one's trust in people, even be they princes. Tomorrow, God willing, we will think on the important proverb Isaiah 41:10 in the introductory verses for the Fourth Sunday after Epiphany. "Fear thou not, I am with thee, be not dismayed, for I am thy God." My our merciful Savior bless me with these precious words in my present trials. We have indeed a great and loving Savior who commands the seas and the storms and who is all-powerful in heaven and on earth and who has promised to be with us to the end of the world. May He strengthen our faith so we may behold His glory which He pleases to reveal to us in times of need and tribulations.

FEBRUARY

Sunday, the 1st of February. Mrs.Driesler returned to me our chalice, which we lent to her late husband several years ago for use in his small congregation.[1] At the same time she sent me a very kind letter in which she mentions her lingering illness and the lack of charity as well as the heartless conduct of the people in Frederica. She also tells of a great fire which destroyed many soldiers' quarters and some other houses. She is asking me to send her some medicine for her sickly condition; however, we are short of medicines ourselves. She is living in the house of her granddaughter who married some time ago a good Reformed man, a grocer who is prospering and has a good reputation.

Wednesday, the 4th of February. Mrs. Kalcher, who was close to death before Christmas, has recovered enough to be able to do light chores and once again to attend public service (one of her most favorite activities).[2] However, she is still subject to sudden onsets of faintness, even in church; and then she must be conducted home. Yesterday God saved her dear husband from a great calamity, which might have cost him his life. The same happened to me, too, for which undeserved goodness I humbly praise Him. He punishes us with measure.

Thursday, the 5th of February. A German servant in Savannah wrote me a very fine letter from which I can easily judge his good state of mind, even though he is known to me already as a well-meaning person. He wishes to obtain Arnd's *True Christianity*[3]; he assures me that he wishes to peruse it for his own and his wife's salvation, and he asks my help in this. I wish to give him my one and only copy rather than have him lack the book. Perhaps God will grant us several copies soon.

Saturday, the 7th of February. Today our rangers started to receive their backpay. They were paid for two years, which amounts to 132 pounds Sterling. Their constable, Thomas Bichler, obtained this money from Frederica for one year, seven months, and 24 days; and in the very near future the rangers are to be paid. We started and finished the distribution of money by praying and praising God, as is proper, since we must regard the money in these hard times as a gift of God. In this sad time of war God is not only giving us peace: He is also letting us benefit richly in spiritual and secular matters. We have no billeting of troops and no war taxes; and our rangers, or town dragoons, get their pay to their own benefit as well as to that of the community and without any hardship to the community. In that way money which is much needed comes regularly into our settlement. We can indeed say with dear David in Psalms 31: "I will be glad and rejoice in thy mercy: for thou hast considered my trouble; thou hast known my soul in adversities." One of these men gave me 10 shillings Sterling of the bounty bestowed upon him by the Lord so that I might refresh some of the poor among us so that they too, like him, be encouraged to praise the Lord.

Monday, the 9th of February. We strongly feel the loss caused us by a hypocritical man without any conscience within our community and in Charleston:[4] Because of him my dear colleague, constable Bichler, had to spend a considerable sum of money in Charlestown as well as on his trip there and back. Up to now I have been unable to lessen the loss to our community; since the woodwork done here and the good boards cannot be sold except for a few thousand shingles and barrel staves which were sent to Charlestown by a merchant in Savannah who was to pay for them but has not yet done so. This sad happening is a great punishment for us; may God in His Goodness let it redound to our own good.

In our prayer meetings and weekly sermons we hear now, from the beautiful prayers of King Solomon, about God's wise and gracious intentions when He sends us various trials in answer to our sins and when He impresses upon his people that they may repent their sins and turn to God, acknowledge His name, pray to Him privately and in meetings, and let themselves be guided onto the right path. He would then hear their prayers in heaven, be merciful with the sinners, lessen their well-deserved common and special tribulations and let them benefit again from His Goodness. Such is His fatherly way, according to Jeremiah 18: 7-8. It is a great consolation that God is willing to hear our prayers in our need and accepts our penitence, provided it is not a legalistic and hypocritical penitence;[5] Habakkuk 4 v.2: "In times of misery thou showest thy goodness." Tobias 3 v. 14: "When thou art angered thou still showest mercy and forgiveness and in misery thou forgivest the sins of those who call upon thee." Thus, sinners who are ready to repent acknowledge the Lord's name according to the instruction of His word and from their own experience as well as that of others for the awakening and strengthening of their faith. They also learn that all things, even physical punishment and tribulations, are in their own best interest. Praised be the Lord every single day!

Tuesday, the 10th of February. Yesterday afternoon Mrs. Kohleis sent her only daughter, six years old, from her plantation to the orphanage, on an errand for Mrs. Kalcher. On her way home she missed the right road to the bridge and got lost in the woods. That night, rangers were sent out immediately to look for her; next morning they were joined by more who were dispatched from the plantations and from town to search for her on foot and on horseback. In the afternoon, she was finally found in the little pineforest. Neither the intense night frost nor the many wolves which roam these forests had done her any harm. She is alive and healthy and slept through the night without any special fears or anxieties. While in prayer, I remembered Matthew 18:14.

Wednesday, the 11th of February. Brückner is a Christian-minded and obliging man from Salzburg. Since his conversion to God he has been making himself useful like Onesimus, and he runs his household well. Although he has recovered from his dangerous illness, he is not yet quite well and is unable to do heavy work. He has planted a great number of mulberry trees and is planning to produce silk, if God preserves his life. He is well content with His ways even in the face of misery and sorrow. A Frenchman in Purysburg, from whom I have purchased young mulberry trees, brought me three different kinds of silkworm seeds this morning. From these, reportedly, one can harvest silk from three to four times, until August; the last cycle, however, is said to yield only small balls because the mulberry leaves turn harder and harder during the summer and no longer provide the worms with enough nourishment. From the experiment which has been planned in our settlement for this year, we will be able to decide whether or not such repeated cycles of silk production are practical and profitable. In the course of summer cool rooms are necessary, and most people lack such.

Thursday, the 12th of February. Much joy and praise of God has arisen in our community since the lost girl was found. A devout woman told me that, while in prayer, she found much joy in thinking that our merciful and all-powerful God would protect this child in the woods from cold, wolves, and other harm just as easily as He protected Daniel in the lions' den. The child's mother gets much pleasure from her little girl. Among other things, she taught her the following verse: "My Friend is mine, and I am His, who dwells among the roses." Now the child always calls Lord Jesus her friend and prays to Him on her knees. One time she said unexpectedly to her mother: "My Friend has been to see me, and He has told me that He wanted to give the heavens to me and His whole treasure of bliss." These words she had heard from her father on the way to church the previous day. The mother feels the manifold effects of the Holy Spirit's grace in this little child much to her joy and the praise of the Lord. This devout woman is visited by God with various sorrows, difficulties in her household, and physical weaknesses. She prays that her Heavenly Father continue to cleanse her and make known to her the innermost recesses of her evil heart, and fullfil His good purpose. I told her that God sends tribulations to His children also in order to prevent and prohibit them from lapses into sin, excesses, etc., since He knows their hearts better than they do themselves. However, she feels that they could serve God better and lead a Christian life more easily if they were not so sick, infirm, poor, etc. Surely our wise and merciful God would not hinder them by such sorrows if He did not foresee the opposite. Therefore we must be content with His ways.

Some start to doubt their penitence and the forgiveness of sins because of His punishments. Because they do not innocently believe in the gospel but adhere to the rules of the Old Testament, they divest themselves of the great comfort which is granted so generously in Holy Scripture to all those who bear the cross.[6] Precisely such matters were addressed in yesterday's evening prayer, occasioned by the mention of the plagues detailed in Solomon's prayer. For the non-believers these plagues were a punishment for their sins; for the believers, however, they were fatherly chastisement. Their prayers and supplications rise upwards and press beyond the clouds and the heavens and enter into the presence of God's glory, where their Intercessor and Champion has gone to comfort them. How powerful is a penitent and faithful prayer!

Friday, the 13th of February. Yesterday evening I learned to my sorrow that not only all sorts of evil people in Savannah and Frederica, but even our N. are slandering me in an irresponsible manner and have interpreted the way I dispatch my duties which have been assigned to me by my superiors and which I assumed out of love for our community most maliciously and unkindly. May God forgive them and especially poor N.! If my enemies had knowledge of any misconduct or abominable deed of mine they would certainly not hesitate to make it public joyfully; but they lack such proof and therefore slander me because I take care of our community and its every single member and attend to their spiritual and material needs and do not willingly let them be subjected to violence or injustice.

The bitterness against me stems mainly from the fact that I and my community are regarded as being responsible that others may not bring blacks into the country. In this, however, they are quite wrong. As far as N. is concerned, who is friendly to my face and who indeed has reason to be grateful to me, the root of his animosity and slander lies in his own domineering nature, which I attempted to curb. In fulfilling my office, as well as my conscience and the wish of our dear Fathers, I could allow no one who may have wanted to establish himself as the master, to rule my dear Salzburgers wilfully and tyrannically. Therefore I had to check this N.'s thirst for power, which, however, I did at all times with love and Christian arguments, and all sorts of services. My enemies are often all too eager to despise and slander my spiritual office; therefore I have been turning over in mind for some considerable time the idea of appointing, as soon as possible and in God's name, somebody more suitable than I for dealing with official affairs and matters for the authorities.

God will continue to hold His hand over us and see to it that no harm comes to our honest Salzburgers. I, on the other hand, will be even more able to see to my spiritual duties, which, through the goodness of God, is my greatest pleasure. On the other hand, such a neglect of one of the duties of my office fills my conscience with considerable anxiety. At the moment I am reading again the *Watchman's Voice* by the late Grossgebauer, and in it I find many a passage for my humiliation.[7]

Saturday, the 14th of February. Since the new moon two weeks ago a great number of white and Spanish mulberry trees have been planted in the town and at the plantations. Our rangers were a great help. In the course of three years the trees usually grow to a size where the leaves can be used for feeding the worms. The Spanish variety has quite large, delicate leaves; and those trees grow much faster than the others. People are also planting all sorts of useful trees along both sides of streets, which are 60 feet wide; likewise in public places outside the town, on the banks of the Savannah River, and right in the middle of town, which will be both pleasant and useful in time. May God bless this work!

Sunday, the 15th of February. Although it rained all day today, we received a good deal of goodness and blessing. Similar to the rain outside, there is a spiritual rain through which God lets us partake of His good treasure by preaching His Word; and He has given us much edification from that. After our late morning sermon Veit Lechner's little daughter, to whom his wife had given birth last night, was baptized publicly.

It was also announced that three weeks from tomorrow, God willing, our yearly memorial and thanksgiving service would be celebrated and at the same time Holy Communion would be given to those who would register for it and behave with the necessary dignity.[8]

Monday, the 16th of February. Yesterday, old Mr. /Theobald/ Kieffer from Purysburg was here, and he told me that his oldest son, Jacob, who had been suffering from consumption for a long

time, had died on the 5th.[9] Towards the end, on his own and on
his father's plantation near Purysburg, he had to endure much
suffering from his ravaged body; among other things he had
said to his family: If he were to convert only now to God, it would
be difficult because of the great pain. He was afraid of his own
feelings and that maybe he could offend his Savior by being im-
patient, but no sign of impatience could be detected in him. Finally he asked to be read to: "Jesus, my refuge" and "My Savior is
alive", etc. He commended his soul to God, bid farewell to his
family, and died in peace.

Tuesday, the 17th of February. Mrs. /Elisabeth Catharina/ Zettler is awakened to a new sincerity in Christianity by the death of
her brother, /Jacob/ Kieffer. A year ago, then still in her old
house, God had already shown her His goodness on the occasion
of the dangerous illness of her husband; she has, however, not
practiced faithfully and steadfastly the three little words (which
are difficult for some), namely, praying, being on guard, and
struggling.[10] Therefore she had to endure several pangs of conscience and lost almost all joy in prayer to God. She herself was
recently again close to death's door and eternity; and, because of
her severe doubts concerning her soul's state, her troubled conscience had pained her more and deeper than her sickness. Her
late brother, when he was here last, had spent several weeks in
her house; then she could tell many beautiful things of his genuine remorse over his ill-spent wild youth, his great patience in
the face of his suffering, of his complete resignation to the will of
our Heavenly Father, and of his confident prayers. She praises
God that He has led her and her family to believe in the Gospel.

Wednesday, the 18th of February. It is always a great joy to me
when I hear our Salzburgers extol the great blessing of emigrat-
ing from their papist fatherland and praise our wonderful, all-
powerful, wise and merciful God, as a pious man and woman
did in my room today at noon. Though we are living in very
hard and trying times and although several among us are more
destitute than ever before in previous years, pious people consider it a special act of God's goodness that they are living here in
blessed solitude where they can be prepared for eternity without
interference from anyone (except if they wish it).

Some who emigrated have heard only little of God's truth; yet it took root like a good seed. Nevertheless the Word turned into veritable spikes and nails for them and wounded their very hearts so that they had to leave their fatherland and were utterly confused. Now they marvel at God's great power, which worked wonders in their hearts occasionally through a single, often only half-heard verse from Holy Scripture. At times they themselves compare quite cleverly the deliverance of the Israelites from Egypt to their own from their earthly unenlightened fatherland: and God our Lord has revealed His glory in the latter as well as the former case.

Thursday, the 19th of February. I am not willing to spend more money cutting lumber before the ample supply in Abercorn, at the mill, and in town has been sold. However, since several Salzburgers are now adding land to their plantations close to the mill and since the beautiful trees on these lands are being donated to the mill, I do not wish to let those trees just rot but rather have them brought to the mill and cut. At present our mill is used by those people in our community who are bringing their own lumber to the mill and having it cut there: For this service they pay a good price to the man running the sawmill and also get their building lumber inexpensively. Kogler, the man who runs the sawmill and who also does all sorts of cabinet work, wants to cut lumber from white and red wood and make various things to sell from it. We have all sorts of nice trees in our neighborhood which yield delicate and attractive wood; However, they grow commonly in low-lying areas and are so far away from the mill that they can not be transported to the mill without great expense, therefore this is not a sound business proposition until a sale is fairly certain.

Friday, the 20th of February. Yesterday evening, I got word from Savannah that Mr. Whitefield, who has returned to Bethesda from his stay in Charleston, is making ready for his trip into the northern colonies, from which he expects to return in a little over a year. He has made good connections there among people of various walks of life according to newspapers from Pennsylvania and Carolina.

I visited N.N. on his plantation and found him in ill humor

although he has reason enough to be grateful to our Lord for the manifold spiritual and physical benefactions he has received in this country. He has a good number of cattle and plenty of wheat and rice, which he has been able to sell at a good price. If she[11] were of one mind with him, then he would probably leave this colony soon, but certainly without improving himself by such a move. He is a worldly-minded person; and the worries about food and the trouble caused by that prevent him from listening to God's word, which he hears only very infrequently. Yesterday in our evening prayer hour we used Solomon, who was not only a great king but also like his father David, a godly ruler, as an example; and we demonstrated how Christian parents and superiors must care properly for their children's and subordinates' salvation. They have to make a beginning in themselves and must achieve in themselves a genuine love and fear of God; then they will be able to guide those entrusted to them, for whom our Lord Jesus paid so dearly, not only by beneficial admonitions but also by setting a good example, diligent supervision, and zealous intercession.

Sunday, the 22nd. of February. Rottenberger, a very sensible man who is skilled in all sorts of things, has been ailing for some time; he thinks his lungs might be affected and that he might not be with us for much longer. A short time ago he remarried, and God gave him and his three young children a pious and virtuous helper, who was raised in our community to do good; and he has established himself well on his plantation close to town. We need him very much since, next to the sawmiller Kogler, he is the most skilled man. People like him are well off in this country, better than in any place in Germany, where there is a surplus of craftsmen and good workers. This Rottenberger is otherwise a good-natured and orderly man; However, in his days of full health he does not exhibit the seriousness in his own Christianity and that of his family that is necessary for finding bliss in God's word. Therefore, God will have to come to his aid with a bitter cup. I hope he will never forget the death of his first wife, who was saved like a brand from the fire. If I remember correctly, he mentioned this himself in a letter to his good brother in Krausendorf in Prussia.[12]

Monday, the 23rd. of February. A poor, old Englishman visited me today. He has a plantation in Abercorn and wishes to build a small house there, but he can not afford it. Because he shows us much loving hospitality day and night whenever we come to Abercorn from Savannah, and since he also is in charge of the lumber stored there, we will give him as a present twenty boards as well as twenty-five finished, and twenty-five unfinished slabs for outside planking.[13] He will receive the boards in Abercorn; but he has to fetch the slabs from the sawmill here; and today he started to get them. Some time ago we stopped finishing the slabs with axes. Rather, the outermost bark is sawed off the tree trunks; and what is sawed off next are very useful slabs, which can be sold inexpensively. Our sawmill, in many ways, is of great benefit both to the people living in our community and to people from other places, even if we have so far not fully profited from this benefit.

Tuesday, the 24th of February. Up to now there has been a bell on my house under a little roof, which, however, has caused a great deal of trouble and expense because it had been difficult to replace the broken rope. Today two strong posts were built next to one another and the bell was fastened to them; that is now very convenient and practical. The posts are thirty feet high, and a small roof will be built above the bell. God be praised for the benefit we derive from this bell, may He grant us another one in His time at Zion Church!

Wednesday, the 25th of February. This morning I visited Mrs. Lochner,[13a] who had just been delivered of a child. In the presence of her husband and Mrs. Lackner I repeated the most important passages from God's word, which we had heard in our latest prayer meetings and on Sunday in our sermon. Mr. Lochner, whose body and soul are growing stronger and stronger, gave me the opportunity for that. This man knows well how to bear his poverty and various tribulations; he praises God's goodness and benefactions for which he is ever grateful. I told him something about our Lord Jesus' precious words: "The cup which my Father hath given me, shall I not drink it?"

Thursday, the 26th of February. The old tailor, N.[14] and his wife do not have a good marriage at all, which is primarily the fault of that strong-willed and quarrelsome woman. According to them, they have moved here from Purysburg for the sake of God's word and in order to be prepared for eternity in their old age. They attend public service and our daily prayer meetings regularly, but they do not make any progress beyond what they hear. Through their own fault they belong to those who are mentioned in Hebrews 4:2: "The word preached did not profit them, not being mixed with faith in them that heard it." It was explained to them and to others in simple and clear terms, not only on Sexagesima Sunday, in the prayer meeting on the above mentioned introductory verse, but also in the prayer meetings of yesterday and the days before, using Solomon's prayer 1 Kings 8:41 ff. as an example of how they must receive God's word and public service, if God's purpose towards salvation shall be fulfilled as is written in Acts 26:18. They must indeed not be lacking in proper attention (Acts 10:33) or proper meditation and contemplation (Luke 11:19, 51) or frequent prayers before, during, and after comtemplating the divine word.

If faithful listeners pray to our all-knowing and merciful Father devoutly and in the privacy of their own closet, then God will reward them for it publicly, both at public services in church and in their daily work and occupations among men so that they may not be robbed of the treasures gathered by them but rather that they may offer edification to their fellow men in word and deed. In Solomon's prayer, chapter 1, we learn that strangers or heathens will hear of God's mighty name; they will let themselves be lured by it to public service at Jerusalem. They will be brought to true recognition of God and they will fervently pray to the Lord and apply the granting of their prayers towards a genuine fear of God for their own as well as for their families' salvation. Therefore, for our listeners and others who can avail themselves readily of the means of salvation, it is most irresponsible if they do not attain a true and living recognition of God and Jesus Christ as well as filial love and fear of God.

Saturday, the 28th of February. Last year we received in the shipment from Augsburg, among other things, so many copies of *Christian Guide for God-pleasing Confession and Holy Communion*,[15] revised and edited by the late Ambrosius Wirth, that we could afford to give a copy to each head of a household and to each unmarried adult. This beautiful and well bound book was distributed to our congregation on Good Friday, and now we always refer to it among ourselves as the beautiful book which was distributed on Good Friday. Through it, and especially through the thorough examinations of conscience concerning the Ten Commandments and the rules for life according to the Ten Commandments, God gives our listeners much benefit, which they acknowledge frequently. At that time we also received *God's Sacred Heart and a True Christian's Life* by Pastor Starke.[16] This book is also valued highly by me and by those to whom I could give a copy, and it is blessed richly by God for my and my family's edification.

The worthy man who produced this very useful book announced in its introduction the printing of a second volume, called *Sources of Consolation for Souls in Distress and Fear of their Salvation*,[17] which I also would like to have. If our dear God in heaven would bring it about that I could get several copies of both volumes then I would be able to do much good in our community and in this colony by distributing them.

MARCH

Monday, the 2nd of March. One of the patients in our house, the orphaned daughter of the widow Anna Kurtz,[1] has for a long time now wished for the Savior and her own blessed end. Her desire to die increases as her strength diminishes. When she heard that I was going to Savannah, she cried, for she values my company. She also requested that I write a note to dear pastor Mühlenberg, in whose company she herself, her mother, her late stepfather, and two stepsisters, had come overseas, in order to thank him for the love he showed them and his support, as well as to show him the condition of her heart with the following words:

My heart's already left this world
Heaven is its house of joy;

There, it lies on Jesus' breast.
My body wants to be redeemed
Of sins, distress, and pain.
It cries out in this worldly desert:
Jesus, Jesus! How I await you, how anxious am I, poor soul;
Come, come, have mercy on me.[2]

Thursday, the 5th of March. Mrs. Kurtz' daughter had to endure many pains in my absence, but she also received much refreshment of her soul, especially on Monday evening when our
Lord Jesus richly presented her with heavenly joy of which she
spoke so eloquently that others were greatly edified and moved.
When I visited her after my return from Savannah I imparted
these beautiful words to her "I have a desire to depart, and to be
with Christ; which is far better." She said, this was true for her
and that she had seen Him already in her faith. I asked her
whether she was not afraid of being denied heaven because of
original sin and the sins committed by her. She answered completely composed: No, because all was forgiven. She likes to hear
of nothing better than of Christ and death, and she hopes soon
to be with her dear Savior, as is her greatest wish.

Saturday, the 7th of March. A friend in Savannah wrote to
Philadelphia and New York for twelve bushels of flax seed,
which, however, will arrive too late. Otherwise, the people here
would plant flax this spring. Last year worms damaged the flax
plants when they were quite young; and because of this we have
only few seeds. We are all being tested in manifold ways, but our
dear God still shows us His good protection. His goodness
reaches as far as the heavens, and His truth as far as the clouds.

Sunday, March 8. Our dear Lord has shown most kindly His
mercy to quite a few women in our community so that they excel
their husbands and outshine them. Indeed, a few have to put up
with being humiliated and subjected to indignities by their husbands. This, however, has not impeded their righteous nature
even though, under these circumstances, they are deprived of
beneficial formal expression of their faith and proper Christian
spiritual support. It is therefore a great joy for them when we
come to visit, talk of God's word, and pray with them. God's word

becomes very sweet, clear, and real to them despite their outward and inward misery; and their previous life of sin before
and during marriage is held up to them earnestly in order to
humble them and guide them to accept fatherly chastisement
willingly. Despite all shortcomings, their hearts lie only in Jesus
and His dear deeds; and their minds see through all that is dark
and muddled into the perfect calm which is promised and ready
for God's people. Some arrived already this evening from their
faraway plantations and, on their knees, took part in today's
prayer service in which we sought to prepare ourselves for tomorrow's memorial and thanksgiving celebration.

Monday, March 9. This day was devoted to the solemn observance of our yearly memorial and thanksgiving celebration:
and for that purpose the entire congregation had come together
in the Jerusalem Church in order to take part properly in public
prayer, song, and the preaching of God's word. Sixty-four people went to Holy Communion in a Christian and edifying manner. I preached on our Lord Jesus' dear and consoling words
about the love of our Father in Heaven for His children here on
earth: Luke 12: 32: "Fear not, little flock; for it is your Father's
good pleasure to give you the kingdom." As introductory verse I
had chosen John 16: 27: "For the Father himself loveth you, because ye have loved me, and have believed that I came out from
God."

My dear colleague had as his introductory verses Psalms 103:
17–18: "But the mercy of the Lord is from everlasting to everlasting upon them that fear Him, and His righteousness unto
children's children. To such as keep His covenant, and to those
that remember His commandments to do them." As his text he
had chosen Psalms 26: 6–7: "Blessed be the Lord, because He
hath heard the voice of my supplication. The Lord is my
strength and my shield; my heart trusted in Him, and I am
helped: therefore my heart greatly rejoiceth; and with my song
will I praise Him." He explained these verses and preached on
God's gracious protection of His church.

Usually, in our memorial and thanksgiving celebration we like
to remind our listeners, adults and children, generally and specifically, as much as possible of the spiritual and material benefits

which our Lord God has showered on us so richly right from the beginning in this country of our pilgrimage. We like to remind them so that, like David, they, together with us, may praise, in song our all-powerful and all-merciful God, who confers on us all benefits. To some extent, this has happened today already in our sermons; but it was planned especially for today's repetition hour when I had sufficient time to go into this matter in depth. In this I was greatly aided by the beautiful and edifying introduction of Part Two of the Ebenezer reports, which have God's Georgia as its topic: 1 Corinthians 3: 9; I read almost half of it aloud, along with various proper comments and explanations; and I plan to continue with this in future evening prayer meetings.

The same subject will also be my dear task in my next weekly sermon in our Zion Church. This is also God's expressed wish and command according to Psalms 78: 4, that we should make known to our children God's glory, His power and the wonders He hath wrought. May our all-merciful God richly bless everything which was read, sung, and preached. May He also be pleased by our public and private thanksgiving for His many benefits which we received in the past and present as well as by our eager and dutiful prayers on behalf of our dear and esteemed Fathers, benefactors, and friends. May He be pleased for the sake of Christ, in whose name we have acted! In our case, just as in the case of God's ancient Israel, benefits and tribulations go hand in hand and we exhort each other: Give praise and honor to the name of your God, for He will come to your aid! Amen. Ebenezer: So far the Lord has helped us, Halleluiah.[3]

Wednesday, March 11. Sick Mrs. Glaner is improving steadily. On her sickbed she is filled with praise for the Lord and His mercy past and present. Much to her benefit, she remembers the edifying cases of devout dying persons in Salzburg and takes them as her example. Two pious widows, Mrs. Zant and Mrs. Graniwetter, are her neighbors to the left and the right of her house; both received much spiritual and material benefit from the righteous Glaner and his devout wife.

The sick young girl in my house is growing weaker by the day, and her desire for her Savior and her own blessed death through

Him is growing stronger. She admonishes her mother gently and cleverly; it is easily seen that she is quite competent to distinguish falsehood from truth, and nature from grace. She prays to the Lord on behalf of her two sisters, who just now are preparing themselves for Holy Communion in order that He may well receive and enlighten them. She dearly desires Holy Communion, which was given to her this morning after praying, reaffirming her baptismal promise, and administering the last rights.

Thursday, March 12. Zedler,[4] the shoemaker, and his wife have had to endure a great many tribulations lately; not only in that they had to suffer through their own ill health but also through the sicknesses of their two children as well. They also were subjected to lack of food. However, they are accepting their situation in a proper Christian manner. I happened to have with me the profound and edifying *Meditation on the Providence of God over Men* of which a good number of copies were sent to us a few months ago from Memmingen via Augsburg.[5] I read from it a passage dealing with the topic of our conversation with both husband and wife and afterwards presented my copy to them as a gift.

A few days ago I impressed upon my listeners, among other things, this important verse: "That He died for all, that they which live should not henceforth live unto themselves, but unto Him who died for them," etc. See Romans 14: 7–9. The fall and actual arch-sin, which is mostly not even recognized as such, lies in that man neglects his Creator, Savior, His God who blesses all and makes himself a God which can result in nothing but misery and chaos. If, through God's grace, man succeeds in abandoning his willfullness and learns to put his trust completely in our all-wise and all-merciful God, then he will become His child and servant and will be easily content (though not without a struggle) with whatever our Father and Lord allots to him.

Friday, March 13. In the winter of 1745 all children in our area developed a very hard and persistent cough which now once again is affecting our children and which is on the increase.[6] Both times the cough started in Savannah and then spread to our district. Otherwise the Lord has mercifully saved us from dangerous and contageous diseases in this country. May he continue to give us His fatherly protection! I got word from Savannah that the Council members unexpectedly received *Sola Bills*[7] in the amount of 500 pound Sterling from the Lord Trustees and indeed at such a time when money and other necessities were greatly lacking. These *Sola Bills* were found in a ship which had been captured by the Spanish and transported to St. Augustine some time ago. There, the mere pieces of paper, which can only be validated by signatures in Savannah, were worthless and about to be thrown away or burned. An English prisoner, however, bought them all for one duplone ransom and brought them to Charleston after he himself was ransomed off and released. This, too, shows God's merciful care for our country.

Today, at 3 o'clock in the morning, the 15 year old daughter of Mrs. Kurtz took her leave of everyone in the house and died, although after a difficult agony, in joy and with her heart well content.[8] Her life and death is an edifying example for all who knew her: and I consider it a privilege that she was sick in my house and died here. I hope that her frequent and faithful prayers may benefit me and my household. For the edification of us all I made public some details of her blessed life and sickness, as well as of her death filled with faith and hope, both in the school at the plantations and in my weekly sermon at our Zion Church.

Saturday, March 14. Mrs. Zimmerebner, whom the esteemed Senior Urlsperger may still remember by the name of Margaretha Berenberg is, by God's grace, in a quite different frame of mind from the one she was in before and after her journey here. She recognizes that God showed her a great kindness through her marriage to the righteous Zimmerebner, a hardworking and dedicated miller, who is a blessed tool for her soul's unburdening and rebirth by word and example. She told me, among other things, that recently he had said these words to her: "My dear wife, nothing would give me more joy, not an entire kingdom, or even the whole world, but to find that next time when Holy Communion is held, you should show signs of proving yourself to be worthy to receive this sacrament."

Another pious woman, who lives in Zimmerebner's neighborhood and who is to give birth shortly, told me tearfully that God gave her so many children and that she was so unsuited to raise them properly to His glory. I quoted two Bible verses to her: "Lo, children are an heritage of the Lord: and the fruit of the womb is His reward!" and further: "If any of you lack wisdom, let him ask of God, that giveth to all men". In Germany she had not learned to read; and, although she would have liked to learn how after she was married, sickness, various duties, and having children prevented it, which she greatly regrets. I told her how she could and should apply the time she spent with her small children and her domestic chores very usefully to God's praise for her children's benefit and her own soul's salvation even in her husband's absence. Some of the people here who have quite small children are tested more severely than others at this time, by having to care for them and clothe them and by other things: However, God always helps them mercifully through their difficulties.

Sunday, March 15. Quite unexpectedly I received a letter today from Mr. Whitefield, which he had written six days ago, in Bethesda, the orphanage in Savannah, when he went there from Carolina for a few days. Soon after that he returned again to Charleston, where he will spend fourteen days; and then he will travel on into the northern colonies. He shows in many kind words his earnest love for Ebenezer; he promises to get for us such things as I would ask of him from either Pennsylvania or New England. He regrets not having been able to talk to me again before his departure, for which, however, I am not to blame. He had already left Savannah and Bethesda before I learned that he had returned from Carolina. The last time I came to see him, in Bethesda at his invitation, he promised me two or three work horses and some harness for our poor farmers. Now, however, he informs me that one of his best horses took a fall and that he will need the others on his plantation in Carolina for plowing; therefore he can not help us in this matter at the moment.

He finds that he cannot get enough farm work done at the orphanage with white laborers for sufficiently maintaining the orphans and the people who were hired to keep things in order.

Because Negroes are not permitted in this colony, friends in Charleston advised him to buy a plantation in Carolina and to work it with Negroes or black slaves. Several rich people, who had been won over by Mr. Whitefield's sermons, contributed money. He hopes that not only Bethesda, but also Ebenezer, will profit from this plantation in time; and he asks that we give thanks to the Lord of Lords, who shows to us daily that His grace is everlasting. He is sorry for me that I have so many problems and so much unrest through all sorts of affairs, which are part of my duties, and he adds: "What is there to say? We have to undergo so many tribulations before we may enter God's kingdom. Therefore, dear Sir, be of good cheer! A single glance at our Christ's countenance will end all misery and pain. One day will make up for many."

At all times he thinks very highly of our esteemed Fathers in London and Germany. On their behalf, he made the following request of me: "When you write home, I would be grateful if you would give my most sincere respects to Professor Frank, Mr. Urlsperger, and Mr. Ziegenhagen. I pray God that He may grant their souls abounding grace, mercy, and peace." Since my letters to these servants of God were sent off yesterday and the day before, I cannot accede at this time to Mr. Whitefield's request. However, I wanted to include it in this diary, which is even more important.

Monday, March 16. The two good men who were in charge of the rafting of a large number of boards to Savannah last Wednesday returned before daybreak yesterday. God helped them to complete their task successfully and they delivered the boards properly to the yard of the honest merchant Mr. Habersham for sale. They say that rafting the boards downstream was easy, but bringing them up the steep hill or bank at Savannah was very difficult. I don't know yet how our Lord, who is all-powerful, will bring it about that an easier way of handling such boards be found.[9] If something could be constructed it would cause more expense even if the Council in Savannah would give its permission. We always aim to progress modestly; and we pray and believe firmly in what is written: "For that He is strong in power; not one faileth." Yesterday evening a pious

Salzburger told me something about how his prayers were answered and about God's merciful watch over him; and he added: "My Father in Heaven provides advice and assistance in all things."

Tuesday, March 17. Today, in our Zion Church I finished my reading and explanation of the very beautiful introduction to the second part of the Ebenezer reports. In it, we and our children are reminded in this time of our memorial and thanksgiving celebration of God's mighty works among the Salzburgers in general and within our Salzburger community in particular. We are reminded not only clearly and expressly to praise our great and merciful God, but also of the strengthening of our faith in these hard times and of our intercession for our known and unknown benefactors in Europe. Again, I impressed upon my listeners the important words from the 78th Psalm, vs. 3–4 and vs. 6–8.

Wednesday, March 18. Most of our widows try to continue to live on their husband's plantations as well as they can. They have a few cows, and they sow some wheat, rye, and barley; now they are busy planting Indian corn, beans, and squash, in which I aid them as much as possible by hiring workers to do their plowing and other chores. Those laborers receive either lumber from the mill or cash for their food. If wishing helped any, I would wish for each widow one hundred white well-grown mulberry trees surrounding their homes on the plantations, just as at the orphanage and my house. But only widow /Anna Christina/ Müller in town and widow /Sibilla/ Zant on her plantation have a number of such useful trees.

Several other widows either have none or only very small mulberry trees, which they regret now that it is too late. What trees they had were destroyed by crabgrass, which is very damaging to trees and all good greenery. Last February, for the benefit of widows and orphans, I had one hundred fifty young mulberry trees planted in a straight row and so far apart that it is possible to plow in between them and destroy the crabgrass and other harmful weeds. By doing this, the growth of these trees can be assured easily. Maybe others will imitate this method, which would benefit them and their descendants.

Friday, March 20. Mrs. /Maria/ Lemmenhoffer has been a widow for more than a year now. She was ailing frequently; however, she has felt our Heavenly Father's care for her spiritual and material needs keenly. Like other pious widows among us, she is a true devotee of God's word both in meetings and at home, she prays often and loves quiet and solitude. She derives much benefit from the Holy Bible, the blessed Arndt's sermons on Christ's passion, and the blessed Wirth's book on confession and Holy Communion,[10] in the latter especially from the sections on examining one's conscience and the rules for proper living according to the Ten Commandments.

The passage dealing with first duty according to the First Commandment she rereads often and is greatly impressed by it, much to her benefit. The wording is as follows: "Fear thy all-seeing God as thy loving heavenly Father, who is powerfully present at all places and judges without respect of persons, each according to his own works. His eyes are brighter than the sun and see everything that men do and peers even into the secret corners. And remember that He carefully examines and knows all thy thoughts, along with thy speech, deeds, and doings and will one day call you to account."

Saturday, March 21. God is providing us with a very pleasant spring and good weather for growing. A few days ago night-frosts stopped; during the days, so far, the temperatures have been mild, nor was there any lack of warm rain for making our fields properly fertile. Our European crops, such as wheat, rye, barley, oats, and peas are doing very well; from these we expect, with God's blessing, a good harvest in a few months. The white mulberry trees are fully in leaf. However, the Spanish variety which has quite large but also delicate leaves, is just now starting to foliate, and this shows that both kinds of mulberry trees are necessary if one wants to make a success of silk production. In some cases the silk worms emerged already eight, ten, or twelve days ago from the seeds; they would not have any suitable feed if people had no proper white mulberry trees but only the Spanish variety.

This Spanish variety, however, is very useful because of their large leaves, which in size almost equal wild-growing mulberry trees, when during the last fourteen days the worms require large amounts of leaves day and night. These can be quickly collected from the Spanish variety and last long. The Spanish variety is also popular because it is fast-growing and grows taller and wider and has better tasting, larger black berries than the white variety. But they are hard to come by, because only a few of the berries contain viable seeds. During February many branches of this variety were planted in fertile and moist soil and many of them sprouted leaves. Experience will show whether or not they will take root and therefore can be propagated by cuttings like the white mulberry trees. Last year I had branches of Spanish mulberry trees grafted onto the ordinary variety, but they all died.

Sunday, March 22. When I visited Mrs. N. yesterday afternoon on her plantation I found her with her book, passing her time pleasantly with reading and praying in her husband's absence; the husband regards this as a neglect of her household duties. Since God started the work of conversion in her, she likes to spend a good deal of time on spiritual exercises. Because of this, however, she has to suffer somewhat from her worldly-minded husband. I told her that she could show her Christianity also in obedience towards her husband and in attending conscientiously to her household chores; she could think of God while working; then her husband would be convinced most effectively that her Christianity was no threat to his homelife, but rather an advantage. I also told her something of the pious maiden in the midst of popery of whom the blessed Mr. Scriver tells in his *Soul Treasure*[11]. Her hard service did not allow for any special outward spiritual exercises, rather, while working physically, she thought of her dear Savior constantly and thanked him most heartily for His great love.

Monday, March 23. Because we do not have any schoolhouses yet in town or on the plantations we keep school during summers partly in our churches, and partly in Mr. Lemke's and my house. In winter we move from the Jerusalem Church into the orphanage and on the plantations into the houses of Steiner and Brandner, both from Salzburg. There, as well as in other places, the children enjoy the warmth. In my mind I am ready, with

God's help, to put an end to this moving back and forth of the school. We now have boards, lumber, and shingles and from the Society I hope to receive soon the fifteen pounds Sterling which certain dear benefactors outside Germany have donated to us. With this money a spacious schoolhouse, with two rooms, shall be built in town, as soon as I can get the men to start construction.

Our dear God will, in His good time, take care also of the school needed on the plantations. Although this sizable contribution was originally intended for another useful building, since it did not arrive before the spring and a solution was found in the other matter, we will go ahead and build our schoolhouse with it as planned.

Tuesday, March 24. Widow /Christina/ Müller's youngest daughter /Maria Magdalena/ caused her mother great sadness by her disobedience. She told me of it in tears. I remonstrated with the daughter in her mother's presence and instructed her on the sin of disobedience. I quoted the third chapter Sirach to her; and God's grace allowed her to recognize her sin and to repent and she asked forgiveness of me and her mother. Later I learned that she was prostrate and showed several signs of remorse. She is among the children of whom I have high hopes that they, after the present generation is gone, will live piously in Ebenezer. Her mother, who earnestly and seriously employs all means of Salvation, instructs her well in all that is good in Christianity and in the proper running of a household. The daughter is kept in strict discipline, which she will appreciate as a great benefit only later, once she has reached maturity and full reason.

Wednesday, March 25. During this time of the Passion we do not concern ourselves with texts from the Old Testament, but with the text of all texts, the gospel according to John. We study, section by section, the description of the bitter Passion and death of our most dearly beloved Savior and Christ who blesses us all. Our sermons Sunday mornings are also on this same topic; and, instead of the usual concluding and introductory verses, the regular gospel is used for our edification. Our merciful God grants me to feel His gracious aid most richly in this and He blesses my heart with this dear Gospel of man's reconciliation;

and I hope He will bless other hearts, too, so that they may clearly recognize their sins and His anger earned by such sinning as well as the precious reconciliation and redemption through Christ. May they learn to accept willingly the order of grace and salvation, in which sinners receive reconciliation, through the effects of the Holy Spirit's grace.

Thursday, March 26. Schäffler's three year old son, whom he begot in his marriage to the late widow Ernst, lay sick for a long time and has now died. God has sent much misery to Schäffler so far, but he recognizes that God has his best interest at heart.[12] At the funeral service we made good use of the fourth contemplation contained in the beautiful book by Senior Urlsperger for the sick and dying, which deals with being a good patient.[13] God allowed me to derive much benefit from this. It is a topic which is not only extremely timely just now during the Passion but also applies to the various sufferings and tribulations to which our community is subjected. A pious woman, who finds much edification and spiritual nourishment in this book, said to me recently that there were so many important thoughts contained in its observations, prayers, and songs that she wished all members of our community were familiar with this book.

Friday, March 27. This spring several men from our community tried again, on foot and on horseback, to bring back to our herd some cattle which ran off a few years ago into the lowlands behind Abercorn, which are densely overgrown with cane. As in previous attempts, they were completely unsuccessful again. These cattle, which ran wild, have increased in number significantly during the past thirteen years; and not only the Lord Trustees, but also our community and others who live in this colony and the district from Savannah to Mount Pleasant and who have lost some heads for some years can lay a claim to these unbranded cows, steers, and calves. Our people are harmed most by this because, when their cattle wander off into this area, it is either impossible or very difficult to bring them back again. The Lord Trustees and other rich people who own large herds do not feel the loss as keenly as we do. Others probably shoot a few head, which, however, is against the wishes of the authorities and against one's conscience, and which none of our people would do. Others own very good horses for rounding up their cattle; and we lack these also.

Monday, March 30. Old /Theobald/ Kieffer in Purysburg, who had lived with his family here in Ebenezer for some time, bought three Negroes, or black male slaves, motivated by desires mentioned in 1 Timothy 6:9. He had to incur debts for this purchase and suffered great loss from it, serving our people as a warning. One of the slaves drowned himself, another one died, and the third ran away in winter and the cold and wet afflicted his legs to such an extent that they will have to be amputated. Finally, he sold him for the price of a cow, but it also died. Because this Kiefer is so old and in such great need, his son, who is quite well-to-do and who is still living here, lent him some money in order to buy another Negro together with a woman; they work both on the plantation in Purysburg and also on his plantation across from us in Carolina.

These Negroes begot a boy; and father and son desire that I baptize the child, which they adopted and intend to raise as their own in a true Christian manner. The Negro, as father, would like to see this happen also. On the condition that old Kieffer and his son give their promise that the child would not change hands and that they would see to it that the child was raised as a Christian, I could not and wished not refuse Holy Baptism to the child. Since, however such a practice is somewhat unusual in our community, I instructed my listeners in our repetition hour yesterday; namely, that one may not deny baptism, the means to rebirth and the right to enter Christ's kingdom of grace to heathens or children of other disbelievers, when they come into the power of Christians and remain in such. I proved this by quoting Matthew 28:19: "Go ye therefore, and teach all nations, baptizing them in the name of the Father, and of the Son, and of the Holy Ghost." And further: "Teaching them to observe all things whatsoever I have commanded you."

I offered more proof from Genesis 17, where God commands that even purchased servants and their children be made part of the Holy Sacrament of Circumcision, and thus of God's covenant. I also mentioned what we were told by Saint Augustine how several pious and noble ladies bought small children from

heathens and disbelievers in order to lead them toward our
Lord Christ through Holy Baptism in their tender youth.

Just now we have frequent mention in Christ's Passion of how
our dear and precious Savior had suffered from Jews and heathens and thus had assumed mankind's sins. He reconciled the
whole world with God and earned for everyone God's kingdom
and all treasures of grace: and in accordance with His kindness
and wisdom He granted God's all-encompassing grace and love
and His own all-encompassing benefaction not only to adults,
but also to children through special means of grace, for example, Holy Baptism, which He Himself ordained. He calls out on
the cross, breathlessly: "Look unto me and be saved all ends of
the earth."

This morning, at the Jerusalem Church, the Act of Baptism
was celebrated solemnly. Our schoolchildren, and some other
people were present, as well as the father of the child, at his own
request. We proceeded, as we usually do among ourselves at children's baptismal ceremonies, according to the edifying ritual
prescribed by the London German Chapel.[14] Only this exception was made that the child was referred to as heathen child
when it was mentioned during the baptismal readings and
prayers. Likewise the baptismal witnesses, who, as proxies for
the child, abjure the devil, all his works, and his nature and confirm as representatives of the child its belief in God and the Holy
Trinity and its desire to be baptised in this faith, were addressed
as follows:

> This child shall not only at the present time but also later, when it
> has gained in years and reason, be guided towards the Lord
> through proper instruction; and, because its heathen parents are
> incapable of doing so, this charitable and Christian duty will de-
> volve upon you as its Christian baptismal witnesses. Therefore, I
> ask you before God whether or not you are willing, as long as you
> shall live and as much as possible before your own departure from
> this world, to see to it that this child, who is now to be baptized as
> you have asked, shall be raised in a Christian manner and shall be
> instructed from God's word to lead, by God's grace, such a life as is
> warranted by Holy Baptism. If this is your expressed will, an-
> swer clearly 'Yes'.

The baptismal witnesses were: Old Kieffer, his son, and Maria Kieffer, young Kieffer's wife. They agreed joyfully to aid this child on its path to eternal salvation inasmuch as God would grant them sufficient grace and wisdom. I prayed to God in church yesterday, and today before the baptism in Kieffer's house, that He may fulfill in this child what He had said in the parabel of the leaven regarding the nature of God's kingdom and its increase, which progressed secretely, unnoticed and often by humble tools, not unlike a discarded piece of leaven. Matthew 13:33. On this occasion I remembered the blessed Mr. Aaron in East India, whom God also turned into a blessed tool among his people.[15] There the following occurred to me: "Despise it not, for there is a blessing in it."

APRIL

Friday, April 3. Kogler from the sawmill told me that three Englishmen from Savannah arrived two days ago in order to have some work done at the mills and also to take a look at them at the same time. A short while ago they moved into this colony from Virginia, and their plantations are on the Ogeechy River. One of them is quite a skilled builder who is familiar with the construction of mills, and he commented on our mills and his knowledgeable and Christian opinion of them was highly complimentary. The same man mentioned that C**s,[1] together with another drifter, Fr. B*ck, and a German shoemaker, had shown up at his place in Virginia and that the three of them had traveled on to Pennsylvania. He had pretended to own several thousand acres of land near Savannah Town, for which he wanted German settlers. That was the reason, he said, that he was on his way to Germany via Pennsylvania. He had also told this man many good things about Ebenezer and our mills. May God cause this poor man to repent before His terrible judgment overtakes him.

Saturday, April 4. A wheatfield was shown to me on the land of the Salzburger Gschwandel; this wheat is the best that has been planted here so far. It is quite high, the stalks are strong, and the plants are starting to come into ear. Wheat on other fields by comparison is hardly more than one foot above the ground. Other crops look promising, also. Our people plant wheat and rye usually shortly before Christmas or a few days or weeks thereafter; because we don't get any snow here they are afraid that, if they did their sowing any earlier, the seeds and seedlings could be killed by one of the major frosts, which we do get.

Another consideration against sowing and planting during late fall was that their wheat might blossom and come into ear too early the following spring, when hard night frosts might damage or destroy the plants. Now, however, Gschwandel's wheat showed these fears to be unfounded. He sowed it at the end of August and, although it seemed that the extreme cold during the winter had destroyed it, the following spring showed that only its leaves were damaged superficially, but not the roots; to the contrary, it made the plants stronger in the spring. The ears did not sprout too early either; this is happening just now after all danger of frost has passed. One of the Salzburgers said to me: "In two matters are we to be punished: first that we refused to plant our wheat as General Oglethorpe had instructed us regarding the time of sowing; namely, at the end of August or the beginning of September (because he quoted from the *Columella*[2] that our wheat had to have *duos soles,* or two suns); and second, that we did not plant mulberry trees as he instructed and encouraged us. Now we can see the loss.

Sunday, April 5. After her husband's blessed departure from this world, widow Graniwetter has had to endure various hardships on her plantation, which, generally speaking, is otherwise in good order. Her two children are still small, a circumstance which makes fieldwork and regular attendance of public service difficult for her. This causes her considerable conflict and sadness. One of her hired help, a young boy who otherwise is a good worker, has been suffering from problems with his feet for the past two weeks. I am greatly troubled by her difficulties, as well as by those of other widows; and I hope that our all-powerful and merciful God will be mindful also of this beautiful promise of Christ: "If the poor man cries out unto me I shall hear him, for I am merciful."

Tuesday, April 7. I visited widow Graniwetter's hired lad on his sickbed. I quoted the little verse: "Call upon me in the day of trouble" and reminded him of his earlier misdeeds, lies, and other sins, which he will have to recognize and regret sincerely and for which he will have to ask our dear God's forgiveness in Christ's name. He will have to strengthen his faith if help for body and soul shall be forth coming. I also showed him how he could confide in God, simply, as others have done, confess the miseries of his body and soul, and await help patiently.

Widow Graniwetter told me that, in her tribulations, our dear Lord reminded her often and, seemingly directly from heaven, of the remarkable words which she recalled in her heart during sicknesses while fully aware of her sins: "I shall not forsake thee as long as ye remain faithful in your love unto me". She strives to understand this fully and asked me to guide her in her efforts to fulfill this duty of loving her Lord. She arrived at this conclusion: Since God has not deserted her so far in the tribulations of her soul and her conscience, which are much more severe than physical miseries, He would not desert her now in her present physical trouble and sadness. Some time ago, on the way to church, I had reminded her of this, and she had asked God to give her a sign in church and to instruct her in the meaning of these words, which were in her thoughts constantly, so that she could fulfill her duty in loving her Lord. To her great joy and edification, this has happened indeed, for in church we sang the song: *Sey getreu in deinem Leiden,* etc.[3]

Friday, April 10. This morning, at three o'clock, I left Savannah and arrived at Ebenezer healthy and happy at noon. On Wednesday, shortly before I left on this trip, I felt a fever coming on: however, our dear God let it take a benevolent course. In Savannah a short letter from Mr. Verelst was waiting for me. In it he notifies me that some time ago a large and a small chest arrived for us from Germany; both chests had been sent on to the governor in South Carolina. The chests were brought here by Kiefer's boat and delivered to me. There was no letter included, only a shipping notice. Our merciful God be thanked also for this blessing, which He sent to us in these lean times when clothing and other things become more and more expensive. However, I would have treasured a letter from our dear Fathers in Europe or from our esteemed friend, Mr. Albinus.

Saturday, April 11. The skillful and hard-working N. fell suddenly dangerously ill; and because Mr. /Ludwig/ Meyer, whom he usually consults, felt poorly himself, he was moved from his plantation to the orphanage. God affects this man's conscience deeply with sicknesses; he humbles himself before God, weeps and cries out to Christ for help. As several times before, he has the best intentions for the future: afterwards, however, he usually slides back into indolence and lack of faith. May God strengthen his heart this time right properly![4]

Sunday, April 12. Yesterday afternoon the two chests were brought into my house; and, since the lid of the smaller chest was broken in many places, I had it unpacked as soon as possible. It contained books which were given to our community probably by several benefactors from Switzerland. We plan to use those books in accordance with the praiseworthy intentions with which they were given if our dear God grants us sufficient wisdom and strength. Since our community is not lacking in good books, we will joyfully share this beautiful gift with other good people in this country, as we have done in the past. The aforementioned chest contained two kinds of books: namely, Part One of the catechistic *Childrens' Bible* by Pastor Abraham Kyburz, and a spiritual *Flower Garden* by an anonymous author.[5] There were thirty copies of the former and ninety-four of the latter.

It seems that a few books, before they reached our hands, had been pulled out by unkind people. There were two boy's shirts, made of strong handwoven linen, at the side of the chest to fill up the space. There was no inventory included; also, this chest of books was never mentioned in any of our letters from Europe. May God be praised for His goodness, through which He remembers us and blesses us. May He bless also our known and unknown benefactors abundantly!

Monday, April 13. We count, and most justifiably so, the large chest from Augsburg, which was unpacked today, among the blessings which our dear Savior earned for us on the Cross and which He bestowed on us so unexpectedly. It contained not only uncut white linen, bed, and table linen, a large and a small pillow, childrens' clothing, black and striped uncut linen and other useful things, but also beautiful books and treatises; we have much occasion to praise God for these gifts and to pray for our dear known and unknown benefactors, especially in these lean times.

The large chest and the one we unpacked yesterday had not been mentioned by anyone; we did hope that the chest from Halle, which was sent to Mr. Lemke and which, a year ago, was in the possession of dear Senior Urlsperger would be the first to reach us. We are still waiting for it; and we pray God that He may send us this chest as safely and as undamaged as He sent us these two chests. The Schauer's balm contained in the second chest and that which was sent in the chest from Augsburg is likewise a very pleasant gift.[6] God be praised for everything!

Tuesday, April 14. From Christ's Passion, John 19:23, we learned and were thereby instructed and consoled in these times of need that our dear Savior and Christ, who blesses us all, knew how those feel who are very poor and suffer the lack of clothes. Our Savior suffered and was tempted and, as a merciful high-priest, He can help those who are tempted so that they may follow His example and be patient, be content with what God sends them, be calm at His wishes, and put their trust in God despite of all they lack. Hebrews 2:13. In His greatest poverty He did not forget His dear, poor mother, a widow, but took care of her most lovingly, and directly through the services of His disciple, who loved Him and who was loved by Him. He is still steadfast, just, pious, and faithful into all eternity; and, while He is on the throne of joy, just as when He suffered disgrace, He is a loving friend to those who sin (as well as to widows and poor people).

He proved this again, as often in the past, at the beginning of this years's Passion Week because He awakened John and blessed loving people in Europe, especially in our dear Augsburg, people who, through His grace, come as His willing tools to the aid of our poor, especially of our widows and orphans, by sending their kind gifts in the aforementioned chests to us. In this sermon, I still remembered what we had read in church on Sunday, in sequence, from 1 Timothy 4 on the subject of Christian widows, about their good qualities, and about how to take care of them. I reread these lines aloud again on this occasion, and I commented upon the text for my listeners' benefit. It is a remarkable word of the Lord: Psalm 3, "Honor widows that are widows in deed."[7] They have prayed and hoped with me so far: now they will be full of joy together with us and they will be encouraged in the praise of God and in heartfelt intercession. Those among us whose hearts are filled with goodness will be joyous on account of our Lord's merciful care; and they will commend their own beloved ones to such a kind Lord in life and after death.

Wednesday, April 15. The esteemed Mr. Johann Brunnholz, whom we regard very highly, gave me much joy again by writing a short, but very lively, letter which was dated February the 24th. In it he mentions several letters which I had written to him in the past; from one of those he learned of the damage done to by the devious C**s with his cunning tricks and under the cover of God's name. He consoles me heartily, quoting Romans 8:28 and Psalms 37:39–40. He also gives us the pleasant news that from the last few letters from Europe, they again recognize the love of our Lord of the Harvest, for Pennsylvania, namely, that two righteous men, Mr. Thomson and Mr. Handschuh, who had been a laborer in Salfeld,[8] would be sent to aid His servants.

Dear Mr. Brunnholz is severely troubled by the heavy debts which he incurred through the construction of the two new churches in Philadelphia and Germantown. I know from experience how one feels who is in debt for the sake of his community. The construction of our mills, in which matter I was guided by the Lord Himself, after all, has put me deeply in debt. However, things will work out, even though so far neither I nor any other friends have been able to make the expected profits from the sawmill. The Lord's word keeps reminding me: "Cast not away therefore your confidence, which hath great recompense of reward.". But it takes patience, too.

Thursday, April 16. In both Jerusalem Church and Zion Church we held our annual sermon on Holy Communion, as is customary among us on this so-called Maunday Thursday. In the afternoon we had the pleasant task of sorting through the charitable gifts which had arrived so that tomorrow, as soon as possible, they can be distributed in an orderly fashion and without undue haste to our widows and orphans, poor people, our schoolmaster, and several people who have assisted our community, as well as to some widows in the neighborhood. May God strengthen our faith by this latest demonstration of His fatherly care; may He lead us all to repentance and may He reward our dear benefactors in Augsburg and elsewhere in this pilgrimage richly for this and other kindnesses.

Good Friday, April 17. God be praised! Today, as in every year, we celebrated with many blessings this day of the suffering and the death of our great Highpriest, solemnly as a day of reconciliation of the New Testament. At the same time, Holy Communion was given to sixty people. In my opinion, not all of the children who had been preparing themselves for Holy Communion were as ready as they should be in theory and practice, to receive Holy Communion: Therefore, I had to postpone their confirmation and admission to the Lord's Table. Just as last year, when our dear God granted us the joy of being able to distribute the edifying book by the blessed Ambrosius Wirth for Confession and Holy Communion to our entire community, so this year also we could partake of a similar joy.[9]

About thirty-nine people, our widows, orphans, and other dear persons, who had proved helpful to our community, received the charitable gifts which had arrived here at the beginning of Easter Week, namely, shirts, aprons, material for jackets and trousers, kelsch, bed linens, covers, childrens' clothing, headwear, tablecloths, etc.; and therefore we distributed those items with joy and praise of God after our afternoon services. All members of our community, old and young, received edifying books and treatises, among those also two well-bound Erfurt Bibles. Just as the two dear men, Joseph and Nicodemus, as we heard this afternoon in the description of Christ's burial, had wrapped the bare, holy body of Jesus out of love and faith for the Lord, our dear known and unknown benefactors did the same today for the destitute members of our community. May He let them hear these words of grace from His transfigured mouth: "Inasmuch as ye have done it unto one of the least of these my brethren, ye have done it unto me."

Under these circumstances, I find the 8th verse of the instructive song about Christ's burial especially impressive and blessed: *Als Gottes Lamm und Löwe entschlagen und verschieden,* and we benefit greatly from its example of Joseph and Nicodemus. Christ shall be honored now that He lies dead; we shall embalm and wrap Him and His poor limbs; and likewise, we shall clothe the naked and come to the aid of those who are forsaken.

Saturday, April 18. We have had no rain during the past few weeks: today, however, our merciful God refreshed our soil with it. Even in this we are strengthened in our hope that He will grant us various kinds of fruits of the field and a blessed harvest. May He allow us to accept His gifts and kindnesses with a humble, grateful, and obedient heart. May He never let us forget the dear price which our Lord Christ paid for our misuse of the gifts of God, which He gave to us for the purpose of our refreshment and daily sustenance; a fact which we pondered especially in yesterday's reading of the Passion.

Sunday and Monday, April 19 and 20. God showed us much grace in these two days; we celebrated Holy Easter with reading, singing, praying, and the public preaching of the Divine Word on the victorious resurrection of our Lord and Savior, Jesus Christ. At the conclusion of the festival all of us together praised our merciful God in the name of Jesus Christ in a public prayer hour; and we gave thanks for the great kindness which allowed us to enjoy the celebration in peace, solitude, good order, and pleasant weather.

Tuesday, April 21. Several people here are busy making silk, and the weather is very pleasant. So far we have not had any hot days: it is still tolerably warm during the days and tolerably cool at night. If it had been too hot during the time when the worms are about to start forming cocoons then there would not have been enough fresh air in the houses and rooms of our people; in other years the worms turned yellow and many died, very much to the disadvantage of the people. Today we sent our first silk to Savannah: I was told and shown this blessing, namely thirty-six pounds.

Wednesday, April 22. Our dear Mr. /Ludwig/ Meyer is suffering from various physical weaknesses; and, since his dear wife is also sick most of the time, he has a heavy cross to bear. May our merciful God strengthen him further. So far he was blessed and he has served our community in many cases very conscientiously with his beautiful gift and experience in the medical and surgical arts. He also used to instruct the children in our school each day for two hours; but now he thinks it necessary to stop the work at the school because his weak body would not be able to stand up any longer to such rigorous work. We and our community are indeed in need of his health and prolonged life; therefore we are quite willing to release him from his duties at the school as he requests. We wish most heartily for him to receive our Lord's blessing for his soul and body for now and all eternity and to recompense him for his work and his love for our children and other people. May God send us a well suited person for the position of schoolmaster in town for our children's benefit and also to help us with our various official duties.

Friday, April 24. The pious Mrs. N. had, for quite some time now, much to suffer from her husband, who was given to drinking. Today, however, she came to me at the Zion Church and thanked me formally for my efforts to stop this vice as well as the various unpleasantness resulting from it, in which matter God gave me his blessing. Her husband was a musician in Salzburg and he was a hard-drinking man in Germany, too, so that drinking became a habit with him. I expressed my joy concerning this outward change and gave him to understand that, if he would continue to conduct his life in an orderly manner and if I received sufficient proof of his change for the better, that I would be happy to contribute something to his food supplies and for his household.

Saturday, April 25. Yesterday afternoon our dear Father in heaven brought us a great joy. Major Horton not only wrote to me most kindly after a long period of silence and that is earnestly starting payment for his four hundred boards, barley, and other things he received from Ebenezer, but he also sent me a package of letters which had arrived for me from London. Mr. Verelst wrote me very kindly and assured me of his good will and assistance in our affairs as well as those of the Lord Trustees.

Dear Mr. von N.[10] received the silk which was sent off last summer, together with a small box of souvenirs. I was somewhat shocked, however, to learn that he had to pay the extra postage for the latter. In the future, I will have to arrange the sending of our packages better. The letters from our most esteemed Senior Urlsperger, dear Mr. Albinus, and Mr. von Reck pleased us especially; we have to praise our merciful God for those most heartily and humbly. Also, a noble personage wrote to me in such an edifying and loving manner that I consider myself quite unworthy of such a favor. Praised be the Lord for His eternal goodness which he shows to our Ebenezer and which can be seen readily from the manifold gifts of love which have accumulated in the keeping of dear Senior Urlsperger.

Mrs. Balthasar Bacher met me yesterday on the road between the plantations and town and thanked me for the blessing which God had sent her yesterday through His words in the Zion Church. She gave her best wishes to me, God's poor and most mortal tool. I pointed out to her, however, that all praise for the spiritual and physical benefactions which we derive through one of God's tools belongs to God alone. She is well content despite her poverty and various tribulations; she considers herself quite unworthy even of minor blessings because of her previous life of sin, especially her disobedience towards her parents. She wishes only that the Lord may continue to provide for her soul. She also said that, since we blessed her home with God's word, she could feel the Lord's grace keenly.

Sunday, April 26. The worthy Mr. N. did us a favor, among other things, in that he reported to us the sad, but important, news of the oppressed circumstances of the Protestants in N. and N. The matter was brought before His Majesty, the King of N. and the Prince of N.; and it seems, to the advantage of our persecuted brethren in faith. Yesterday, in our evening prayer hour, we benefited from this news, with God's grace; namely, first, in letting us know the spirit of persecution better and better; and, all of us, praise God with our hearts, with words, and with our conduct, for saving and protecting us from it, and, second, in letting us realize how much better off we are than our oppressed brethren in faith, since we live with God's Holy word, the Holy Sacraments, and well-ordered services in both churches. Both of our schools are well established, we live in total religious freedom, and we can act freely and according to our conscience. We can be well content with what God provided for us, and we remember what some of us once promised our dear God that we would be glad to live in extreme poverty if only we could live with God's pure word.

Third, we realize what great blessing it is that we Salzburgers had the freedom to emigrate, which others are not permitted to do, although they would have wished to leave, as we have heard several years ago; fourth, because of these sad tidings, we will most heartily and lastingly intercede for our oppressed and persecuted Evangelical Church. Also, we should be reminded not to misuse the priceless jewel of religious freedom and the freedom of conscience, as the ancient Israelites misused their manna and other great blessings, and in doing so be punished severely. Also, it is very important that we are not affected here by various schisms and disputes within our religion.

Monday, April 27. The captain of the fort or stronghold Mount Pleasant sent his Indian serf to me with a letter in which he asks for wheels made by our wheelwright. Frequently I have to waste time with such minor requests from other places, and such letters of unimportant content have to be answered, too. I can not afford to be short with strangers' requests because such people could easily turn into enemies of our community. But, if those people do not get what they want exactly as they want it, then I am involved in unpleasantness. I try to deal with everybody, present or not, lovingly and with friendliness; and I disregard complaints. Our few craftsmen, such as shoemakers, wheelwrights, coopers, etc. can hardly keep up with the needs of our own community, let alone requests from others. After all, in addition to their craft, they also have to be farmers and tend to their fields and stock. There are too few craftsmen and farmers in our colony, and too many in Pennsylvania.

Tuesday, April 28. A very strong and very cold wind came on with the new moon, and it dried out even more the dessicated soil. If it were not so late in the spring, then this wind would bring us, as has happened in previous years, a severe frost, which would have damaged the young plants in our fields and gardens and the leaves of our mulberry trees. God knows what is best for us! This shall always be our motto: "Whatever God wishes, that shall be my pleasure."[11]

Wednesday, April 29. The people in Germany are told quite clearly, before they are admitted as colonists for Georgia, that farming and raising stock are the foremost occupations in Ebenezer. A few, after living here for a while and after accepting support from the Lord Trustees and our community, become unwilling to continue with the work to which they are not much used: so they sell their plantation and their animals and other things they have gained here and use this money to finance their move to Pennsylvania, which shows how ungrateful these people are and how they disregard God, His blessings, His care and His provisions.[12]

It should be made a rule that only farmers and craftsmen could come here. It drained the financial resources of the Lord Trustees significantly that, when this colony was founded and for a few years following, Englishmen and Frenchmen, who were either bad craftsmen, bad merchants, drifters, or ignorant of farming and also lacking the will, strength, or ability to work hard, were sent here, supplied for several years with food, and aided in building up their herds and establishing their farms. Those people accepted support willingly enough, but worked little or not at all in return. As a result, they finally fell into poverty and gave this area a bad reputation by leaving or writing letters of complaint. Also, the finances of the Lord Trustees were such that it became impossible to aid those of the emigrants who worked steadily and hard.

Soon, some arrived who planned to establish plantations such as they existed in the Carolinas and wanted to work their land either with laborers whom they had brought with them or employed here, but paying them the same amount of money as was paid to Negroes. The workers, however, either died, or ran away, or were set free; and such settlers got poorer instead of richer. They came to the conclusion that the land could not be worked except with Negroes; but it never had been the intention of the Lord Trustees that this border colony should be turned into an opportunity for such plantation owners, but rather a refuge for poor, hard-working people who would eat their bread by the sweat of their brow.[13] Colonies do exist in America within the English territory where Negroes are allowed, and so our area could well be spared this. It is also a great shame that our community has lost all the children who were born here in the beginning and who would be by now twelve or thirteen years old and could be of some help to their parents in many ways, all died.[14]

Thursday, April 30. Brückner, a Salzburger, has been suffering for several years now from various physical afflictions. However, since both he and his wife fear God in their heart, they learned the truth of the saying: "They who fear the Lord shall not want any good thing." Although the husband is not able to do any hard work at all, they nevertheless do not complain of their poverty, rather, they praise the Lord for blessing their household. Today I gave them some advice on how to improve their diet and certain other things, which they took as a sign that God had heard their prayers, since they had asked His advice in just these things and had been content to leave matters in His care. It is quite to their advantage that, a few years ago, they planted white mulberry trees. Making silk is an easy and pleasant work for them, which this time is going to bring them at least two pounds Sterling profit. On one of the roads at the plantations I met a young girl who was carrying a little box to town on her head. It contained twelve pounds silk, and she herself had done most of the necessary work.

MAY

Friday, May 1. Today Public Court was held in Savannah, as is customary every quarter. Since Col. Stephens wanted me to come for various reasons, I made the trip in our large boat, in God's name. I shall stay here through Sunday to preach and to hold Holy Communion for the German people of our faith here, if God will give me the necessary grace and strength. I had to take our large boat this time in order to make it easier and less expensive for our people to bring their silk to town. Last week thirty-six pounds were sent; then another one hundred-seventy-two pounds raw silk, which had been cleaned carefully of the woolly fibers which the worms produce at first, were transported in my boat to Savannah so that the Lord Trustees could dispose of it. May God be praised for this great blessing! How pleased the Lord Trustees, our kind authority in this country, would be, if all cultivated land and plantations had made a start in silk production, which proves to be so useful.

Many Germans live around Savannah, especially in two places: Acton and Vernonburg. But I did not hear that they planted mulberry trees or intended to start manufacturing silk. At the moment, the Lord Trustees pay for one pound raw silk: (which is two ounces less in weight than the German pound);[1] a woman by herself or an older girl could, if there were enough trees nearby, easily process forty to fifty pounds raw silk; which, after all, is a sizable profit. However, most people are too lazy to do it! It is a pity that we do not have more mulberry trees in Ebenezer.

Saturday, May 2. Today, I traveled with a guide to visit German settlers on the White Bluff, called Vernonburg.[2] There, the people from Vernonburg, others from neighboring districts, and even some men and women, feeble from sickness, gathered, willing and eager to listen to the words of grace which I preached on a short, but very important text: "Peace be with you." God gave His blessing to these souls, who were as hungry for God's grace as dried out earth is for a refreshing shower of rain. I noticed this both during my sermon from their tears as well as later from their own testimony. In Savannah I prepared some of the people who live here and others from near-by plantations for Holy Communion and confession, using as text the 23rd Psalm. To my joy I heard that the older population, for whom I had carried out my office for several years, abandoned their old prejudice and dislike of me, as if I had been too hard on them in my preaching, and feel now all the more love for me.

Sunday, May 3. Many Germans are physically weak and will not be able to come to town in order to listen to my preaching and to take part in Holy Communion: They have asked me, therefore, to give my sermon and to hold Holy Communion in the village Acton, which lies between Savannah and Vernonburg. I was most willing to oblige them and travelled there in the morning with a guide, as soon as was possible; several Germans from town had arrived there, also. I chose the beginning verses of the 23rd Psalm for my introduction: "The Lord is my shepherd." For my text I used the beautiful gospel passages: John 10–12 ff. about Jesus Christ, our good shepherd, and I made good use of this welcome opportunity to preach on the goodness which flows into us poor sinners through Christ's threefold office of intercession and through which we are drawn towards Him, so that each and everyone can say from his own experience: "Lord! It is good to be here." It was, however, not easy to give a sermon in the assembly house we were in, a former barn, and it was not really a proper place for holding Holy Communion; however, our dear God gave me the strength to conduct the services in good order and to the edification of everyone present.

A young preacher, Mr. Zübli, was also there; he and his family showed me much loving care.[3] He held a sermon and prayer meeting one hour after our services had concluded. I was asked for good books several times by Reformed people and members of our faith; I gave them some, and I plan to send some more in the near future. Some items they wanted, I do not have, for instance, *Bibles*, Arndt's *Christianity*, or the *Treasure Chest*.[4] God clearly blessed them in what good books I had given to them as presents in previous years and which they had exchanged among each other.

In the evening the people from town gathered for a prayer hour; we made good use of the beautiful song: *Ihr armen Sünder kommt zu Hause etc.*, which impresses upon us who we are, who Christ is, and which is the right path to Him and salvation.

Monday, May 4. Already on Friday, I had taken care, to the best advantage of our community, of the matters that required conferring with the President and other members of the Council.[5] Therefore I was able to leave Savannah early this morning, around nine o'clock. Wind and water were fine, and I reached home healthy and happy under God's guidance, together with Mr. /Ludwig/ Meyer, via Habercorn (or, as it is actually pronounced by the English, Abercorn).[6] My dear colleague, his family, and mine, we all, to our mutual delight, are healthy; and our community's affairs are in good order.

Mr. Verelst's last letter to President Col. Stephens had the pleasant effect that he and other council members were quite willing, 1) to deliver to our people who arrived with the last transport all pigs and chickens or poultry that we have not yet received; 2) to reimburse one of my friends in Savannah for the money I had borrowed from him for last year's silk; 3) Also, they promised to pay as soon as possible for this year's silk. I requested their assistance also in another matter and found them willing and helpful. They plan to continue with the construction of their church this year; and they intend to buy from our sawmill the boards necessary for the inside panelling, the flooring, and for their pews. No firm order was placed, however.

Wednesday, May 6. We have not had any rain for quite some time now, the soil is therefore rather dried out. In some of the fields the wheat is starting to turn rusty; the same thing happened two years ago, and it is doing considerable damage to our poor farmers. However, plenty of rain must have fallen elsewhere, because water level of the river first rose quickly, and then fell again quickly. Clouds formed several times and thunder could be heard, but it did not rain here. The Lord will give us all in His good time; and, since we turn to Him in our need, He will no doubt give to us what is good and beneficial. The weather is fine for the barley harvest though; our barley is now being cut and brought in. The miller told me that last week and this week he milled new barley for Eigel, who had run out of flour for baking bread, and that the flour had been of very good quality.

Thursday, May 7. This morning our miraculous and merciful God consoled me in my distress, namely, that I wish I could aid our poor, hard-working, and pious people with advice and assistance, but can not. I took heart unexpectedly upon reading from Schinmeier's *Treasure Chest*[7] and I became quite hopeful again that, after enduring our tribulations, all will be well with

us here in Ebenezer. The dear words which gave me such blessing are contained in the aforementioned booklet, namely, in
Part One, p. 150; Matthew 7:7–8: "Ask and it shall be given you;
seek, and ye shall find; knock, and it shall be opened unto you."

It would not be surprising, and it should well be, that a Christian pray to God and not forsake Him, since He so graciously
listens and speaks to us without interruption and says, "Ask, see,
knock," Oh, if we were only so diligent in praying (at least with
sighs from the heart as God is in inciting, alluring, commanding, promising, and compelling us to prayer. Alas, we are too
lazy and ungrateful. May God forgive us and strengthen our
faith, Amen!

The wheat of some of our farmers, which was planted before
Christmas, is turning rusty, and the wheat grains are staying
small; our people call that "mildew." Gschwandel's wheat,
however, which, as I mentioned earlier, was planted early in the
fall, stands better than any other wheat crop in our area has ever
done before. All the ears were full of grain before the great heat
and drought set in; now it will be ready for harvesting soon. This
is beginning to convince our farmers that the wheat is not being
ruined by either the soil, climate, weather, or (as they think) by
poisonous dew, but mostly by untimely planting and the lack of
proper care for the fields.

The same is true, I think, of our fields of Indian corn, which
were planted by plow in the little pine forest and which are
weeded regularly; it stands very well while other fields on very
rich clay soil, which were planted by hoe because of the numerous branches and roots, are almost completely dried out.
This obvious experience, which we could observe now over several years, will shame those who used to say bad things about the
pine forest and sinned thereby. A few farmers got some *Veesen* or
spelt and planted them with their wheat. They have not yet come
into ear and probably will also have to be planted in the fall,
which, however, will not be possible this year. Our Fathers,
friends, and benefactors have to be informed about everything
here so that they may use this knowledge to their advantage before God and men. Therefore I see no reason not to include
these things in my diary.

Friday, May 8. This afternoon several of our people were paid again thirteen pounds, nine shillings, and one and one-half pence for silk which they had sent to Savannah; altogether one hundred-thirty-four pounds and nine ounces. This money also was distributed under prayers and the praise of God. Two young girls have been very busy since yesterday in spinning some of the silk in order to gain more practice and experience in this useful skill; the machine which was put up on our farm last year is well suited for this task. This year, compared to last year, the spinning of the silk is being accomplished much quicker and more successfully; the person who tried it first last year is getting especially good at it.

Saturday, May 9. By coincidence I learned that certain married couples and neighbors are not at peace with each other; therefore their prayers, Christianity, and daily progress in their households suffer. God does not bless disorder; and sin, where it is rampant, is (not only is going to, but really already is) in a very real sense people's undoing. We had a hearty talk; I pointed out to them that outward manifestations of sinning are signs of an evil inward attitude and explained to them the necessity of a genuine change of heart. I also made some suggestions as to how they should behave towards each other, according to God's will and the command of His Word, if they should partake of the three beautiful things, which please God and people well: Sirach 25:1–2. They took it all well.

Tuesday, May 12. A German good-for-nothing from Vernonburg, who had taken service in the fortress at Savannah Town, abandoning his wife and children, came to me. He told me of his bad luck and of his miraculous salvation by God. According to him, he had obtained permission to visit his family and got lost in the woods for a few days. Finally, an Indian gave him a boat, in which he intended to come here: however, dangerous currents in the river brought him to a spot where several accidents had happened in the past; he was caught in the thick branches of a tree, which jutted out of the water, and had to spend eight days there, unable to either reach the bank or to free his boat, living off a few pieces of biscuit. He would have perished if God had not arranged it for some men from our community to come along there yesterday in order to collect honey from certain trees; they freed him with great effort and danger to them all and brought him here. He left today and joined a party going down to Savannah. This man was at first Catholic, then half Reformed; then he joined the Herrnhuters. Finally he turned towards our church, used the means of salvation diligently, and led an orderly life. Afterwards he went to Charleston together with a German shoemaker and enlisted in the army for three years.

Wednesday, May 13. It still pleases God Almighty to keep the heavens shut and closed so that rain can not fall. Thunder could be heard in the distance A few times and clouds formed so that we hoped for rain; but the wind drove the clouds away again each time. We implore our merciful God in this time of great drought to water our furrows, to wet our plowed land, to make it soft with rain, and to bless our plants. Our dear people will have a poor wheat harvest this year. Because of the ongoing drought, just as two years ago, the stalks turned rusty, and the wheat grains themselves stayed very small. We don't know yet how our rye and other European crops will turn out. The barley stands well: but people did not plant as much of it as last year. People were worried that what had happened earlier might repeat itself; namely, that late frosts killed most of their barley.

This spring plenty of Indian corn was planted by plow; in these fields the plows are also used to cultivate the soil and to keep it free from weeds; the ground is well suited for this and only one horse is necessary for such work. Indian corn, as well as beans and squash, usually grow very well; nor is as much time for harvesting and thrashing needed as is for European crops. For these reasons our people will most likely start to prefer these crops; especially since they realize that planting and weeding by plow is much easier, quicker, and more advantageous than using the hoe, which our people used mainly in the beginning. It must have rained heavily at other places, because the water level of our river, which was quite low, is starting to rise again.

Thursday, May 14. An English woman in our neighborhood asked to have her daughter instructed in reading and other things and wanted to board her with us for that reason. The good people have no idea how busy we are; for that reason I cannot instruct even my own children in English and other things as thoroughly as I might wish. We could use an English schoolmaster with a talent for teaching and a Christian heart: so that by and by all our people and our youngsters could learn the English language well. If anything here has to be written in English, and there are many such trifling matters, people come to me with it; the same happens when something written in English arrives here or if Englishmen come to us; this increases my duties a great deal. But I do not complain about this, because our dear God gives us strength and aids us in all things.

My dear colleague, who assists me willingly in many things, will be in charge of the mills from now on, managing them and doing the accounts. This eases my workload somewhat. Things do work out by people working together, after all. If only our dear God could send us a righteous schoolmaster who likes children and who could instruct them well and also keep the right balance between school and work. If the children have to spend too much time going to school, they cannot help their parents with their work as is necessary, and this would cause problems, since people here have no servants. They have other opportunities also, to obtain a sound foundation in their Christianity, namely, through sermons and reading their catechism, as well as weekly preachings and prayer hours, in which a good deal of catechism is taught. We have in our public meetings our sheep and our lambs always before us. The older children also receive more instruction while they are preparing themselves for Holy Communion.

Friday, May 15. After the weekly sermon in Zion Church young /Georg/ Meyer's wife had someone ask me to come and see her in order to talk about her present spiritual condition, which she did under many tears. It pleases our dear Savior to bow her down mightily under His cross; this, however, as she knows from experience, is for her own good, for her soul's salvation. A short time ago He assured her through His word and spirit anew and most emphatically of His precious grace and the hope for everlasting life; but at the same time He wanted to prepare her for more grief and tribulations.

At my previous visit I had left her with the beautiful words: "But I am poor and needy; yet the Lord thinketh upon me: thou art my help and my deliverer." Psalms 40. Our dear God blessed these words for her and consoled her; for that reason I had to go over them again. Her mistakes are making her wise. Another young woman told me also that the cross of her marriage is more beneficial to her than the previous good days.

Our dear God has given me not only the strength and the time, but also the means to write a few long, but hopefully not useless, letters to the esteemed Mr. von N. and to a few others of our dear known and unknown benefactors in Europe: I put them together into a package with letters to S. U.[8] and Doctor Francke, as well as a letter to Mr. Verelst. I also included in this package a little box containing white and yellow spun silk, so that Mr. Harris can send all this to London.

Sunday, May 17. This morning, as well as last Thursday, God refreshed our soil with such rain as we had been wishing for. Our people are working with eagerness and devotion for themselves and their neighbors; and it is a great joy for me and a source of praise for God when I see how they work not in vain, so it seems, but rather thrive under God's blessing. The rain did not deter them from coming to our public services, in which our loving God granted us much edification.

A young woman from Salzburg, who loves our Lord Jesus with all her heart, was rather hard on her young neighbors after learning that something was amiss in their household. Although she meant well and tried to move them to seeing and acknowledging their wrong and to repent before God, she set in her words and gestures no good example either for these young people, who had come to her in a neighborly and right Christian frame of mind, or for their parents, either. I could not condone her behavior, because it is against the example and blessed teaching of our Lord Jesus Christ, who praises those who are peaceful and those who make peace with others and who admonishes His apostles as follows: "Keep peace with all men"; also, this exhortation applies: "Let your light so shine before men," etc.

What the blessed Friend of Man said in seriousness and

friendliness to the two, who got carried away although they also thought they had the right on their side, is written down in Luke 9:55–56 in order to instruct us. After these dear people realized their mistake, there were many tears and much praying; and our dear Father in heaven answered their prayers so that all ended for the best and in Christian peace between her and the two aforementioned neighbors, as she reported to me yesterday with great joy and praise of God. She learned her lesson also from the blessed Luther's exegesis of today's epistle James 1:19–21.

Tuesday, May 19. This year God gave his special blessing to silkmaking, and therefore our people have been encouraged to devote their time to this useful enterprise. Today the last batch silk was delivered for spinning and I wrote down the entire amount we made: Four hundred and thirty pounds. We sold three hundred and sixty-six pounds and seven ounces to the Lord Trustees' silk filature in Savannah for thirty-six pounds twelve shillings and ten and one-half pence Sterling. We kept sixty-three pounds and nine ounces here for spinning, and we will soon finish with it. The silk which was spun by two young women here is of varying quality because it had been intended to experiment with different methods of spinning in order to gain more experience. However, the quality of the silk balls which people received towards the end of the silkmaking was not the best, at least not as good as the first balls we made. Therefore, spinning off those proved more difficult; but, in our opinion, our spun silk turned out quite well and we hope that the Lord Trustees, to whom it will be sent, will be pleased. Also, as I had requested several times in the past, I hope that they will indicate to us blemishes in this silk and advise us as to improving the quality.

Some silk strands consist of eight to ten threads, some however of four threads, and we shall see which will be preferred. Out of lack of experience as well as of better opportunity, our people produced some doubled silk: two or even three worms were spun in one ball, which does not give them any profit but causes loss for our buyers. Because this kind of silk is not only coarse and impure, it is also difficult to spin and takes probably twice as much time to do as pure silk would take. Our spinning women have to gain experience in this also, and this silk as well was sent to the Lord Trustees for their evaluation. Silk worms are almost like sheep in that everything about them is useful.

In addition to the silk, very fine wool can be made from the material with which they cover their ball-shaped cocoons, and what is left after the spinning of that as the most coarse and of least quality can also be used instead of flax. The dead worms left in the containers are high grade chicken and duck feed, and there is plenty of them. Even the withered leaves and stalks left over from the worm's feed, together with their droppings, supplies us with an excellent fertilizer for our gardens. During the last fourteen days alone, when the worms consume a great quantity of leaves day and night, this amounts to several large baskets and bags for people who make about fifty or sixty pounds of silk.

Last year the worms were killed by baking them in ovens, because they could not be spun off in time; this year however, those silkballs, where the worms were made to bite through, were placed on slate roofs at noon and left there for about three hours. After they were taken down they were put in empty barrels and covered very tightly, so that the worms suffocated quickly, even when they were protected by thick, double-layered silkballs. This is a much safer method to kill the worms and leave the silk undamaged than by baking the silkballs in ovens, as is done in Savannah. This area is in every respect extremely suitable for silkmaking, and our people regret it now that they did not all follow the repeated advice to plant mulberry trees. This is probably true for a few other things, too. What people were not used to seeing done and doing in their native country, they did not want to trouble themselves with here, which was their loss.

Wednesday, May 20. Some time ago a shipment of charitable gifts arrived from Halle for us, and we had the pleasure of experiencing our heavenly Father's merciful care for us in this time of need and to praise humbly His goodness, which we do not deserve at all. Our loving Father in heaven gave us such joy through these gifts of love which he sent into the hands of Senior Urlsperger. We took heart and were consoled and strengthened not only because of these considerable gifts for our community's different needs, but also because of the heartfelt and moving good wishes and the encouragement which were sent along at the same time. We shall use everything according to our most esteemed benefactors' wishes and suggestions; for which task I pray to God for wisdom. May He accept our poor thanksgiving for this recent and special demonstration of His fatherly care in the name of Christ; may He answer our prayers for our esteemed known and unknown benefactors and reward them richly in this life and the next for all their gifts which they shower on Ebenezer.

Our most esteemed benefactors do not ask to receive any gratitude for their abundant gifts of love. Therefore they send their gifts to Augsburg and Halle without mentioning their names, which, however are well known to God. Nevertheless, frequently I wished, when I received their gifts, to thank them through a public letter of thanksgiving in my name and that of our community and to express to them, simply, and with an open heart, our wishes to God for His invaluable goodness on their behalf, as we are in the habit of doing. I was however unable to express myself to them properly, and not because of a lack of means but rather out of lack of ability and enterprise. Now, however, I have attempted it, and I intend to include in this package a simple, but well-meaning letter of gratitude and to send it to all of our most esteemed known and unknown benefactors in Europe, may our Lord bless them in His unending goodness!

Thursday, May 21. I went through the thorough and edifying *Compendium of the Entire Christian Dogma,* using the method of questions and answers, with the children on the plantations who are preparing themselves for Holy Communion.[9] Our dear God assisted me insofar that I was able to finish at the beginning of this week. Our merciful God strengthened me in body and spirit for this task, which is so dear and useful to me and which I carry out for the older children and a few apprentices every Tuesday and Friday two hours before my weekly sermon. I have much cause to praise the Lord for His goodness, which I do not deserve at all.

The older children understood well the theoretical and practical truths of God's word, after being taught the aforementioned material; and God allowed me to observe some of the fruits of my labor, both while I was teaching and later from the behavior of some of the children. They are all willing enough; their lives are well ordered, and they use the means of salvation eagerly both publicly and privately.

One of the boys, who had come up from Savannah,[10] gave me much joy by his eagerness, attention, careful rereading, his prayers and pious conduct, as well as his affection for God fearing people and his eagerness in seeking their company. At holy Whitsuntide I hope to admit those children to confirmation and Holy Communion. A few gifted children from town will attend, too; these come to my house four times a week for instruction to prepare themselves and are also taught the aforementioned material. For the time being I will review all articles of faith with the children on the plantations summarily. In town, however, between now and Whitsuntide, with God's help, I will continue to preach as much as possible on the blessings of grace, the means of grace, and the order of grace.

Friday, May 22. At the beginning of this week I wrote a letter to the Council in Savannah. In it, I asked for the speedy payment for our silk, for the surveying of the fertile land located on the Mill River towards Abercorn and across the Ebenezer River which was donated to us, and for the culling of a herd of wild cattle in a low-lying area. Also, in Mr. Lemke's name, I inquired whether or not it was true that Germans had to serve longer than the three years stipulated in their contracts? Our esteemed friend, Mr. Albinus, wanted to know that because German servants, through Mr. Driessler, had complained about their contracts being broken. A friend to whom I had sent my letter so that he could deliver it personally wrote to me that the Members of the Council were meeting in Savannah, and that, if I came quickly, they could answer my letter right away. Therefore I traveled there immediately but found yesterday that they no longer were together for their meeting.

The President, Col. Stephens, had written a letter to me and sent it via Old-Ebenezer, so that I received it only on my way back. In it he writes that he presented my letter to the Council and that the Members wanted to discuss the various points raised in it before Captain Thomson left; however, since they could not discuss the details of my letter in my absence, they requested me to come to a meeting on Monday. After I delivered to my friend in Savannah the little box with our spun silk, together with the letters to Mr. Verelst, I and my Salzburger companion prepared to travel back and we arrived this morning around 8 o'clock at Zion Church, so that I can still teach school today, hold the usual weekly sermon, and baptize a child, which was born to Mrs. Hässler this morning.

On my way down I had been in some danger in the small boat (since taking the larger boat is more expensive and I do not wish to burden our community), for a strong wind was blowing towards us and night had fallen. Normally this wide stretch of the river is dangerous even without such difficulties. However, God aided us and, by combining our efforts, we reached the other side without mishap and were able to praise God's protecting and blessing goodness. Because of the wind and the dark we did not want to proceed any further, and for a while we could not find a proper spot for landing the boat or finding a convenient shelter for the night. Finally, we reached a house where I bedded down on the hard floor and my companion stayed in the boat until daybreak. I slept on the floor with all my clothes on, with part of a chair and my traveling hat for a pillow, and, under my Savior's wings of grace I slept so soundly and well as the emigrant Jacob on his journey, Genesis 28.

Saturday, May 23. From morning to sundown the heat is great; and, because it did not rain as much around Savannah as it did here, their crops are said to have almost completely dried up. Praised be the Lord that He aided us insofar that we were able to harvest already two crops: 1. our silk, which brought our people forty-six pounds Sterling in cash, which I paid out to them already from an advance made to me by a merchant; 2. our European crops, namely, barley, peas, rye, and wheat; this bounty from God is just now being harvested, although on some fields the cutting makes only slow headway because the farmers lack help with the work. We hope to harvest Indian corn, beans, rice, potatoes, and squash at the beginning of fall; towards winter the beets will be dug up.

This country has many advantages over others; it is to be hoped that it will be settled with Christian people who will eat their bread in the fear of God and by the sweat of their brow. There are many malcontents in this country and a few even in our settlement; may God make them repent, before His judgment and severe punishments overtake them.[11] We work faithfully and by God's grace with such people among us: however, some remain lazy and indifferent, despite the use of the means of salvation, Revelation 3:16.

At the moment, we are still contemplating the eighth chapter from 1 Kings and we learned in our last prayer sessions as well as in our weekly sermon from vv. 46–51 that God finds it necessary to work various kinds of judgment even for those who, according to their outward confession, are part of His people and members of the true church. Among those, the spiritual judgments are the most dangerous, because they are the most difficult to recognize. 2)[12] That the cause for such judgments and of perdition is none other than sin itself, which arouses the wrath of God and finally moves His justice and truth to fulfill His fulmination. Sin is the downfall of people.

How little, however, do those who are careless and deem themselves safe among us also recognize sin in its ugliness and perniciousness: even though we try hard to remain aware of it by being mindful of instructive Biblical verses, noteworthy examples, and especially of the mirror of Christ's inward and outward suffering. We remember those expressly in order to convince people and instill in them a beneficial awe, remorse, and shame; and we seek refuge in Christ, our sole Helper. In these times of need, if people here suffer from sicknesses, poverty, and lack of physical nourishment, then they complain about the hard times, and they are not content either with this country, or the authorities, or with themselves.

However, these people do not better their circumstances by such behavior; rather, they fall deeper into sin and invite God's punishments. Therefore, 3) we show them further from the cited work what God's intention is in sending them punishments, judgments, and tribulations; namely, a. that they may accept these as the bitter fruits of their sins; b. that they may mend

their ways, Jeremiah 1:3; c. that they seek forgiveness for their
sins from the blood of the Intercessor by humble prayers; d. that
they ask humbly for a lessening, and even averting of their
punishments; e. that they remind our dear God humbly of the
convenant of grace entered into at Holy Baptism, and try to live
according to it and to remember gratefully His great deeds
which He worked for the sake of our salvation and protection, to
His praise, to the strengthening of our faith, and for the faithful
hope that He will not forsake us in our present plight.

O! May our dear listeners follow this and similar guidance
from our living God's true word: how easy it would be then for
our merciful God, who prefers life and goodness, to free us
from all punishments and tribulations and to give us His manifold blessings, since we have so many dear intercessors and willing benefactors in England, Germany, and outside of Germany.
Some people among us, because of their unrepenting hearts and
their restless minds, which crave change, desire to move to other
places, which, they are told, are easier for the flesh than
Ebenezer. Some men (like S. S.), could not even find themselves
better provided for at other places; yet they seek change nevertheless. My eyes, however, are directed towards the Lord in all
things.

Sunday, May 24. Today I received a letter from Mrs. Driessler
from Frederica, which contained, among other things, these
words: "Our Germans are moving away one by one, because we
have no pastor here. O! You won't believe what a pity it is; on
Sundays we don't even have a prayer meeting, not to mention a
sermon, neither in English nor in German."[13]

Monday, May 25. Major Horton recently increased the
monthly pay of our seven rangers, or town militia, from fifteen
to thirty shillings Sterling: and I suspected that they would,
from now on, have to spend more hours on duty and that therefore their fieldwork would suffer. To my great joy however, he
wrote to me that he would not change the arrangements made
by General Oglethorpe: so that their fieldwork and the running
of their farms will not be hindered any worse than before. The
difference is only that, from now on, each man has to maintain
his own horse, saddle, and musket. In previous years they had

gotten horses and equipment from Frederica, but they had not been well supplied, and they rather prefer to have their own horses. God be praised for this new manifestation of His fatherly care for our community! I regard this advantageous solution a merciful answer to the prayers of the faithful men and women among us. It just now came to my attention that they commended this change, which had taken place, to God's merciful ways, even at the risk of damage to their own households. That the rangers consist of members of our community, is very useful for them, me, and our entire settlement.

Tuesday, May 26. Since I was asked by the Members of the Council to appear before them yesterday afternoon in order to discuss certain necessary details, I traveled yesterday morning via Abercorn to Savannah; and, after we had concluded our business, I returned early this morning at daybreak from Savannah so that I arrived back home again at 12 o'clock noon. Some people in Savannah are unwilling to accept the fact that on some occasions I spend only a few hours, or, as few hours as necessary, there. This is interpreted by some people, who do not know any better, as misanthrophy or dislike of Englishmen. People who are better informed, however, who have sufficient insight into my affairs and duties assess the situation differently. I can not burden even my friends there with a prolonged stay: otherwise it would be very expensive to stay in Savannah, which my income does not permit.

The President and the other Members of the Council resolved the following in response to my letter: 1. That the money for the silk we delivered and which was spun here should be paid to me now; this comes to 43 pounds Sterling. Our poor attempts to improve our silk manufacture, with God's blessing, and my own inadequate suggestions to the Lord Trustees, led to this good result, that not only our people, but also others, will receive cash payments for their silk. 2. Our people received permission to kill off gradually the wild cattle which roam the lowlands around Abercorn and our cowpen; especially wild bulls or bullocks shall be attended to first. 3. The land across Ebenezer Creek can not be surveyed before peace is declared. Another very fertile piece of land along the Mill River towards Abercorn is under consideration; the Council is not yet certain whether it should be turned into a plantation for the benefit of the entire community, or for that of a preacher and schoolmaster in Ebenezer, or for me and my family. 4. Concerning the question whether the Germans who arrived last will be held to the contract they signed in London and will be required to serve three and not four years, I was advised to write to London myself and explain this matter. I am insisting, modestly but seriously, that the chest sent from Halle, which was addressed as per shipping notice to N. N., who has not undertaken anything in this matter, will be sent on to us. I shall see now whether or not some progress will be made in this matter: thereafter I will report the state of affairs in a letter to England.

Wednesday, May 27. This month we did not have a shoolmaster for the school in town, since Mr. Meyer had to stop his work there. My dear colleague, Mr. Lemke, took over all duties at the school during this time and I was unable to assist him in this, as much as I wanted to, because of my many obligations within and without our community. Now we thought of /Georg/ the brother of the surgeon, Mr. Meyer. He has the ability to be a schoolmaster in Ebenezer, and he will become even more suitable if he puts into action what I told him today regarding two verses: "Every good gift and every perfect gift is from above," etc., likewise, "If any of you lack wisdom," etc. He is willing to take on the schoolmaster's job for the period of half a year so that we may be able to judge whether or not is well suited to teach the children. May God give us His blessing!

Thursday, May 28. Today we commemorated the Ascension of Christ, our Mediator and our Savior; and the entire community assembled at Jerusalem Church for that purpose. In town, the weather was dry, but on their way back it rained; however, nobody, whose soul benefited from today's preaching of God's word and who, like us, waited for a fruitful downpour eagerly after the long drought, will complain about that. God be thanked for His spiritual and material blessings!

Friday, May 29. I am rather looking forward to a profitable trade in boards until we can also do business with other kinds of wood products, such as barrel staves, hoops, shingles, etc. Although all of our dear people here have enough to eat, some lack clothes for themselves and their children. All clothing, from shoes to hats, is so expensive here that our dear friends will hardly be able to believe it and a poor man has a hard time of it buying even a few shirts which, even if made of the poorest quality and coarsest linen, cost over four shillings Sterling, that is almost two Reichsthaler. If they all could work their fields with horses, instead using hoes only, then they would have more time to earn some money in other ways. As it is, however, many lack horses (although they have plows, or could get them from me) and any opportunity to earn money: therefore their lack of clothes is even getting worse. As much as I would dearly like to help people improve their situation, I am not in a position to do so, since I am still in debt because of the mills and the congregation. Our people regret it now that they planted neither mulberry trees nor flax; both of which would ease their lot.

Last winter I ordered about ten to twelve bushels of flax seed from New York and Pennsylvania; but it was only a few weeks ago that one barrelfull arrived in Savannah, which cannot be sown this summer. What seeds of flax and hemp we did have and sowed stand very well in our gardens, although we were without rain for a long time this spring. We could weave more linen, cotton, and wool, but we have so few people here, and there is so much other work to do. People always complain about too few doing the spinning. However, since during the summer the noon hour and during the fall, winter, and spring some time in the mornings and evenings could be used for such work, even if it were only one hour each day, I do not understand why every householder, if he had some spun yarn, could not have some material woven each year. "Commit thy way unto the Lord; trust also," etc.

Saturday, May 30. As soon as Mr. Thilo moved into his new house, his wife gave birth to a healthy and beautiful little girl.

Sunday, May 31. Yesterday our miraculous Lord took quite unexpectedly Ruprecht Eischberger's older, ten-year old daughter to Him through temporal death. We, who knew her, were saddened by this, but also filled with joy because she died in Christ and her soul is now in God's hand. She had a pious heart, and she did not bear the other schoolchildren's disobedience but admonished them with deeds and words. Her favorite occupations were praying, contemplating God's Word, and singing. She enjoyed going to school and to church, and she learned with great eagerness the introductory verses for both Zion Church and Jerusalem Church. She considered her ministers to be servants of God, showed them affection, and prayed for them regularly.[14] Whoever could hear her, how naively, lovingly, and trustingly she used her own words to speak to God, her Father, in Christ's name, was edified. She helped her infirm parents in running the household to the best of her ability and aided them also in spiritual matters right up to the end, which came swiftly after only twelve hours. On Friday she was still at school and in church: towards evening she felt a chill, then a great heat and stinging sensation, which tired her out quickly; and, suffering thus, she died in the same paroxysm. Her eyes were directed upwards, toward heaven; during all this; and at the very beginning of her attack she said to her two little siblings, who had misbehaved: "Be quiet, I shall go to my heavenly Father soon." She almost always had an ailing body and never had a healthy color.

JUNE

Monday, June 1. Schoolmaster Kocher is well blessed with a good harvest, and another is ripening in his field. Because he did not have enough room in his old quarters, he had a comfortable little clapboard house built, which was dedicated today with God's Word, song, and prayer, as he had requested. I spoke on the consoling words 2 Corinthians 1:3–4 and demonstrated in a simple way: 1) what God is to us fallen sinners; 2) how He behaves towards His servants and children; 3) how they ought to behave towards God and each other. These beautiful words fitted in well with both the contents of yesterday's gospel passage Exaudi Sunday and also with our present time of being tested and of suffering.

A saddened widow confided in me her wish that I may assist her in a certain matter with her neighbors, who are otherwise quite pious and kind. I did so this afternoon willingly and with good success. Before I left her, I recommended to her to turn to God and prayer in all her affairs and difficult circumstances. I assured her, quoting God's word, that God would send her His counsel and assistance shortly; she ran back into her small room and brought me a torn, printed piece of paper, which she showed me with joy and said she had found it today, on her way back from my house, lying in the road, and when she looked at it, she found God's consoling words on both pages: "I will never leave thee, nor forsake thee" and her faith was strengthened greatly, because it also said: "The Lord hath said," etc.

Tuesday, June 2. Last week, young /Georg/ Mayer attended a meeting to be instructed and to learn the method of teaching, which we introduced here. Yesterday he started work in the school in town. He was introduced to the children, together with the necessary remarks, and a communal prayer was sent to God to ask for his success in tending school. May God bless this new undertaking to His glory and to the chilren's benefit!

Wednesday, June 3. Recently, Mrs. N.'s dangerous paroxysms, which she sees as the signs of her impending death, have recurred. She is preparing herself well for her blessed journey and praises our heavenly Father tearfully, and with all her heart, so that He may guide her, knowing that her days of well-being and health will not be as useful. She is of good cheer and holds her most beloved Savior in the highest esteem. The faith in His name is her formost care and endeavor. Her previous sins, which are of a certain kind, weigh heavily on her; and she has to fight hard, protected by prayer and gospel, so as not to fall again into legalism and fearfulness.[1] Her love for God's word, Holy Communion, and prayer is so great that I would be hard pressed to think of another such example. She brings much benefit to her household, her godchildren and to the entire community (I don't want to mention others) by her prayers: therefore I regard it as a blessing from God that she is still alive and among us. Her prayers are quite childlike, compelling, and edifying.

In the last chest from Augsburg, in addition to the aforementioned three shirts for three orphaned sisters living in Frederica, there arrived also three shirts for an Englishman, who gave lodging to a Salzburger. I wanted to set these aside, until instructions would arrive from our most esteemed Senior Urlsperger, since I had written to him recently in this matter. However, I gave them to three poor Salzburgers, as I was moved and compelled by compassionate love and pity for them; two are true Christians, and the third is a hard-working and goodhearted man, who well deserves compassion. I can assure our dear benefactors that this their gift for the praise of the Lord and for the comfort of Christ's poor limbs, was used (also, even if one of the men is not a true Christian, his wife and his two small children are; and the husband can become a true Christian yet through God's goodness, which may lead him to penitence). These men surely will intercede most heartily for their benefactors and the other pious members of their household will meet this obligation likewise.

Thursday, June 4. Recently, a German of our confession wrote a letter from Charleston to my dear colleague, Mr. Lemke. In it, he is asked to come and hold Holy Communion. Nine months ago he had gone there and performed his office to the best of his ability and without any complaint. However, due to the cunning, meanness, and fraud of K**,[2] this journey cost him so much money, that he will feel its effect for a long time in his household accounts, unless our dear Lord sends some little money above and beyond his salary his way in order to make up for the loss. At the moment, I myself am not in a position to assist him and give him more money than his share of the sum which our dear Lord sent into Senior Urlsperger's hands for the both of us, in accordance with the instructions accompanying the received consignment. The aforementioned man requests also a Bible, Arndt's *True Christianity,* and a songbook. In this, however, we cannot oblige him any more than any of the others who wish the same. Our older children who are to be confirmed in the near future lack also Bibles and songbooks.

Sunday and Monday, June 7 and June 8 were the Holy Whitsunday Celebration. On the first day of the Holy Whitsunday Celebration, Holy Communion was held with seventy-eight people, among them eleven children: namely, six boys and five girls. They are being allowed to the Lord's Table for the first time now after thorough preparation, public examination, renewal of the convenant of baptism, and the act of confirmation. Our dear God gave His blessing to this important step, which adults and children took before His countenance; and He caused much good in them, as is clearly visible from various external signs and indications: for this we must praise His goodness.

In examining the children, I made allowances for our present circumstances, and elaborated on an important article of faith, which is unknown to many Christians: namely the nature and office of the Holy Ghost. As a model for my instruction I used the beautiful *Compendium Theologicum*[3] by the late Pastor Freylinghausen, a work on which I also rely in my preparation hours both for teaching as well as for recognizing the truth leading to blessedness in God. We are living in a country where all sorts of sects and hawkers of strange beliefs thrive, and some places are full of them. For this reason we take great care to instruct our children, especially the older ones, thoroughly, simply, and naively, in the entire Christian dogma.

We guide our pupils patiently so that they themselves may recognize the existence of divine truth, either theoretically or practically. This enables them to to base their faith not merely on human teachings but on God's true word, and they will not come to believe this or that just because they were so taught by their parents, schoolmasters, or teachers. Most of our children benefitted well from this kind of instruction and gave me much joy through their Christian conduct, in school and otherwise. I hope that, by His word, the Holy Ghost laid a sound foundation of true Christianity in them. I hope further that they will demonstrate this in the future by reaping the rewards of blessedness in God and praising God, by edifying their community, and by redeeming themselves.

Those present were cautioned in a friendly manner not to judge a child whom they may have known before, prematurely; by doing so, a great many people fall in error or at least upset themselves and, in this manner deprive themselves of the blessing of their edification.

Shortly before confession, a pious man sent me a note as follows:

"Friendly greetings to Your Worship. I can not express my feelings because of the two children. My heart is heavy. May the Lord grant us His assistance; I will not stand in the way, because I might be afflicted with culpable ignorance. May the Lord bless you, and strengthen the children with His Spirit."

The youngest girl[4] has the reputation of being well brought up and conducting herself in a proper Christian manner. She has a thorough knowledge of our Christian teachings and has edified many with her fine answers in Church. Neither is her older sister lacking in knowledge. Her conduct, however, was not in keeping with Christ's teaching. She improved considerably after going into service with a Christian woman from Salzburg and she now shows much good will and promise. If I had refused to accept her for Confirmation and denied her taking part in Holy Communion, then more damage than good would have been done. Also, our next Confirmation for children is a full year away (since many are still very young) and she would have had to wait a long time to partake of Holy Communion.

In addition to the aforementioned cautioning of the listeners against premature judgments, I reminded all to lead those children towards goodness by watching them, guiding them, praying for them, and admonishing them both with words and with a good example as well as by protecting them from all such company which could damage them. Quite a few of the forty-one children whom I confirmed during the past thirteen years here would have been the better for it if they had not kept bad company. Counting this year's six boys and five girls, fifty-two children have been prepared thoroughly for Holy Communion and were confirmed publicly.

As I usually enter in my diary the names and background of our children who, after Confirmation, were admitted to Holy Communion for the first time, I will continue doing so this time. It is but a small task for me and might be of some use after all.

1. Johann Georg Heinrich, twenty years of age, from the Duchy of Wurttemberg. His father was a righteous man and died in our settlement. God granted him his wish: namely that

all his children be brought to Ebenezer (which he thought to be a great benefaction), including this young man who had served several years at Fort Augusta and after that with our Col. Stephens. His four fine, Christian sisters live here also.

2. Johann Christoph Krämer, an orphan from the Palatinate, twenty-one years of age. His parents died in Savannah a few years ago. His sister, who had married a local man, died in child birth. He was, like young Heinrich, not very knowledgeable. However, God worked His ways in both of them. They were in service with the same master.

3. Adrian Krüsy, eighteen years of age, a young man of fine natural talents and good promise. His father was from Switzerland but died recently. He had charged me with the spiritual and physical care of this one dear son whom he managed to get to us (his wife and other children are still living in Appenzell). He is apprenticed to our skillful master-builder, Kogler.

4. Johann Adam Treutlen, fourteen years of age, the son of a widow in Vernonburg. He arrived together with the last German people and is in service here. He is a pious and good-natured child, and applied himself to Christian teaching with thoroughness and joy in his heart. It was difficult to get him here, because of his mother; but, once he did join us, he liked it all the better.[5]

5. Johann Georg Schneider, twenty years of age, the oldest son of our aforementioned cowherd. He has a good nature; however, his parents are not taking as good care of him as they should as far as spiritual matters are concerned.

6. Georg Kocher, fifteen years of age, the son of our schoolmaster on the plantations, who was confirmed with great emotion and received Holy Communion.

7. Gertrud Klocker, sixteen years of age, and

8. Eva Klocker, fourteen years of age, both orphans and children of quite pious parents who died a few years ago. Their brother, Paul Klocker, died some time ago, at the age of four, also a pious child. Both girls are good workers and quite knowledgeable in domestic matters. They are in service with two families from Salzburg.

9. Gertraud Kurtz, seventeen years of age, and

10. Eleonora Kurtz, fourteen years of age, both orphans, the children of a righteous widow, who is living in my house, and a pious man from Salzburg,[6] who died a few years ago at his plantation and who was survived by three girls. The oldest of these died a few months ago in my house, filled with consolation and hope for life eternal. She left her two sisters, who are good-natured and love Jesus dearly, and also her mother, well-blessed.

11. Katharina Dorothea Arnsdorf, fourteen years of age, a fine young girl. Her stepfather, mother, and three siblings are living here.

Mrs. N., whom I surprised a few days ago in the middle of a quarrel with her husband and in an angry frame of mind, came to me on the first of the holidays, shortly before our repetition hour. She assured me, in many emotional words and quite tearfully, of her remorse at what had happened. She was among the first children who had been taught and confirmed here. Being reminded of this and of her own faithlessness and her sliding back into sin on the occasion of the children's confirmation, she claimed that she had been unable to attend church this morning because of grief, disquiet, and tears. She is truly reconciled with her husband and has asked his forgiveness for her mistakes; and she prays to God in all seriousness that He may not act according to her sins, that He may not banish her from His countenance, but that He may give her salutary penitence to better herself. She regained some faith and the hope that even her thirsty soul could be blessed with grace and consolation from the two precious evangelical verses which Mr. Lemke had chosen for his introductory verses and text on the first holiday in the afternoon: Revelations 21: 6 and John 7: 37–38.

Tuesday, June 9. Major Horton, the commanding officer in Frederica, arrived in Savannah, travelling on land via Fort Argyle. From there he wrote a friendly letter to me, as he usually does, in which he assures me of his affection, of his willingness to be of service to me, and of his efforts to locate our chest from Halle which was not delivered to us. He also sent a letter of credit for sixty-one pounds ten shillings Sterling in payment for some boards he got from us, a horse, barley, horsebells, and a boat. Although I myself will receive for our community's fund only twenty-six pounds and a few shillings of this sum (with which I will be able to pay off some debts), I am pleased that several members of our community will be getting some money, of which we are usually short. Only recently, widow Driessler praised the Major's good will and assistance; now he wrote to me on her behalf as follows: "I have written to Dr. Burton and asked him to see to it that our regimental chaplain try to obtain an annual pension for Mrs. Driessler, our late chaplain's widow, from either the Society, or the Lord Trustees of this colony, or from what source he thinks best." I hope that she will secure such a pension.

The president and the other members of the council replied to my letter which I had sent to them before the holidays, that they are willing to pay, upon my request, to the fourth transport the money for the still outstanding pigs and chickens. That means fourteen shillings Sterling for each family, which is a great blessing for the poor. Our friend, Mr. Habersham, writes me that a certain captain, who is sailing to to the West Indies in a small craft, bought four thousand feet of the boards we have in storage in Savannah. He (Mr. Habersham) intends to countersign for the payment; otherwise I would not have agreed to the deal, which I made sure to mention in my recent letter to him. God be praised for those beautiful manifestations of His paternal care for us in these hard times! Also, He will surely hold His hand over us in this dangerous matter: namely, the Indians up in the countryside, who normally are our friends, are engaged in a very dangerous war among themselves. Allegedly, they also threatened to drive those people off their plantations at the Ogeechy River, who settled higher than the tidal mark.[7] Our Savannah River was not mentioned. Major Horton is trying hard to pacify them, and he will have to use force if he does not succeed.

Wednesday, June 10. The children who were allowed to take Holy Communion on the first day of the Holy Whitsunday Celebration still come to me for instruction each week: those in town for four hours and those on the plantations for two hours. I review some of the material, which we covered already, and I also teach what is still left in the *Compendium*,[8] and also teach what still has to be explained.

Friday, June 12. I paid a visit to Ruprecht Eischberger, who is ailing, and his wife. Both parents are still filled with grief over the severe loss they suffered by the death of their pious and good-natured child, who was a great help to the sickly parents not only in spiritual matters with prayer, intercession, reading aloud, quoting God's word, giving a beautiful example of a most dear love for Christ, patience and sweet disposition, as well as of an abhorrence of all evil, but also in material things, working in the house and kitchen, attending to matters outside the house and helping raise two young siblings.

When her mother fell ill during the wheat harvest, she brought her the necessary medicine quickly, and after that she knelt down in a corner and prayed to God simply and with heartfelt emotion for His blessing, imploring Him to heal her mother, whom she could not bear to lose, and added: "O my dear Heavenly Father! If it be Thy will to take one of us, let it be me, for we need our mother more," etc. At the wheat harvest she also had expressed her disapproval of such people who complained of mildew or rust, which damaged much wheat. She said: it all came from God, and people ought to be content; we were not worthy of what God gave us and we should thank Him most heartily, etc. The two younger children, four and seven years old, feel their dear sister's parting as well and grieve for her; the youngest[9] used to say: "I miss Katharina so much, if I am pious and work hard, I will come to her."

Saturday, June 13. N. has made considerable progress with regards to his constant anger in his present marriage. Last week he also promised me to make an effort to improve his conduct and not give me cause for sadness any more, but his good intentions were of only brief duration. Yesterday evening he got angry at something (I do not know what) and made his wife suffer for it although she had nothing to do with it. Then he fell ill suddenly, complaining of pains in his side and coughing hard. He became afraid of dying then and sent for me urgently. When I arrived, he was ashamed of his ill temper, regretted it much, and cried about it. He prays God He may not yet take him from this world and cast him into the perdition which he so richly deserves for his poor conduct in the past and present as well as because of his latest unworthy taking of Holy Communion. I hope it will be possible for him to be saved like a firebrand plucked from the burning, since he does not try to defend himself by blaming others but rather feels that his evil ways burden his conscience and prays to Christ eagerly. However, the contrary is true in the case of poor N., and I am filled with sadness.

Monday, June 15. Included in our shipment of the charitable gifts from Augsburg is half a guilder, sent by the Salzburger Madleitner for his fellow countryman in Ebenezer. The name of the recipient was not mentioned, but I found out soon that it was George Glaner from Memmingen and I sent the money to him immediately.[10] He told me the secret of why this Madleitner did not mention the name of his fellow countryman and why he had sent such a small gift so far. Rumors were spread in N. that the reports they received from Ebenezer were not true. If, however, the half guilder of the anonymous fellow countryman were to reach the right hands, then he (Glaner) should write back, report truthfully his own circumstances, and mention the gift. In this way, he (Madleitner) would be assured that the letter was genuine and written by no other than Glaner.[11]

Glaner told me that God had blessed him richly especially in this year both spiritually and physically and he would report back with pleasure. He also intended to write as follows: "Even if the cost for the journey back to Germany from Ebenezer were not to exceed the value of the gift he had received he would have no desire to leave." This Glaner is living comfortably on his well-run plantation, although God burdened him with a cross: his wife has been very sickly for some time and came close to death several times. Also, he has two widows as neighbors and spends considerable time on their behalf; their cattle gave him quite some trouble and he had to neglect some of his own work. I will gladly try to reward him for this as much as God allows me to.

Wednesday, June 17. There was such an unexpected and unusual storm on our plantations, as we never before had experienced: wind, rain, and hail. It lasted for half an hour. In town there was a little rain, but no wind. This storm did great damage to our Indian corn which stood well in bloom. On one poor man's plantation below the mill so many stalks were torn off that a large wagon could have been filled with them. Many trees were uprooted and some people were afraid for their houses. In some places, the ground was covered with an inch (the thickness of a thumb) of hail. No injuries of people or animals were reported, though. Our miraculous Lord visits us in many a way; may He let all turn out for the best!

Thursday, June 18. Mr. Habersham, a merchant in Savannah, wrote to me that he intended to go to Charleston and, if possible, wanted to discuss a few things with me. He also informed me (Major Horton had written me the same thing) that the king had given orders to dismiss all additional troops which, up to now, had served in the border fortifications and on reconnaisance boats either as soldiers or as rangers, which had caused a great deal of expense to the king. The regiment stationed in Frederica is to be increased in numbers and will supply the regular soldiers which are to man the border fortifications. The nineteen thousand pounds Sterling, which used to go to the additional troops annually, will be used, it is expected, to improve the conditions of this colony. This change also has the advantage that young men have no longer an opportunity to live a loose life at the fortifications, or on the reconnaisance boats. Rather, they will earn their living in a better way by useful work. Maybe it will be easier from now on to find fieldhands for hire.[12] Those who wish to become soldiers in Frederica have to contract their services for seven years, and they have to be content with a daily pay of six pence. In addition to that they are obligated to work in the fields to contribute to their rations. These conditions will be to the liking of only a few.

Friday, June 19. Tonight I returned from my journey in good health and I thank God for His merciful assistance. I received the money for the fourth transport, which Col. Stephens had paid out to me for the pigs and poultry donated by the Lord Trustees. Each family will receive fourteen shillings Sterling, which is another sign of God's paternal care for us. If only all were to use this money for the purpose of awakening and strengthening their faith!

Saturday, June 20. On my return journey from Savannah I

called on Joseph Watson, the Englishman. I borrowed his diary
from him, which he had offered to lend me earlier. In it, he describes his expedition of 1741 to the Cherokee Indians in great
detail and reports some strange things about the topography of
the countryside, the Indian way of life, Cherokee customs and
superstitions, as well as his own business with them, for example,
his preaching and baptizing. His handwriting is hard to read
and I had to make many guesses as to the meaning. Also, I do
not trust the author's professed reactions, and therefore I am
less inclined now to take the time and the trouble to translate the
diary than I had been some time ago before I got to see what it
was like. He is a Manichean, or comes very close to their evil doctrine, and adheres to dangerous teachings. Among the Indians
along the Mississippi he met a man called Christian Priber from
Upper Saxony, a man with a degree in jurisprudence and he describes in his beliefs, conduct, ethics, and dress as being of such a
kind that he is despised by even the Indians for it.[13]

Sunday, June 21. Recently we had much rain and several severe thunderstorms, which, however, our merciful Lord, as always, let pass without harming us. During today's evening
prayer meeting it started to rain heavily, under thunder and
lightening, and the rain continued long into the night. We hear
that there has been very little rain in Carolina for the past four
or five months.

Tuesday, June 23. This morning, on the plantations, I finished
reviewing the entire Christian dogma as presented in the late
Pastor Freylinghausen's *Compendium.*[14] I heartily praise the
Lord, who has given me strength and His assistance so far. A boy
who is in service with a Salzburger thanked me, with tears, for
the instruction he had received. God's word, which this young
boy accepted eagerly and repeated frequently, did much good in
him. If he cherishes what he has received, he might prove to be a
useful tool for the glory of God in the future and be of service to
his fellow men. He has fine talents and would be suited for
studying, if he were free to do so and if he had the opportunity.
However, God has need of faithful and clever people in everyday life also.[15]

Thursday, June 25. This month we had much rain, especially

during the past eight days. In spite of that, the waterlevel in our
river and at the mill is low. This indicates that in the mountains,
in Creek and Cherokee territory, only a little rain fell, otherwise
we would soon see the effects on the Savannah River. But more
water is to be expected; and, in order to be prepared, I am having the waterway of the first millrun repaired by our carpenters.
Its bottom has rotted away and then the boards which form the
canal or waterway fell apart. All wood on or above the ground
rots very quickly here. A few days ago I observed some damage
on our Jerusalem Church which is built of planed lumber and
which had been well and carefully joined. If I had been able to
obtain oil paint, I could have had both churches painted and
then the rain and humidity would have done less damage.

Sunday, June 27. Our rangers, or town soldiers, have been
very useful to me, on instructions from General Oglethorpe. I
was able to rely on their services on behalf of our community, in
transporting my letters; and, when traveling to Savannah I did
not need to trouble our people. Since they will be dismissed, together with other additional troops, I am forced to hire a servant
who will take care of such business until the Lord Trustees undertake to lessen my burden and make some changes. I do not
wish to impose on any members of our community, since they
have enough troubles of their own. Most of them do not have
servants and they have their hands more than full with taking
care of their fields and household chores. Before our rangers
were stationed here, we had all sorts of difficulties with vagrants
and riff-raff living in our woods. At night they came out and
stole things and probably shot some pigs. Afterwards, we were
not distrurbed by either Negroes nor other runaways.

I believe that God will protect us in the future even if it may
seem that we are unable to take protective measures ourselves.
In our evening prayer hour we hear from 1 Kings 8:56 that Solomon counts peace among the most noble divine benefactions
for which we must praise our dear Lord even if we have to suffer
from various other tribulations. This great benefaction which
we received here in our community without fail during these
dangerous times of war has not been appreciated properly by
all, and now we have been reminded of this our duty. In the En-

glish diary of Captain Watson, which I mentioned recently, I read that the Cherokees threatened to attack Ebenezer because General Oglethorpe did not compensate them to their satisfaction for their help at St. Augustine and for their dead. But God did not allow that. It was and still is said: "The Lord God is a sun and shield: the Lord will give grace and glory: no good thing shall he withhold from them that walk uprightly. Oh Lord of hosts, blessed is the man that trusteth in thee."

Sunday, June 28. Our merciful God blessed us with much goodness again this last Sunday and we praise Him humbly for it. Reading the second article of faith fitted in beautifully with the text of today's gospel for the second Sunday after Trinity. We contemplated the examples of divine mercy, of human meanness, and of divine retribution. This was also the topic of our introductory verses Psalms 81:11–13.

Monday, June 29. N. has been punished by God. She is extremely weak after giving birth. This, however, is for the best as far as her soul is concerned. She is good-tempered, enjoys God's Word and the quiet. She would, hopefully, make good progress in her Christianity if only she had a faithful helper for this in her husband. He is not a spiritually minded man and quite far from a righteous life in Christ. In this man's neigborhood there are some other such unequally minded couples. The wife is very pious, and Maria confided in me some good things, too. But she suffers greatly from her husband, who is hard, angry, and stubborn. Now and then she comes to see me and asks me for instruction and consolation. Usually she returns home with a lighter heart. A true Christian must not be complacent in the face of outward and inward sufferings, but must, before all, praise God. He should know that nothing happens by accident but rather that all comes from His beloved hands and is intended to serve us best. The most severe cross we have to bear makes us most like our Lord Jesus.

Tuesday, June 30. Because of the money for the milling and other things which are being sold and bought here, we are in constant need of small coins. The shopkeepers in Savannah need the few English half pence, the Spanish three and six pence for making change and therefore hold on to them. We lack small coin, and Spanish shillings and pieces of eight are mostly circulated. Our small bills for one, two, four, and six pence had the disadvantage that shopkeepers and other people in Savannah and Purysburg accepted and circulated them also. This led to the result that those, too, became scarce here. Some were torn, and we finally were forced to withdraw them again. Now necessity gave us the idea that instead of bills only checks from the mill account, in our saw-miller's name, Kogler, may be used, and only in Ebenezer. We hope that this will solve many difficulties.

JULY

Wednesday, July 1. Ruprecht Kalcher, a Salzburger, denying his own needs and out of a true love of God and our children, served as the father of our orphanage with great faithfulness from the very beginning, and he was unable to start a plantation for himself and his children. The one he had drawn by lot went to two other hard-working men, namely, the late Graniwetter and Bartholomäus Rieser's son. Now God has given him a plantation quite near town. He can use a plow on it right away, because the people who live on the plantations donated their gardens north of town to him. These gardens were planted before the plantations got started, but then the people on the plantations did not need them any more since they had cleared enough land on their plantations. So the gardens were neglected and the land went to waste. These gardens will now be converted into a plantation and Kalcher will be the new owner.

I myself was present when the people from the plantations were asked for the land, and I was glad to see that no persuasion was necessary (Kalcher, in keeping with the Tenth Commandment and observing God's will, would not have accepted the land otherwise), but they gave him their gardens quite willingly and they wish him well in his new undertaking. There are more unused gardens near town. Bushes and trees grow wild there and I wish that their owners would also be that willing to convert them into a plantation. I also wanted a change regarding the building plots in town. Each consists of only one eighth of an acre and is ninety feet long and sixty feet wide. That is a small piece of land. If a house that is not too small is to be built on it, and further a kitchen, a cellar and a well house, a stable for animals and a chicken coop, then there is hardly any room left to plant a house garden or to raise some fruit trees. Mulberry trees thrive best around the houses, and this is also convenient for taking care of the silkworms. For these reasons I was of the opinion that all building plots should be of a larger size. I may direct this request to the Lord Trustees, since all members of our community are unanimous in this matter. There is still time to make the necessary changes easily.

Thursday, July 2. This year, those of the farmers in our settlement who own horses and plows are not only working their fields easily but also accomplishing a great deal with little effort. This makes the poor wish for horses very much. As long as they have only hoes for field tools, their health is being eroded and they become poorer and poorer and have to go into debt. This does some considerable damage to their Christianity. They begged of me urgently that I should help them find horses or mares at low prices, as I have done in the past for others. I would gladly do so if only I could. However, since the purchase of some horses could do so much good in our community, I will have to attempt to borrow some money. Yesterday, I had to write an important letter to our Court Preacher, Ziegenhagen, in which I brought up this point.

Today I am going to write to Pennsylvania again to our friends there, requesting some spelt and *Feesen*[1]. Our farmers prefer these because they think that it should not be threshed during the summer heat and also that the kernels inside the husks do not get damaged as easily as wheat. Threshing is made difficult and unpleasant not only because of other work for our Indian corn, beans, and potatoes, but also by the great heat in June and July. Still, it has to be undertaken immediately after the harvest or otherwise the kernels will be damaged by worms or small flies. Afterwards, wheat stored in barrels or sacks stacked one on top of another (and probably also in the silos) gets hot and everyone hurries to the mill as fast as they can. We can see this now; people from Purysburg, Frenchmen, and Germans, who have finished threshing their European wheat, are coming to our mill by boat. Since our people need very little threshing, they can be accomodated quickly. If one only knew how to preserve European grains, such as wheat and rye, either in the straw or the kernels themselves a little longer!

It amazes me to think of the wagons and oxen at threshing time among the Jews and other peoples. It seems they threshed their wheat and other kinds of grain immediately after the harvest. Did they do this, like us, out of necessity, or for other reasons? I do not know. It occurs to me that I read about the late Master Seinler in Halle, that he invented a machine for threshing which could do the work of five men. I think, however, if this machine were of advantage, that the orphanage in Halle would use it in their threshing. However, I have neither heard nor read about anything like that happening. Last winter, one of our farmers sowed some spelts together with his regular wheat, but nothing came of it because it was too late in the year.

Friday, July 3. Widow Graniwetter, probably due to the hard work she did in the fields with the hoe, has fallen dangerously ill. When I visited her yesterday she was quite peaceful and content on her sickbed. She praised the goodness of the Lord, who had given her the gift of peace of mind and body. She regards this as a sample of eternal peace which she dearly desires. She is not worried on account of her two small children; she believes that God will take care of them, just as He has of all the other orphans here as well as of three orphans from Abercorn. They will stay with two Christian families and will be better taken care of regarding their soul and body than by their own parents, who had lived in ignorance and quarreled often. If it pleases our dear God to send us more means, then we will bring about even better conditions for assisting widows and orphans among us.

The misery of many children in this country saddens me greatly. However, I can do nothing to save them, since I cannot do all I wish even for my own community. But even the poorest among us have cause to praise God for His mercy. Mr. Mayer had gone to Savannah for some time. When he returned he brought the sad news that a fine and honorable German man who had been in service with Mr. Thilo's in-law had lost his life unexpectedly in the river, with his wife and other people, among them Mr. Mayer, on the enbankment looking on. He wanted to save a pig which had fallen out of a boat, fell out of his own boat, and could not be saved. His body was not recovered. Probably a large crocodile, which was only a few feet away from the drowned man, dragged his body into the deep. His name was Jakob Weissenbacher and he is said to have been a skillful and hard-working tailor.[2]

Monday, July 6. This year people in Carolina feared for their harvests because their was no rain for a long time. Indian corn, which usually costs more or less one shilling Sterling in Carolina, rose to two shillings and ten pence. I did hear, however, that in some places, where the rain did fall in time, the crops (grain, beans, and rice among them) are recovering quickly. One man, whose plantation lies at the Ogeechy River told me that, due to the lack of rain so far, he does not expect his harvest to sell for more than five shillings. Therefore, we have special cause to thank our dear Lord for His benefaction of the good weather. Our fields and gardens are in such a fine condition as one might wish. I think that this year so much Indian corn has been planted here as never before. God has given plows to several of our farmers, which is a great blessing in many ways in this hot but fertile country.

Tuesday, July 7. Today, soon after we left for Savannah, there was a great thunderstorm. The strong rain got us wet almost to the skin. There are not many places on the way to Savannah either by land or by water where one might find shelter from the rain or an opportunity to dry off, one has to be patient almost until Savannah. One sits in an open boat where the rainwater collects quickly, and gets one's head wet from above and one's feet from below, especially since the local boats are such tubs. If it pleased God to improve our situation here, then I would like to be able to make my frequent journeys on behalf of our community in a little more comfort. I am somewhat afraid in boats which rock so much, especially at night. At times there are trees, branches, and pieces of wood in the river, and even the parts of the river which are wider are dangerous in the wind. However, I can not change these things, because it would mean a larger expense to take a larger boat with a larger crew. I myself can not afford it, and neither can I burden the poor members of our community to man a larger boat without pay, although my trips are on their behalf.

Wednesday, July 8. So far, God has given me sufficient health and strength. I do not attend to the duties of my office only, but see to many other tasks, although they are necessary also. Because of this, I have been in a quandry in the past on several occasions. My desire to learn one of the Indian language is still strong. Who knows what good it might do one day? At the beginning of this month I wrote a letter outlining various improvements for our area and community, and how a Christian man trained in the law or a merchant could contribute further. However, this time I did not get an opportunity to sent this letter to Charleston.

Thursday, July 9. After I had taken care of the business I had with the members of the City Council on behalf of our community, I started on my journey back again this morning. Bichler, our constable, had a court case pending involving someone in Savannah, and some of his witnesses were from Ebenezer. They did me the favor, for a small sum, to take a large, wide boat to Abercorn in which, at high tide, the thick boards which were left over will be brought to the mill. From these boards our sawmiller is to build sturdy millraces or channels to the first mill gear and to the rice press. He also wants to make a little dam in the small rivulet above the millrace, where the water threatens to erode the island. I hope that these two projects will not be too expensive and very useful. We had a buyer for the thick boards, but he offered as little money for them as if we had been forced to sell. One matter could not be settled at this time in the council. It concerns some land which was donated to us by the Lord Trustees, and that means that I have to make the trip again Tuesday in two weeks, or on July 18. Yesterday evening I held an edification hour or evening prayer for the German people in Savannah on Job 1:21. "Naked came I from the womb," etc. At the beginning of my sermon I explained, using verse 8, how, in even these poor times, people have to be in order to repeat the words of this holy man in truth, and despite their lack, suffering, and tribulations. See also 1 Timothy 6:6–8.

Friday, July 10. From Charleston the sad news reached Savannah that the French in the East Indies had taken Fort St. George or Madras away from the English. How I and other honest people here wish that this were not true! May God come to their aid, as He has come to ours in the past, and assist them with His wisdom, strength, and mercy. May His work there, even in times of such great tribulations, endure and even prosper! May He let us use wisely the time of rest and peace for as long as we may enjoy it, following the example of the dear souls in Judea, Samaria, and Galilee, Acts 9:31. Besides the bad news, I received good news also. Mr. Verelst wrote to me from London, dated March sixth of this year, that four iron stoves were sent to him from Germany, and he had sent them on to Charleston in four wooden crates. He would have included various other items which he had received for us, if the ship had had the space to transport them. He also renews our hopes for the large chest from Halle, on which he will be able to report with certainty when the next boat arrives. At that time he will learn the contents of the chest from the Court Chaplain, Mr. Ziegenhagen, and will have the chest opened. It is said to be in storage in the customs house and the address is no longer legible.

Saturday, July 11. An old man, seventy years of age, who heads the Anabaptist community in Charleston as their teacher, took a rest in my house today during the heat of noon. Then he continued his journey via Old Ebenezer to a plantation on the Ogeechy River, where he knows a man who is an adherent of his sect, and who had promised to do his best to cure his impaired hearing. He complained of the many Arians, Socinians, and Deists in Charleston and various other places in Carolina.[3] His own son-in-law, a well-trained medical doctor and justice of the peace in Charleston, is a Socinian. The German people who seek diversions in Carolina now and then for the pleasures of the flesh are to be pitied greatly for their own sake and that of their children. Usually they end up asots[4] or fall into the hands of swindlers. Some time ago I thought about the Salzburger Ruprecht Zittrauer and his downfall. I was told he had become

an overseer of Negroes or black slaves on a plantation in Carolina, and his two children are growing up in ignorance and
meanness. His wife, Anna, had received a great deal of help and
support from the poorhouse at Augsburg. However, neither he
nor she was willing to learn something here, and the few prayers
and the little they did remember from their catechism they
probably have forgotten by now. May God have mercy on them!

Monday, July 13. Last winter and again this summer, a man
from Carolina visited various parts of our colony. He can not
find enough words to praise the advantages which the people of
this area have over others in the way of pasture land for cattle
and horses, and therefore in breeding them. If it were possible,
he would bring a herd of cattle for breeding into our colony and
put a family in charge of them. Throngs of people from other
colonies would come to us if only it were legal to keep Negroes
and if they were not so afraid of Spaniards and Indians in this
time of war. It surprises me that these people are so frightened
by three kinds of enemies, namely Spaniards, Frenchmen, and
Indians and still would bring in a fourth, that is, Negroes or
black slaves, into the area.

Wednesday, July 15. Susanna Ernst, the orphaned girl in service with our schoolmaster in town, Mayer, has been as white as a
sheet since her last dangerous illness. Now the reason for her
sickness may have come to light. Secretely she was eating salt,
raw wheat, and raw, uncooked rice, and probably other things
hard to digest.[5] On the other hand, she showed no interest in
cooked and healthy meals. After I was informed of this disorder
I spoke to her in the presence of the schoolmaster and his wife
and talked to her lovingly and seriously, using both promises
and threats, about the fifth and sixth commandments.[6] Then I
prayed to our merciful God for His blessing of what I said to her.
I reminded her of the serious saying: "Whoever inflicts harm on
himself is rightly called an arch villain." Some time ago I heard
in Savannah that some grown people in Vernonburg also ate all
sorts of strange things, such as sand and clay, and damaged their
health considerably. The children in this country do these things
frequently, complaints on that are common. Some of them have
died already, as I have noted in this diary.

Thursday, July 16. Widow Graniwetter has been content for
some time now in her situation as a widow, which God settled on
her. She is blessed in that she no longer entertains anxious or
worrisome thoughts which plagued her earlier. She perceives
blessing in all things and does not fret over her two small children, who are very young but healthy and fine, and her love for
them makes things easy. God has sent a persistent sickness to
pious Mrs. Glaner, the sister of the late Veit Lemmenhofer. She is
blessed with His mercy in this and she is looking forward to
going to heaven more and more. Shortly after I visited her in
her house, she brought me her songbook which contains the
beautiful wedding song of the faithful: *Gott Lob! ein Schritt zur
Ewigkeit ist abermal vollendet* etc. It has become her own, special
song and we had an edifying conversation on it.

Saturday, July 18. For some years now, our carpenters had so
much work to do on their plantations, at the mills, and in the
private houses, that they could not find the time to finish our
Zion Church. Recently they got together and put in the ceiling
or second storey flooring there. Windows and doors were made,
and for each door a little projecting roof to protect the interior
of the church and the beautiful doors themselves from rain. All
that is left to do is make the benches or chairs for the men,
women, and children, as we have them in the Jerusalem Church.
The window panes have to be set into the frames which are already finished. We do not have sufficient money for all of this
right now, however. The benches we have at the moment will
have to do for a little longer, and the panes will be put in before
the start of winter, God willing.

Sunday, July 19. I am seriously concerned to hear from
various members of our congregation, when I go to visit them,
that some very young and some older children, ranging from
three to thirteen years of age, persist in eating strange things,
such as sand, earth, linen, coal, leaves, paper, etc. and can not be
persuaded to stop this practice. Their parents offer them
healthy and well-cooked meals, and good-tasting fresh fruit is
available, for instance, various kinds of peaches and melons. Mr.
Rottenberger has three children who are endangering their
health in this sad manner. I can not give any other advice to the

parents than to recommend the strictest supervision of their
children, stern discipline, and prayers for the Lord's help in ex-
pelling the demon of these unusual cravings who would do
damage to our settlement by depriving us of our young. Mr.
Landfelder's little girl ate not only unripened fruit but even tobacco and is now dangerously ill from it. I have never heard of
anything like this in Germany. May God have mercy on us and in
His goodness avert further injury from us!

Monday, July 20. A pious woman from Salzburg, who has to
make the trip from her plantation to town every day so that Mr.
Mayer can treat her hand, stops at my house frequently. We find
her company, her blessed conduct, words, and works very edifying. She, like the pious Job, fears God in her own fashion. She
avoids all evil and accepts everything, good or bad, alike, from
the hand of her Heavenly Father. Today, in my living room, she
expressed some fine and edifying thoughts regarding her injured hand and the blessings and tribulations sent by the Lord.
It became clear that she had realized her own nothingness as
well as God's dear grace in Christ and His fatherly care of His
children. As always, she praised God. She is more than grateful
for the blessing of her timely expulsion from her wordly and
dark fatherland (namely, at a time when she was ready for such
an important change), and also for the blessing of the gospel and
other means of grace. Her greatest concerns in this world are
that her own soul be saved and that her children, genuinely
faithful, be lead to Christ. Her heart is full of God's promises
and, even though she can not read, she quotes the important
introductory verses which we studied recently very well and uses
this knowledge to her advantage.

Tuesday, July 21. I had asked a friend of mine who was going
on a trip from Savannah to Charleston to inquire at the post office there whether any letters for me had arrived. Yesterday evening, I am glad to say, I received a package of letters from him
which he had found in the post office and we were all filled with
joy at that. We had thought that these letters were lost, because
letters which we had received in September and October of last
year mentioned letters by our dear Senior Urlsperger and Mr.
Albinus, which had been mailed to us in July and August.

Praised be God, who let them arrive here in good condition! I have no doubt that He wanted us to derive His blessing from these letters! This week, in preparation for holding Holy Communion, we have to study some verses of King Solomon's prayer, 1 Kings 8. Afterwards, with the assistance of the Holy Ghost, I intend to read these two letters from dear Senior Urlsperger and Mr. Albinus for my own benefit and that of our community. They contain a great deal of thought for prayers, the praise of God, and for the realization of God's miraculous ways, where He accompanies His servants and children. Mr. Albinus wrote us also something of God's work the in East India and he included a brief notice, printed in Tranquebar, reporting on the progress of the missions in Cudulur and Madras.[7] May God crown this work with His blessing and watch over His faithful servants there like a father.

Wednesday, July 22. This summer will yield large harvests because we had plenty of rain, thunderstorms, and cool winds. The grain in the fields stands tall; and we hope also for a rich harvest of Indian corn, beans, pumkins, rice, and potatoes. During the spring, the corn was plagued by many worms, and it seemed as if they would devour it all. Then, however, God sent us rain and the worms disappeared gradually. Recently I was told that more people would plant rice if I were to see to it that a new building be added to the mill so that the rice could easily be hulled and prepared for the press. We have an opportunity to buy the necessary machine, and it would not be too costly. However, I can not undertake any additional construction work until the sawmill and other mills return more profit than they do at the moment in these poor times with hardly any money around. Our rice press is very useful; however, our people here do not quite know how to thrash their barley. In Germany it is being done properly and maybe God will send us someone who knows how to do that and who can assist us.

Because the weather so far was so good, everything seems to be growing very well. We have several varieties of peaches, which are much bigger, have a better color, and taste much better than the peaches grown in Germany. We have an over-abundance of them, and some are being dried, some are fermented into brandy, some go to the pigs, and some are left to rot. Peach trees of all varieties grow wild here, like willows or thorny bushes. They are not cultivated, fertilized, pruned or kept weed-free. Trees bear fruit in their third year already. If our people had distillation boilers, they would know how to use the many peaches. Fruit dried in the sun or in ovens does not keep well in the summer and quickly gets full of worms. On the other hand, I did hear that some very hard-working people manage to keep them for almost an entire year. Sugar melons and watermelons are good fruits, also. We have figs and apples, too; and, since people can see how well these crops do, they are starting to cultivate more of these trees. This is a blessed country.

Thursday, July 23. I hear that our pious people here, after waiting for so long, are eagerly looking forward to have selections read from Your Worship's letters which arrived recently, and to be edified.[7a] They know that Your Worship and your dear wife are in good health and that our dear God protected her and your daughters from great sadness. For me and for them this is cause for great joy and humble praise of God. People also ask for news of the other dear benefactors of the Salzburgers who resides in the generous city of Augsburg. Their charitable gifts still appear great and wonderful to our pious Salzburgers. However, I have no news which I can share with our people. Our Senior writes of one great benefactor in Germany: "It is true, Mr. ** does much good, and you will see that he intends to continue doing much good in the future."

Friday, July 24. Some of our people would like to have cotton seed, which grows in East India. Yesterday I wrote to a friend of mine in Charleston in this matter. About ten years ago we got some seed and saw that in one summer young trees grew many branches and reached a height of probably eight feet.[8] All froze in the winter because they were not covered. The local cotton is delicate and white, and the plants grow easily and abundantly. There is the drawback, however, that the seeds are lodged firmly in the lint and it is difficult and cumbersome to pick them out. Cleaning the lint of the seeds is much easier with the variety from East India.[9]

In past years, our fig trees usually froze and died. Now we

cover them with straw in the winter and they survive without damage. Sometimes fruit is set and grows under the straw and ripens very early. When the trees are several years old then they are hardy enough and need no longer be covered. Some bear fruit even as small bushes during their first year, others in the third and fourth year, when they have grown into large trees. The fruits are large and very tasty. Orange trees would probably grow here also, as in Charleston and Frederica, if we took good care of them in the winter. Only one man among us, Hanns Flerl, knows enough about trees and successful grafting methods. My own vineyard died because we do not have anyone here who knows how to tend one. I think anything would thrive here, if we only had the necessary time, means, and knowledge. We have not enough workers, no good fieldhands at all, their wages per day and year are very high, and my own income small. Therefore I can not start an orchard or garden to get other people interested, although I have wanted to for a long time.

Saturday, July 25. Some time ago, Held and his wife left for Carolina so he could support himself better as a weaver there than here as a farmer. His wife has returned to visit her sisters and to go to Holy Communion. She reports that her husband does not receive any money for his work there either (cash is as rare in Carolina as in Georgia) but he gets good value in trade so that he can live comfortably. His good work will probably come to an end as soon as the two Negroes or black slaves have learned weaving from him and become able to weave themselves. This is happening throughout Carolina; Negroes are taught every skill and are then used in all sorts of enterprises. This is the reason that white people have such a hard time earning their bread except if they become overseers of Negroes or keep slaves themselves.

Sunday, July 26. Today we celebrated Holy Communion with sixty-two persons. I preached on the gospel for the Sixth Sunday after Trinity on various sins against the sixth commandment. Naturally, with love and empathy, I mentioned our children, who endanger their health by eating things which are obviously bad for them and who shorten their lives in this manner. I admonished parents and people, for whom such children work, lovingly and seriously of their obligations and reminded them to do their duty, spiritually and physically, so that this kind of manslaughter not be on their heads. Every woman who comes to church is taught this lesson, before God and our community: "God will reward you mercifully for the faithfulness with which you raise your children. If, however, you let them stray, then God will demand their blood from you on Judgment Day." If the parents, after being so instructed, do not neglect their children but raise them carefully, correct them in kindness, teach them Christian conduct, and pray with them frequently and regularly, then they will not lack the spiritual and physical blessing they need for raising their children in a Christian manner.

Wednesday, July 29. Several letters from Philadelphia arrived via Frederica. The news is that Mr. Whitefield is dangerously ill, and Mrs. Whitefield reports further that several Herrnhuters or so-called Moravian Brothers from Philadelphia were headed for Georgia. Whatever their intentions may be will soon become apparent after their arrival here. I am surprised that I did not receive any replies to my numerous letters to our dear brothers, the Lutheran ministers in Pennsylvania.

Thursday, July 30. This year we can not complain about too much heat during the dog days. Several days now it was as cool after sundown as is usual for the fall. People who work up a sweat during the day and get chilled in the evenings and during the night can easily contract all sorts of sickness and diseases.

Young Mrs. Lackner is a very pious, patient, and well-content young mother in her lying-in and she probably dignifies her physical condition at all times with God's word and prayer. While I was at her house in order to talk and pray with her, Mrs. Glaner, sickly but honest, came for a visit, just as is written in Luke 1 of Mary and Elizabeth. As is the custom among our neighbors, she had brought along a token of kindness. Mrs. Glaner, since she has no children of her own, is raising a little orphaned girl lovingly, seriously, and properly. I, as well as others who know this, are filled with joy at that and are guided by her example as a wise, careful, and hard-working mother and guardian who labors lovingly and seriously.

Friday, July 31. Yesterday, in our evening prayer hour, for the

praise of God and our own edification, I started to read aloud
dear Senior Urlsperger's letter which I had received last week.
Tonight I continued, or rather repeated and explained again,
what I had read yesterday. The various points which our Senior
made in the first part of his letter to the esteemed Court Chaplain Ziegenhagen are very important to us; namely his and his
family's tribulations as well as other physical and spiritual matters. I was able to use this material for all sorts of beneficial and
necessary comments. Today I was kept from holding my weekly
sermon in the Zion Church by a downpour and another adversity. Otherwise I would have read aloud this letter there also, as I
had promised to do. I will do it, God willing, next week.

AUGUST

Sunday, August 2. On this first Sunday of the last month of
summer we remembered publicly the many spiritual and physical benefactions which God our Lord showered on us this year so
richly, although we did not deserve it, from near and afar. He
gave us these blessings in this desert, just as He did to the many
people in the desert as is set down in today's gospel Mark 8:1 ff.
Today, in our regular evening prayer hour, we thanked Him for
it on our knees. Today's Sunday gospel gave me a good opportunity to explain His good counsel to the poor and His rich consolation for them, a well-suited subject matter for our poor community in these hard times. As introductory verses we
contemplated the beautiful and edifying words Tobit 4:22 "Do
not be afraid," etc. From this, our dear people here may learn
how they can be full of hope despite their poverty and their
many worries, as everything will turn out well. See also 1 Timothy 4:8. We are often reminded of the Israelites in the desert on
their way to Canaan to whom God sent not only many spiritual
and physical blessings but also several salutary tribulations.
However, God our Lord failed to fulfill His purpose in many;
they were striken down in the desert and it was their own doing
that their escape from Egypt was of no avail, but, rather, caused
a greater judgment. May this be a warning to us, Hebrews 4:11.

Monday, August 3. Almost every day we have rain for several hours, and this is a disadvantage for our people in making hay, which is needed in large quantities as fodder for their cattle and the horses which are kept on the farms for plowing and riding. Hay is made, weather permitting, once during the summer and then again in the fall, partly on the fertile island on the other side of the Mill River, partly on the fields for barley, rye, and wheat. Some of the hay is stored in barns or other outbildings, part is put around wooden poles, arranged in a pyramidal shape, and left in the fields throughout the winter. Portions for fodder are removed then as needed. Raising stock, either horses or cattle, is easy and very useful in this country. If only we went about it in a more sensible way, many of our farmers would be much better off.

Every year, many calves are sold in Savannah; people say that they are forced to sell in order to buy shoes or other clothing or to get some money to pay the doctors' bills, etc. Other people in other settlements do not sell their calves but wait patiently for them to grow into adult cattle. An ox fetches from two pounds Sterling up to possibly two pounds and ten shillings. Those who raise their calves can expect a good herd of cattle in a few years. One of the main reasons for selling the calves is that people need the milk for their families and for making butter as well as for obtaining lard. Our Salzburgers, as was the custom in their fatherland, are used to butter and lard but not to eating the meat.

Our cowpen assists people's efforts in many ways, but each quarter I have to contribute a great deal, if things should not come to a halt. The annual salary for our cowherds is twenty-five pounds Sterling, but not everybody pitches in and some refuse to help carry this burden. That means too large a sum would be required from each contributor, if I did not help out with some pennies and share God's blessing. If our dear people followed the good advice which they received yesterday from God's word, then God's merciful guidance would ease their difficulties. May God show the intractable among us the error of their ways before the measure of their sins is full.

Tuesday, August 4. Steiner, an honest man, has various problems in his household and is burdened with several tribulations.

His formost concern, however, is his soul's salvation; and for that reason he considers his being tired and sleepy in church a serious obstacle and nuisance. He fights it as much as he can and uses all sorts of methods, even things, but he is not succeeding to his satisfaction. He dearly loves the Divine word and he suffers greatly from his sleepiness. I offered him instruction and consolation from God's word and warned him not to let either the realization or the thoughts of his shortcomings make him desperate or despondent and be diverted from Christ, the Savior of poor sinners. The more he recognizes his faults inwardly and outwardly, as well as his complete helplessness, the more he should humble himself and remember and cherish the great benefaction, namely that God gave us such a powerful Savior who blesses us all and use this knowledge to strengthen his own faith. It is said: "Fear not, just believe."

I have no doubt that God sent him this plight just as He sent to the Apostle Paul the thorn in his side, and that He has not removed this tribulation yet for a good purpose. It is also said: "My grace is sufficient for thee, for my strength is made perfect in weakness." His wife tells me that, although he has to fight his sleepiness in church, he remembers and repeats to her and the children a great deal from my weekly sermons and our Sunday services. The prayers in his home are held properly, and regularly and are quite edifying. He keeps our community's distilling kettle on his farm and works many hours, often well into the night, making brandy for people who bring him peaches. His honest neighbor, Brandner, helps him in this. We have an incredible quantity of the best and most juicy peaches here. Many are used for making brandy, others are dried in the sun and in ovens, others are fed to the pigs, but probably half goes to waste. In such wet weather as we have at the moment, they rot quickly. Peach trees grow wild here, like willows, and need not be cultivated, in even the poorest soil. The pretty and fine-tasting water melons grow well also; yesterday I was shown one which weighed fourteen pounds.

Wednesday, August 5. Mrs. Kalcher dearly loves the Divine word which she reads often and with enthusiasm. She also listens to it and repeats it and prays a great deal. Her children benefit from her eagerness, and she teaches them in a pleasant manner the beautiful and pithy verses which we have examined publicly in the *exordium* since the church year 1743. She repeats them with the children frequently, and they are setting a good example for adults and other children by their skillful reciting of such verses. Even her youngest daughter, at the age of three, likes to learn and quickly memorizes both short and long verses and repeats them all day long in singsong. When I visited yesterday, she sang "Teach me thy way, o Lord, that I may walk in thy truth," and I was impressed anew by these words.

I do this in all my preaching: Each time, I choose as my introduction an important verse which contains the main topic of the sermon I have planned. I explain the various lines in a simple manner and demonstrate their literal meaning in words which can be easily understood; then I apply the divine truth contained in the verse to whatever listeners I have. Although this goes beyond the limits of the usual *exordium,* I disregard this fact because so far our dear God has blessed my methods of teaching and has let the people benefit from it. Usually, our listeners are waiting eagerly for those introductory verses on Sundays and holy days which they themselves selected in church, made a drawing of, learned themselves and taught their children. Therefore, there is probably not one family living in Ebenezer in which the children are not encouraged by their parents or the people for whom they work to learn such introductory verses. By doing this, they collect a great treasure of the divine word in the easiest manner possible.

Friday, August 7. Mr. Kocher, our schoolteacher, is a weaver by profession; and in Germany he used to make both coarse and fine linen. Our dear God has assisted him in putting together a new loom and, little by little (because every beginning is difficult), he managed to assemble the tools needed for weaving, partly by making them himself and partly by having them made. The money which I pay him for teaching our children has helped him both in getting his equipment as well as in building his new little house. Yesterday he sent word to me through his son that he has begun to weave and that he is making good progress in his work. He got some spun flax and wool yarn from Mr.

Whitefield's orphanage in order to weave some wool and linen cloth for winter clothing. I hope to obtain more flax from Pennsylvania and sheep's wool from Carolina: and, since we have our own modest supply of both here in Ebenezer, I hope that this hard-working and clever Mr. Kocher will, in time, get even more work to do.

Saturday, August 8. We have finished the reading of Senior Urlsperger's letter and were reminded not only of the various tribulations which had befallen us but also of God's powerful care for us, and this will benefit those who fear the Lord. God sends us, rather than others, so much goodness at times, that, when we consider this fact and compare our situation with that of others, we are overwhelmed with surprise and exclaim: "Our Lord is God, our Lord is God, praised be the Lord!" He could easily remove our present tribulations, as He has done with other difficulties in the past; and He could make everything well if only all of us would accept His order and let Him fulfill the purpose of His Divine benefactions and tribulations.

I have taken care to memorize the following edifying verses well: "Blessed is everyone that feareth the Lord; that walketh in his ways. For thou shalt eat . . ." etc. "It shall be well with thee." Also: "He giveth his beloved sleep." However, I have to bear witness, lovingly and seriously, that those few among us who followed their call and were sent to Ebenezer at great expense and who are so well taken care of here both spiritually and physically and who daily enjoy more benefactions from the Lord's hand through the service of His tools both near and from afar commit a serious sin if they move away from here and, for the sake of their own comfort, turn their back on the church, schools, ministers, and benefactors.

Our dear listeners are led diligently to the strange and instructive story of the Israelites. From it they can early recognize God's conduct towards them and their own conduct towards God and His blessings and tribulations. They also see what punishments and judgments are the consequences not only of major sins, but also of a lack of faith, complaints, impatience, misuse or belittling of divine benefactions, the hurting of His servants, or the desires for the fleshpots of Egypt. How often are we reminded, in the writings of the New Testament, of the story of the Israelites? It is God's will that we make use of it in order to be instructed regarding our own circumstances and be consoled and warned. The example of the Israelites applies to us in a very special manner.

Sunday, August 9. The German people of our faith in Savannah asked that one of us two would preach to them this Sunday and hold Holy Communion. Because I have had to travel to Savannah so frequently in the past, my dear colleague, Mr. Lemke, went. Already Friday afternoon he started out in order to have more time to preach God's will and counsel to those who wished to take Holy Communion and to talk to them in private, if the opportunity arose. I myself was strengthened again by our merciful Lord so that I was able to preach here in the late morning, repeat my sermon in the afternoon, and hold our public prayer hour in the evening. I spoke on the gospel for the Eighth Sunday after Trinity, dealing with Christians and proper Christian conduct toward false teachers. For my introductory verse I had chosen 1 John 4:1. Our listeners were dutifully admonished to encourage their children not only towards genuine piety but also to make frequent use of our community's good opportunities to be thoroughly instructed in the articles of faith of the Lutheran religion, in God's word and the symbolic writings of our Lutheran church, in a country where all sorts of dangerous sects and heretics abound. Some of our people are somewhat tardy in this respect, and today I put great emphasis on the dangers threatening their own as well as their children's souls.

Tuesday, August 11. I like to visit our widows and orphans as often as I can and to console them with words from the Holy Bible. Our dear God has shown me His blessing in this. Mrs. Graniwetter has two small children; and, since it is virtually impossible to find good fieldhands, women servants, or nurses, she has a hard time running her household. But in all her adversities she finds strength in the Lord our God and she is convinced that God, who created and sustains heaven, earth, and all things, will take care of her children, too. Since she accepted her call and came to Ebenezer, she has been constantly reminded of the verse: "We must pass through much tribulation into the kingdom of heaven." At that time she had said to her late husband, "We must not expect an easy time but rather be prepared for a great deal of hardship which will befall us in Ebenezer. However, let it be, we shall enter into God's kingdom eventually." Now, she thinks often of those words and they are a great blessing for her.

Wednesday, August 12. At the orphanage I was shown some quinces of a remarkable size. About twenty of them had grown in Mr. Mayer's garden on a smallish tree which was only three or four years old. When they are ripe they can be peeled and eaten fresh, and they do not pucker one's mouth as do quinces grown in Germany. They taste almost like pears. My own are not ripe yet and will not be as big as Mr. Mayer's. I have no other explanation for this than that his and mine are of a different variety. In this country it is possible to grow a nice orchard in a few years; almost all kinds of trees bear fruit in their fourth year. I have heard that apple trees in Germany must be several years old before they bear fruit. Here, however, apple trees shoot up from their seeds all by themselves and grow wild; and, if they are grafted carefully and cultivated, then they will bear very good apples within three years. But the trees do not get as old as in Germany and do not grow as big and tall.

Now, more often than in the past when many were content to have only peach trees, which need no care at all, some of our people are starting orchards. My own vineyard, which has been very promising for the past few years, died off almost completely this summer. The people who did the annual pruning and tying of the vines for me insisted on doing it the way it is customary in Germany which, however, as General Oglethorpe told me, is not practical in this country. The vines should be trained up to a height of seven or eight feet and tied to stakes or poles, forming little rows and arches. Otherwise, the grapes hang too low and the heat reflected from the soil ruins the fruit.

Thursday, August 13. Mrs. Müller, a widow, is well content in her situation. She thanks God gratefully for all the blessings, both spiritual and physical, which He has granted to her in our community. She does good works frequently, as the needs of her fellow men occur. There are a few ungrateful and discontent men and women in our settlement, but many others deem themselves unworthy of all the good things which our dear God has sent them and pray regularly for the dear benefactors who have helped them and wish them God's blessing. A few days ago, a pious woman was reminded of God's miraculous ways which she had encountered in Augsburg. She wished with all her heart that our merciful God may allot many more years to our esteemed Senior Urlsperger, despite his advanced age, and that He may reward him a thousand times for his fatherly love and good deeds. Some among us do not thrive, and this is their own fault, for they remain in their unenlightened condition in spite of God's blessings. They and their families, and probably their friends and acquaintances as well, live against God's word, giving way to their human urges. This is the reason that God and His blessing is not with them.

Friday, August 14. Up to now we waited every day for the letters from Philadelphia. Yesterday I received a letter from a lieutenant in Port Royal in which he writes that he had some letters from our friends in Philadelphia for me, but that they had been taken from him, together with some of his things, by the Spaniards near Charleston. This person, Peter Grung,[1] arrived with the second transport and settled at first in Old Ebenezer, then joined Mr. Weissiger[2] and moved to Pennsylvania in the hopes of becoming a tradesman there. As a soldier he served at Carthagena,[3] with the rank of ensign, and was recently promoted to lieutenant. I wrote back and admonished him lovingly not to neglect his soul in his dangerous profession. As a sign of my love for his soul I sent him the beautiful little book *Dogma of the Beginning of Christian Life.*[4] I also included a letter to Pastor Brunnholz, which he promised me to forward.

Saturday, August 15. Our dear God sends me much edification and spiritual enjoyment while I am rereading the symbolic writings of our Lutheran Church. Indeed, God's grace must be admired humbly and praised highly; His grace with which the faithful adherents of Evangelical truth and through their work, many thousands of people are blessed.

Sunday, August 16. Zittrauer, the carpenter, told me that God had shown great mercy to his wife, who was in considerable danger during childbirth. We must praise our dear God (as I have done, as well as the father of the child, and the godparents before Holy Baptism was held in my house); for, in His goodness He averted the danger and misery to which many a mother and her child were close at the time of birth. Oh! How many spiritual and physical benefactions does our merciful God shower on us here! We discovered this again today while examining the gospel for the Ninth Sunday after Trinity. We learned about the damnable misuse of God's goodness and patience, and for my introductory verse I had chosen Ecclesiastes 8:11, "Because sentence against an evil work is not executed speedily."

Monday, August 17. For the past few weeks there was hardly a day without rain. Despite this, our fields look good, but the people who are making hay are inconvenienced greatly by the unreliable weather. But Christians say: "I accept it as He giveth it."

Wednesday, August 19. The elderly German widow who moved here five months ago with her two sons and one daughter seems to have abandoned her considerable prejudice against me and our way of holding church services. While she was in good health she listened to God's word eagerly; now she is dangerously ill, and although she did not summon me to her house, she does not dislike it when I visit her and talk with her about God's word. Despite her learning, she is quite blind where God's counsel regarding human blessedness is concerned. However, she is content and consoled and therefore I have to be very careful with her, if I do not wish to make her angry at me again, which would lessen her opportunity for enlightenment. Before she came to settle here, someone had given her the beautiful book *Scriptural Instruction for the Sick and Dying*.[5] She likes it to be read to her and praises it as a very edifying book. Her two daughters, who are married to local men and who have developed a thorough spiritual insight as well as a genuine fear of God, offer her Christian consolation frequently. With God's merciful assistance, if she continues to trust me, I will at least succeed in preventing her from sending her two younger sons, ages eleven and fourteen, to a blind and mean man in N. but rather get her to allow them to stay on here with us and be raised towards spiritual and physical goodness after her death. That is also her daughter's serious wish.

Thursday, August 20. Yesterday, around noon, we were over-joyed to receive several packets of letters from our Fathers, bene-factors, and friends in London and Germany. They were dated partly from the end of last year and partly from the beginning of this year and so, once again, our merciful Father in heaven sent us renewed proof of His special care for us and our dear listeners in these poor times; He strengthens our faith and we praise His great and magnificent name. God awakened not only the hearts of the Lords Trustees anew but also those of several other dear benefactors in Germany, to aid us in our present pov-erty with advice and assistance. May they help us endure the damage done to us by that aforementioned deceitful and fraud-ulent person (it happened just a year ago), with love and kind-ness.[6] May our merciful God be a rich Rewarder for that now and in eternity!

The day before yesterday, in our weekly sermon and prayer hour, we examined the following beautiful words (concerning the eager and generous sacrifices of Solomon in 1 Kings 8:63): "He who hath mercy on the poor honoreth the Lord: He will (there is not the least doubt of that) compensate him with good."[7] Therefore, the gifts which our most esteemed benefac-tors send to us as true agents of Christ for our churches, schools, and our community in Ebenezer will not be lost to them, but are being lent to the Lord who, when He pleases, will reward them with His goodness. For this we thank Him kindly.

May the Lord be also praised especially for inclining the most praisworthy *Corpus Evangelicorum* in Regensburg[8] to pity and mercy toward our Ebenezer congretation. And for letting such a considerable help come to us from there in this expensive and miserable time of war. May He also be praised for His assistance in physical matters which, this time, is being sent to us through the hands of our dear Senior Urlsperger and Doctor Francke from the Lord Trustees, from several new dear benefactors who do not reside in Germany, from the most praiseworthy Society, and from other most dear friends. May He be praised and may He keep them in health! May He bless them eternally!

Friday, August 21. Pious Mrs. Glaner is still sickly, but she can leave her house now and she runs her household as well as can be expected. Her dearest task is to go to church, and nothing in this world gives her more joy than our Savior and His Holy words which sustain her daily in her pilgrimage. The memory of her late brother, Veit Lemmenhofer, and his partaking of the eternal joy in heaven, as well as a feeling of her own misery, make her sigh and desire a blessed parting from this world. She showed me her material blessings, her wheat, rye, barley, and wheat flour. She praised the Lord eagerly and proclaimed her own unworthiness. She also confided in me that it makes her very sad and causes her much pain when she hears that someone wishes to leave our settlement, this quiet and blessed island, where God talks to us with so much kindness and provides for us so well in spiritual and physical matters. She was happy to learn that Senior Urlsperger celebrated his sixty-third birthday yesterday, and she praised God together with me. Yesterday, publicly and privately, we asked our merciful God and Father in Heaven (and we have more than a thousand reasons for doing so) that He may bless His faithful servant both spiritually and physically and reward him for all the fatherly love he has shown to us so far. May God strengthen his body and soul and add many more years to his life, to honor him and his Lutheran Church in Augsburg and other places both near and far, as well as for the benefit of both his and our families. May God grant us this for the sake of Christ!

Today, in the Zion Church, we finished the very important, edifying, and blessed eighth chapter from the first Book of Kings and examined verses sixty-three through sixty-six. From them, we derived much blessing, sent to us, once again, by our merciful God. I will elaborate on this somewhat.

We learned, 1. that, at the dedication of the temple and throughout the entire year, an amazing number of sacrifices were offered to the Lord. Despite this, the people did not lack food because the service of God does not detract from physical nourishment. The more the faithful and honest servants of God worship Him, the more blessings may be expected to flow from His grace. "He giveth his beloved sleep." Our listeners have to remember this well if they do not want to let the temptation gain a foothold, that time spent in public and private service is a loss of time, 2. In the New Testament we hear of only two kinds of sacrifices. The first one is unique. It is the complete sacrifice for reconciliation, offered by Jesus Christ on the altar of the Cross, when He cried out: "It is finished." The second kind is offered to our dear Lord daily by true Christians, namely spiritual priests. Indeed, it is not the Papist mass, which violates Holy Scriptures, but rather a faith-filled giving of thanks, as is written in Romans 12:1–2. The center and nature of proper evangelical Christianity are contained in these two principles: namely, that a sinner who repents and hungers for grace reaches out, through his faith, to the dear sacrifice of reconciliation and makes it his own.

This leads to the forgiving of his sins, to peace with God, and, surely, to the giving of thanks. It is said: "I would give thee a thousand worlds to compensate you for true love."[9] Where the latter is lacking, the former must needs be absent. 3. Among the reasons for offering so many precious sacrifices (because, all together, they were sacrifices of great value) to the Lord at the time of the temple dedication and then throughout the year the foremost was that these sacrifices should foreshadow the preciousness of the sacrifice offered by Jesus Christ. These are the words contained in the second article of our beautiful catechism, and in 1 Peter 1:18–19, and again in 1 Corinthians 6:20.

If all people were to offer all the world's, or even a thousand worlds', pure sacrificial animals to mighty God, and if all people and angels were sacrificed also, it would be nothing compared to the most precious gift which God sent to us in His son. How could this gift be anything less than everything to us? Perhaps someone among us who gave to God twenty-two-thousand oxen and one hundred and twenty thousand sheep (which is the number of Solomon's sacrifices) might say that God loved him dearly. However, how allencompassing must His love be which made Him sacrifice His Son for our sake, His Son, the Lord of Glory! Oh! how despicable is our damnable lack of faith which nests in everybody's heart, and which manifests itself in misery and sadness.

How great is the love of our Heavenly Father for us, He who gave to us His Son and, with Him, all things: His gospel, teachings, churches, schools, food, and now also so many benefactions from England and Germany! He sends us misery and tribulations to show to us what is hidden in our hearts. Do we value the supreme gift over material wealth? If all of us were to accept this supreme gift then He would give us lesser ones, too, in abundance and to our advantage. The last verses of chapter three, "They blessed the king" was explained as follows to our listeners: Solomon was a great benefactor to his people; he blessed them, prayed for them, prepared beautiful services for God, and worked hard to improve their spiritual and physical well-being. They recognized what he did for them; they blessed him and wished him well. They enjoyed the blessings God had sent to them, to the royal house of their benefactor, and to the entire community. In this we should imitate them, especially since we are in a similar situation now.

We have the most praiseworthy *Corpus Evangelicorum;* and our Fathers, benefactors, and friends in England and Germany have contributed as much as possible, and probably frequently to their own disadvantage, to our spiritual and physical well-being, to our churches, schools, mills, and to other matters in our community. This is demonstrated once again by new gifts arriving from the Lord Trustees, the most esteemed *Corpus Evangelicorum,* and other benefactors in Germany and other countries. When goodness is shown to an entire community then each of its members should be happy, praise God, and bless their benefactors, as is written also in Job 31:20. Those on the other hand who show themselves to be ungrateful and rebellious shall not prosper. Our dear Senior Riesch, from Lindau, wrote a very beautiful letter to Mr. Brandner, a Salzburger (whom he had helped to obtain a share of his inheritance), in which he mentions that he has become old and feeble since the Salzburgers left. In part, this is also true for our esteemed Senior Urlsperger. It is not a small sin if these reverend fathers are saddened and disappointed by people's obstinacy, their lack of faith, bad conduct, or by their leaving our community. These people will not prosper, as our dear Senior Urlsperger himself called to our attention, quoting Hebrews 13:17.

Saturday, August 22. Doctor /Ludwig/ Mayer's brother /Georg/ has been our schoolmaster in town for the past three

months now. He fulfills his duties so properly and with such eagerness that we are well satisfied with his services. This position
is a great blessing for him, since he does not have a strong consti-
tution, and his wife, like him, is sickly also, and they would not
have been able to earn their livelihood by farming. Indeed, he
derived much spiritual benefit from this sign of God's care for
him; it is quite apparent when I speak with him. Some months
ago, Doctor Mayer was tempted to move to Pennsylvania;
however, as a true Christian, he did not consider his own advantage only. He has tested the will of our Heavenly Father and was
able to recognize from various examples of His merciful goodness that he should not move away but rather stay here and use
his talents in the best interest of our dear community, which is
his calling. In this way he will earn his livelihood. He and his
dear wife have no children and their needs are few. I hope that
our merciful God will bring it about that he will become a helper
to me in taking care of our community's everyday matters.

Our foremost problem is that my dear listeners had to work
very hard up to now and I wish it may be possible for them to
earn their bread in an easier way; we might be able to improve
upon our methods of farming, of breeding animals, increase
our silk making, and start some people in trade. Then they
could lead quiet, happy, and honest lives, and be blessed in God.
God's word could be preached frequently and the Holy Sacraments taken. I myself have no talent for practical matters although, through God's goodness, I do not lack the will or the
desire to improve things in our community. Therefore, I would
be very grateful to my Lord if He would bless my humble suggestions which I sent to the esteemed Court chaplain recently. I
am not asking to do less work myself nor do I seek to live a comfortable life (which would not be as good for my health as my
work in the service of the Lord and our community); rather, I
want our dear people to have an able man to lead and to guide
them, since that would be in their best interest.

I always believe that God will arrange things for a beneficial
outcome! We can see this just now from the very special demonstration of His fatherly care for us through the Lord Trustees,

the most esteemed *Corpus Evangelicorum,* and other dear benefactors in Germany and other countries, who elected to remain
anonymous although they contributed greatly to our spiritual
and physical well-being in Ebenezer. However, they are well
known to the Lord who uses them as dear instruments of His
fatherly care, and as angels on earth for His goodness. It is a
great joy for us to mention their most esteemed persons, their
houses, and offices to the Lord in our daily poor prayers. I also
have to remember one of the well-known songs of our blessed
confessors: "Reason cannot comprehend it. She says (when tribulations seem to get the upper hand), 'Everything is not lost'; yet
the cross has reborne those who need thy help" and, especially,
also: "Help us not to vacillate; reason is fighting against faith,
she will not grieve about the future, when Thou Thyself will
comfort."[10]

Tuesday, August 25. Our rich harvest is a beautiful sign of
God's care for us. May He also, for the sake of Christ, hear our
poor prayers for a long wished-for and permanent peace between England, France, and Spain! Then we would have more
reason to hope that our dear, worn out people could get reliable
servants from Germany. If that will not be possible, and they
have to continue without help, then the hard work will bring
them to their graves prematurely.

Thursday, August 27. In my present poor circumstances I rely
on God's dear word as well as on the edifying letters from our
fathers and friends which we are reading publicly, to our community's benefit, great consolation, and comfort. I was touched
especially by one short letter which a little schoolgirl had written
to me, and in which she dedicates to me the words from Isaiah
49:23.

Saturday, August 29. Hanns Flerl and his wife are deeply devout people; and their blessed, quiet, and humble way of life is
edifying for everybody in our community. I consider especially
their frequent prayers and intercession a great benefaction for
me and the entire community. But to them applies the saying:
"Whom I love I chasten and scourge", etc.

This week, God has sent to them another hard and very painful cross to bear. Recently, helping to make hay, the wife, who

was in the last stages of her pregnancy, worked too hard and very sad consequences followed. The child in her died and the mother was close to death. She had already taken leave of her dear husband and would gladly have passed on, since, filled with faith, she had recognized her Savior who blesses us all. God however, who hears our prayers, strengthened her quite visibly after some of our excellent Schauers's balm was rubbed on her. Now she seems to be out of danger again. I myself witnessed signs of God's swift and merciful granting of our prayers. I will report to our most esteemed Senior Urlsperger the details of this, which are highly significant.

SEPTEMBER

Tuesday, September 1. This morning I and our community, in all humility, proceeded to make good use of the letters which arrived recently; and our dear God strengthened me greatly in this undertaking. Since I have to leave on a not very pleasant journey to Savannah this afternoon, I needed this respite. The letter from our most esteemed Senior Urlsperger contained this ominous and hopeful sentence: "The more our enemies envy the spiritual and physical growth of God's kingdom in Ebenezer, the more it will increase in size."

Thursday, September 10. Our miraculous Lord has sent much suffering to Glaner and his wife, a pious couple. However, by His goodness, they benefit from their trials spiritually. For a long time now, the wife has been weak and sickly, and she can attend to only a few chores. He has assisted faithfully two widows in his neighborhood, Mrs. Zant and Mrs. Graniwetter, and has worked so hard that his feet have become afflicted and now he can hardly walk. God's word and prayer are their daily food and drink, and they praise His goodness more and more and never complain about their misery. They yearn for heaven; and our dear Savior means not only a great deal to them, but everything.

Veit Lechner is in a similar beautiful frame of mind, although he is still troubled by old sins he committed in Salzburg and Germany after falling in with bad company. Occasionally he finds it hard to believe that God will bless such a sinner as himself. My words of consolation to him were well received; I quoted from the gospel which is to be preached to the poor, and we held our communal prayer in his house. He has very little, on account of the long drawn-out illness which God sent to him, and from which He, miraculously, granted him recovery, when neither he himself nor his family and other people believed it possible. He is in need of assistance, which is gladly given to him. He is one of those who consider having come to Ebenezer a great and undeserved blessing. Here in Ebenezer we have an abundance of the means to salvation and prepare ourselves for eternity in solitude and Christian simplicity.

Lechner asked his stepson, N. /Schrempf/ why he wanted to move to Carolina when his earnings were quite good here. The answer he got was that there he could eat meat three times a day. He is like those who yearned for the fleshpots of Egypt while they were being tested in the desert. I consider this dangerous and self-centered change of this poor man a great punishment by God. He not only sinned heavily against his father and mother during the journey here but also after arriving in Ebenezer and has not done any penance for that so far. He has also forgotten that God sent him a disease which made him rant and rave during the time of the Spanish Invasion and that He blessed our poor prayers and the medicines we used for healing him.

He had been doing various work and received from me two pounds and eight shillings Sterling in cash for it. He charges a high price for his work. I wish with all my heart that he, his wife, and his two small children may prosper in body and soul! I am saddened and disquieted by the self-centeredness, ungratefulness, and disobedience of people like him, as well as by some other things that happened in our community. However, prayer, contemplation of the divine word, and talking to my dear colleague and other pious listeners give me new courage and console me; and I hope that everything will turn out for the best.

Saturday, September 12. Already on Monday our large boat left for Savannah in order to fetch the things which arrived for us from London. It returned without mishap this afternoon. The four men who brought our things here transported thick

boards to the church in the same trip. An unusually high sand
dune is located directly at the landing site in Savannah and it is
not possible to use a winch for pulling things upwards. Boards
such as these, two and three inches thick and about fifteen feet
long, have to be carried up, which is very hard work and takes a
great deal of time.

May God be praised most heartily for the many benefactions,
especially those from England and Germany, which He has bestowed on our entire community, on our poor, the sick, and our
widows as well as on our families. Our merciful God has sent us
also oil paint for our churches, two mill stones, chains, and ropes
for our mill, medicine for Mr. Thilo and our families, stoves and
beds for the sick, books for everybody in our community, and
many other beautiful and useful things. The mill stones were
not brought up here on this trip but they will be fetched from
Savannah when the water is high enough to reach the mill directly by boat.

Sunday, September 13. Our miraculous God, our Benefactor,
has been sending several severe tribulations to N.N. for the past
few years; but as yet His purpose has not been fulfilled. Quite to
the contrary, as far as his Christianity is concerned, he has worsened. His household is in great disarray, he is raising his children very poorly; and virtually all his affairs need to be put in
order. Today he reported a new disaster to me which has befallen his wife under certain sad circumstances. I took the opportunity to show him that sin is the root of all evil and, with
kindness, I encouraged him to repent sincerely and to remember his promise to God, to me, and to his pious brother in Prussia, namely, to strive for his own blessedness in awe and fear. Finally, I prayed with him to our Lord to have mercy on him, his
wife, his children, and the household he let go to ruin. How well
this man could do! He has such ample opportunity to earn sufficient money! But he proves the truth of the saying: sin is the
people's perdition!

Monday, September 14. A friend in Savannah wrote to me,
among other things, that the harsh and unfair opinions which
some people in Savannah held of me have subsided and that the
members of the city council speak of me now in no other but

loving and respectful terms. I put all such matters into the hands of the Lord; and I have reported the necessary details to the Lord Trustees. Otherwise, I have kept quiet and ignored short-sighted and ignorant opinions. Although I am being mistreated here, I find myself all the more refreshed from afar; namely, by all the beautiful books, letters, medicines, and other consider-able gifts which our dear God has sent to us and which were un-packed recently.

Wednesday, September 16. A pious Salzburger offered to sell me some produce of his various crops and also some hay. He told me that God had blessed him with a rich harvest and that he wanted to earn some money by selling part of it in order to buy heavy winter clothing for his family. What the esteemed gentle-man von N. remarked in one of his very important letters is quite true in this case; namely, that almost nothing proves more disheartening for a hard-working farmer than the fact that prosperity eludes him because he finds it impossible to sell his crops for money. It is therefore of the utmost importance that the Lord Trustees make some provisions for the sale of some of the products which are either grown or made here.

This Salzburger is a well-contented man who, among other things, said: "I am not nearly as poorly off as I am willing to be for the sake of the gospel, just as I have promised to our Lord my willingness to suffer. I can not understand how it is possible for some Salzburgers to leave Ebenezer and not even consider their children's welfare, after having come here for the sake of God's word." I then quoted to him the verse Romans 1: "And even as they did not like to retain God in their knowledge, God gave them over to a reprobate mind, to do these things with are not convenient. Because they did not . . .". Such people as these, who are not willing to be genuinely converted and who refuse to forego their wordly comfort and their desires of the flesh will be punished by God's judgment and, as a consequence, suffer a dis-torted view of things: what is good they will perceive as evil and black they will see as white.

The large chest from Halle which I have mentioned fre-quently in the past because it failed to reach us here in good order has not arrived this time, either. It contained a large quantity of linen for our community; however, our dear God sent us many beautiful gifts: bedding, linen, shirts, stockings, and thread and ribbons for sewing. These gifts had been sent to Augsburg from many places and were collected there; among the things we received were some ready-made clothes from London. Today these blessings will be put in order for distribution to our people. Mr. Thilo received an impressive bounty of medicines from Halle, and both our families enjoyed similar blessings due to the loving care of our most dear father in Christ, Doctor Francke. Praised be God! May He reward these and the many other benefactions which we have received so far most richly!

Thursday, September 17. An old Salzburger thanked me in the name of our dear God and told me that He had done more for him and his physical well-being than he could have asked for or could have understood. He is sixty years old, and a few months ago he suffered from a great weakness, especially in his hearing, so that he became almost deaf. He remembered that he had complained to me of his misery some time ago on his way to church and that I had given him this answer: "God who has helped you in the past can, and will, help you again, for His mercy is undiminished." Our merciful Lord blessed this my consolation for him so that he will never forget it. I reminded him to use the short time of grace left to him well and to work hard towards preparing himself for eternity. In particular, to be on his guard, pray regularly and especially fight his main sin, avarice, worry for food, and greed.

Friday, September 18. Widow Reuter praises God in many ways and recounts the good things that have happened to her since she was widowed. She and her two small children (the youngest is still nursing) enjoyed good health, something which she lacked almost entirely throughout the years of her marriage. God blessed her work in the fields and her cattle so that she was able to pay off her husband's debts as well as buy more clothes and food than while her husband was still alive. She has quite a good harvest of European crops, as well as others, such as wheat, rye, Indian corn, beans, and squash. She sees God's blessing at work everywhere and thinks herself completely unworthy of it.

Her neighbors assist her in several ways; and this summer I hired a worker for her for six days for threshing and making hay, and another one for two days to do the plowing. She herself did all the other work in the fields. God granted us also various gifts from Europe which benefit widows and orphans especially. Our merciful God takes care of even the weakest among us in so many ways!

Monday, September 21. This morning we gave thanks and held our annual harvest service on Deuteronomy 8:10. The text encouraged us to show our gratitude, in word and deed, towards the Lord's spiritual and physical blessings from afar and near. Afterwards we started to distribute the gifts from Europe which our merciful Lord had granted us this time. Tomorrow, God willing, we will continue in good order. Yesterday, it being the Fourteenth Sunday after Trinity, we covered the gospel text dealing with the lack of gratitude for received blessings, which is a sin that greatly displeases the Lord.

Today we considered the verse: "When thou has eaten and art full . . ." regarding the gratitude for received blessings, which is a virtue that greatly pleases the Lord. Although I am troubled these days because of several problems in our community, our merciful Lord did strengthen me remarkably, both physically and spiritually, while I was preaching His word. He is honoring me at present by sending me various tribulations; and my soul as well as my office, I hope, will benefit from this. I completely believe in the verse: "In returning and rest shall ye be saved." May our Lord continue to grant me hope and courage!

Tuesday, September 22. Rottenberger and Kogler's wife have been suffering from physical weakness for some time now. It is God's intention to assist them by offering this bitter cup; and the consequences of His grace and the Holy Spirit are becoming apparent in a miraculous fashion, although their physical condition is very poor indeed.

Wednesday, September 23. Quite early this morning word was sent that Rottenberger needed to see me. On my way there I met a man who was going to work in town. I asked him what Biblical verse he had chosen as his motto for the day? He said that indeed he had prayed together with his wife and had read for a while in the *Treasure Chest*[1] but just then he could not think of a single word, which embarrassed him greatly. In the evening, as I hurried back for our prayer hour after seeing Rottenberger and Mrs. Kogler, I met him again; and, he told me with tears in his eyes, that he had certainly felt the damage done by his spiritual negligence during the day's work. He gave me some of the details and added that from now on he would keep to his new resolve to meet each day well fortified by faith. Thereafter he chose as his motto the verse: "Whom I love I chasten and scourge."

Thursday, September 24. Rottenberger, in his sickness, is using his pains to his soul's advantage. He regrets his former faithlessness towards God, who had worked His miraculous ways in him for a long time; and he is praying seriously and frequently. He also welcomes it when other people pray with him and talk to him about God's word, and especially about Christ, our Savior. He believes himself to be the worst of all sinners; and he humbly marvels at the wealth of God's patience and tolerance towards him. He reminds himself as well as others frequently of the verse: "Haste thee, and save thy soul." In the past, the company of some of his fellow workers sometimes hampered him; and he violated his conscience out of fear of appearing unpleasant.

Friday, September 25. Mrs. Kogler, who is also sick, was doing very poorly several days ago. She was quite agitated, and from her words and gesturing it was easy to see that she was filled with fear and greatly troubled in her conscience. She had to be held down and watched at times so that she would not jump out of her bed. Afterwards she became quieter but could not describe what condition she was in. When I visited her today, she told me at length and with great emphasis that our Lord had shown her much mercy, for she had prayed to Him fervently, asking him to reveal all her sins to her and to grant her a penitent and believing spirit. This the Lord had done and, beyond that, He had almost forced upon her His merciful forgiveness for all of her sins. Furthermore, He had assured her of His grace and had sent her peace of mind and soul. Now she need not do more than reach out, receive His blessings, and be filled with joy. Dying seems a pleasure and great benefit to her now.

This turn of events has awakened her husband's spirit. Yesterday and today he prayed and, greatly moved, praised the Lord. Already some years ago I had started to see the effects of goodness in Mrs. Kogler; also, she had always shown a great love for God's word and prayer. There was some lack of the necessary sincerity, however; and that prevented her from giving herself to our Savior completely and genuinely so that she had been unable to reach certainty regarding her state of grace. The conduct of her husband, who used to be somewhat irresponsible as well as harsh, contributed to preventing her from achieving complete goodness. Now that she has received grace and has overcome her fear, she is advancing him on his path to goodness; and, in contrast to earlier times when he was less willing, he is now eager to mend his ways, since he has witnessed her blessed change and her great joy and has been greatly impressed by it.

Saturday, September 26. Around noon, Mrs. Kogler sent word again asking me to come and see her at the mill plantation where she lies sick. As soon as possible I hurried there. Again, her mind at peace, and with well chosen words, she told me that our dear Savior had helped her out of her soul's great pain and had calmed her spirit. Earlier this morning, her certainty of His grace and sweet love had vanished, and it had seemed to her that she had only imagined His forgiveness of her sins as well as her great joy of a few days ago. She thought that it had all been lies what she had told me of her state of grace, and this seemed a great sin to her. She had humbled herself, thinking of herself as a most miserable worm which belonged entirely and completely in hell's fire and damnation, and she had held to her belief in our dear Savior's word so steadfastly that once again He had sent a ray of His love directly into her heart. Now she felt as alive and full of joy as before her doubts. She then said: "Often I have heard, but never fully understood the verse: "Unless thy law had been my delights, I should have then perished in mine affliction." We then sang the song: *Meine Seel komm in die Wunden* etc., prayed, and praised the Lord. After that this blessed sufferer received Holy Communion. She thought the verse "Behold, I stand . . . etc." quite remarkable because it describes in detail how our Lord Jesus prepares the soul before sharing Holy Communion with it.

Sunday, September 27. Since I have not received any word or letters from our dear brothers in Pennsylvania[2] in such a long time (because their letters were on a boat which was captured and brought to St. Augustine) I have to be content with whatever printed news of God's work there I get sent from Halle. Reading these today edified me greatly, by God's grace. Anew I feel encouraged to praise God most heartily and ask for His intercession. Mr. Mühlenberg and Mr. Brunnholz are two dear men, whom our Lord has equipped with special talents for serving Him. This irritates some, especially members of the various new sects. However, to my great joy, I read how our Lord opens the eyes of those who are blind. Our dear God has sent us again a great deal of edifying printed material, among it news, vitae, and short essays which He usually has blessed in me, our listeners, and my own family. The *Glaucha House Church Order*[3] is an inspirational little book and is especially well suited for our naive listeners.

Monday, September 28. It pleases our wise and miraculous Lord to try and test dear Mrs. Kogler in various ways, and to subject her to misery and tribulations. She remembered that several years ago she had treated someone unfairly in our orphanage, and this caused her great anxiety and fear. Everything, even her best qualities, suddenly seemed sinful to her and she is willing to suffer any pains for our Lord if only our dear Savior will not forsake her but will receive her in grace. She expressed her desire for grace with so much sighing, gesturing, crying, and sobbing that I cannot find words to describe it. I instructed her that Christ's merit applies to all, and I told her that she had done penance for her sins long ago, had paid what she owed, and was included in the order of salvation. Then I recited for her some good gospel verses, with which she was familiar, and advised her to confess all her sins sincerely, together with me, both her known ones and unknown ones, to our Lord Jesus.

After that she was to accept absolution, which I would pronounce to her in my capacity as a servant of the gospel in His name and in obedience to His command. She was to accept my words as if they had been spoken by Jesus Himself: "Be of good comfort, daughter, thy sins are forgiven thee." Because He had said: "Whatever thou shalt loose on earth shall be loosed in heaven." Then I knelt down at her bedside and prayed a prayer of penitance, which I felt befitted her circumstances according to the ten commmandments; and she prayed along, crying and sighing. After that, in the name of God and the Holy Trinity, the merciful forgiveness of her sins was announced. She sealed this with a heartfelt "Amen" and seemed filled with faith. I told her also that feeling was different from believing; otherwise it would be written: "Without feeling shall I trust."

She feels that a genuine change has taken place in her, she truly abhors all sins, desires Christ and His grace with all her heart, and fully intends to spend the short remainder of her life glorifying Him. I therefore do not have the least doubt that she has a place in the order of grace, that her sins will be forgiven, and that she will partake of the entire treasure of blessedness, as Jesus taught us to preach penitence and the forgiveness of sins.

Saturday, September 29. Kocher, the schoolmaster, suddenly fell ill, as did his wife and son. All three became sick at the same time; they suffer from the same symptoms, and apparently the cause of their sickness was a soup they ate. Since they have an open kitchen, it is possible that something poisonous flew or fell into their food. Doctor Mayer, too, has fallen dangerously ill, and our dear God has sent me a sickness also; I came down with a cold fever after yesterday's evening prayer hour, and I was unable to hold our weekly sermon in Zion Church today. Mr. Lemke stood in for me.

With the proper humble gratitude, I count among the major blessings which our merciful Lord is showing to me and my family the fact that my two young sons are receiving private lessons from my learned colleague, Mr. Lemke and our doctor, Mr. Thilo. In addition to their usual lessons in school they are instructed privately for three hours every day in Latin, geography, history, and vocal music. I am unable to pay Mr. Thilo for his service; however, our dear God and Father alerted several esteemed benefactors in Germany who are willing to contribute to the cost of these lessons. I praise the Lord for this, and I wish and pray that our benefactors will receive God's blessing in return.

Sunday, September 30. Pious Mrs. Glaner has been quite weak for some time now. Her sickness has worsened to such a degree that it was thought she would die last night. When I came to see her today she felt a little better. She is filled with a holy desire to die; she told me she had overcome her remaining worldly ties through Christ's strength, her sins were forgiven, and she could feel our Savior's love in her heart. Her husband cried loudly and bemoaned the loss which was about to befall his household, as well as his Christianity, if his wife were to leave him by her untimely death.

His wife and I both consoled him, quoting God's word. In order to strengthen her very sweet and edifying image of the glory of eternal life, I read to her the beautiful song: *Zu dir erheb ich meine Sinnen,* etc. and sang a few lines from it, despite my present state of impaired health. Our community will lose a precious treasure in her parting from us; she, however, will gain all and lose nothing.

OCTOBER

Monday, October 1. Mrs. Kogler has been desolate for the past few days, and her spiritual condition has deteriorated severely. Only a week ago she was gifted with a droplet of sweet eternity's rain and strengthened by the words of the gospel and Holy Communion. Now she realizes more and more the profound ruin of her soul; and she is learning to see what a serious sin the lack of faith really is, as well as how hard God works at setting to rights again a soul which has strayed from the right path and dirtied itself in sins. She thinks that she would not be sick and bed-ridden if she only were able to believe that once again our God in Christ were merciful towards her. Faith itself and all its main signs are present; what is lacking in her is the feeling of faith. Since all the promises which hold true for those who believe apply to her as well, I could give her hope, quoting from God's word, that in time, by the grace of the Holy Ghost, her battle for faith would end victoriously.

Rottenberger, who was seriously ill, has recovered, and is now strong enough to leave his house and attend to some of his duties. He was not at home when I came to see him, and I quoted to his wife these important words of our Lord Jesus: "Behold, thou art made whole: sin no more, less a worst thing . . ." etc. His soul benefitted greatly from the tribulations that God had sent to him.

Wednesday, October 3. In her present sickness Mrs. Glaner suffers great pain from time to time. She not only endures this with considerable patience, but she also praises God steadfastly. She is ready, by God's grace, for her journey to heaven. Today she asked me what song would be contemplated at the next funeral? I reassured her and she was quiet then and well content. At present, she has a great urge to sleep; soon she will go to sleep in the care of our Lord Jesus.

Sunday, October 7. Dear Kocher has to suffer much pain physically and is preparing himself for leaving this world. The medications prescribed for him until now have not effected the results he wished for and he has decided therefore to do without them. He puts his trust entirely into the hands of the Lord, although he was advised differently, because it is God's wish that we should use the medicines given to us and await His blessing from them.

Monday, October 8. Among the many other benefactions from Germany which we regard most highly, we received a good number of copies of a little hymnal containing edifying songs. We are using it now in our regular prayer hours in Jerusalem Church. The texts of these hymns are very enlightening and the melodies are quite moving when they are sung in proper harmony. A few of these melodies have been unknown to us so far and we are learning them now, for instance: *Mein holder Freund is mein*, etc; also *Mein Schöpfer bilde mich, dein Werk, nach deinem*, etc. Most of the unknown melodies to which the authors of these new, selected songs refer, are contained in our complete songbook from Halle; we do not know, however, from where we will obtain the rest of them which we would also like to learn, for instance: *Fort, fort zu Himmel zu* etc. Yesterday evening we sang with great pleasure: *Jerusalem, mein Vaterland, wenn werde ich dich einmal erblicken?* Next we will learn: *Herr! will ich als Pilgrim wallen?*

Tuesday, October 9. Since our dear God presented us with such a good supply of medications from Halle, I sent a small box of them to Mrs. Driessler; and, at the same time, I wrote a letter to her and included a few edifying pamphlets. Today, these things came back from Savannah, together with the sad news that she had died in the meantime. She had not replied to my earlier two letters in which I had included two gifts of money from Europe, and I assume that she was already sick then. Her grand-daughter married an old Reformed man from Switzerland while the blessed pastor Driessler was still alive, but I never got word of what happened to her after that. A short while ago I received an edifying pamphlet from Wernigerode[1] which describes the conversion and salvation of a woman who murdered her child. I shared this booklet with my dear listeners at Jerusalem Church and Zion Church. Some members of our congregation borrowed it and then handed it on; it pleases our merciful God to give His blessing to reading this text, as I learned through several examples yesterday.

N.N's wife remembered the sins of her youth while reading the booklet and became quite fearful and sad; she started praying fervently and now she shows a genuine desire for Christ, our Savior. She was also very eager to see me and had asked our dear God to send me to her as soon as possible; and when I came to visit her yesterday, her wish had been fulfilled so speedily that the words I quoted to her from the gospel impressed her all the more. Since her conversion to God she had, on several occasions, received tangible proof that our merciful God had granted her forgiveness of her sins. However, when the sweet feelings of forgiveness had worn off, she became fearful again; and, in order to correct these physical emotions in her, I reminded her of the firmer prophetic word, which is the word of God Himself. She bears a heavy cross; she has been suffering from a sickly and weak disposition for several years, among other things; yet she never complains. Rather, she praises the Lord all the more.

Monday, October 15. Dear Mrs. Glaner, who had been seriously ill and near death, has recovered amazingly; to my great surprise and joy I found that she is no longer bed-ridden. She has provided us with yet another example of God's goodness, which He can show to us generously when we ask him for it. She would have gladly died in order to be close to her Lord. However, now, as always, she is content to accept His wishes; and she is trying to use the time left to her to His glory, her salvation, and the benefit of those around her. Kocher, our schoolmaster, had been dangerously ill, also. He is out of danger now, as far as we can tell, and is starting to walk again. His wife and son, who had the same sickness, had improved earlier. God be praised for all the signs of His care and help he sends to us!

Tuesday, October 16. Our dear God has sent some tribulations as well as His mercy to a young woman in our community who had just given birth. She is now happily determined to serve our Lord Jesus at all times and with heartfelt sincerity. I explained to her, in the presence of her parents, how she could spend her days most beneficially during the time she would not be able to work as hard as before. I quoted to her the beautiful song: *Ich will einsam und gemeinsam,* etc.

Thursday, October 18. A pious man who had intended to take Holy Communion on the Eighteenth Sunday after Trinity came to see me this morning. He was troubled because of a sinful dream he had had last night which revealed the malice of his own mind, and he was afraid now to take Holy Communion. I instructed him by reminding him of Christ, that generous and plentiful fountain which washes away sins and uncleanliness; and I did not feel I could advise him to forego Holy Communion because of a sinful dream over which he had had no control and which he regretted with all his heart. We have to bear in mind what is written: "Yea, then come to this flood, come ye children of men! The blood of our dear Jesus purifies sinners. Therefore, ye who are sullied, let yourselves be washed here. This blood can replace the ugliness of your sins."

Monday, October 22. I went to see a widow and a sick woman, and both were in an edifying frame of mind. They are drawn to solitude and quiet; they pray regularly, contemplate God's word and serve those around them without considering their own advantage. They gladly accept their burden of suffering and tribulations, both spiritually and physically, yet I never hear any complaints from them; rather, they praise God all the more and consider themselves to be unworthy of His blessings.

Monday, October 29. Salzburger Brückner has been ill for quite some time now; and, because of his sickness, he is unable to attend to his daily work properly. He gives no sign of this, however, in either his attitude or behavior, nor does he complain or show in any way that he is unhappy about the cross God has sent to him to bear. Rather, he recognizes God's grace in these and other tribulations and continues to praise Him faithfully. He dearly loves God's word, prayer, and edifying books; he is blessedly aware of his Christianity and of the fact that our miraculous God led him from a fatherland steeped in blindness towards the true gospel and sustained him in his belief. He praises God with all his heart and he sets a good example for those who, out of indifference, do not fully realize the precious blessings of salvation and spiritual manna and also for those who, like the ancient Israelites, regard it even with contempt.

Tuesday, October 30. Lately I have been re-reading the accounts of our dear Salzburgers' emigration, and our dear God blessed me especially in this. My love for these people to whom God had shown His grace, here and at other places, but especially for my dear listeners, was inspired anew; and I resolved once more to put all my energies and time to good use by assisting them in their efforts to obtain spiritual salvation. I consider myself quite unworthy of all the goodness, both spiritual and physical, which our merciful God has shown to me among these His people for the past fifteen years (for just at this season, I and my late colleague were sent away from Halle, where we lived at that time, and sent to our Salzburger congregation according to a call from Senior Urlsperger in Augsburg). Soul, remember! What I have written and am now again writing in my letters and diaries which I have sent to our most esteemed friends and benefactors in England about the deserved improvements that were desirable for our physical circumstances here, was motivated by my love which I owe to our Salzburgers. For the same reason I will continue to write and offer my humble suggestions. When we first arrived here, in Abercorn and Old-

Ebenezer, our dear Salzburgers' health suffered, because of poor preparation for living in such a strange country, as well as a lack of experience, together with considerable physical hardships at sea and on land. This caused many to become sickly, weak, and unfit for heavy work, although the country itself is a healthy one. If only there were a way to find good workers and helpers for our farmers!

Wednesday, October 31. I hear that we have so many acorns now, large and small ones, that they can be heaped together by just moving one's feet. People who have the time can gather many acorns very quickly.[2] Something else is different this year, namely, that this fall we have not had any frost during the nights so far, which has many advantages, especially as far as our cattle and the pasture at the plantations are concerned. Our merciful God has shown us many benefactions during this month; and we are in particular thankful that He has taken away the dangerous illness from Mr. Kocher, our schoolmaster, and from Rottenberger, who is such a skilled craftsman, as well as from our dear Mr. /Ludwig/ Meyer. The latter has not recovered fully yet but he is getting his strength back and can leave his bed now and then and attend to some of his duties. During this sickness God showed His mercy to him and his wife, who was also ill, as well as to myself whenever I went to see them, both through His word and prayer. Today we were greatly edified by the dear words: "Commit thy way unto God."

NOVEMBER

Thursday, November 1. Yet another cycle of my office is starting this month; fifteen years ago I was called and sent here to serve this dear community of Salzburgers. We praised our merciful Lord humbly and most heartily, both in public as well as in private, and thanked Him for all the benefactions, spiritual and physical, which He has sent to me and this community. We also confessed our sins of omission and commission in the name of our Lord Jesus. For our public service today I used Hebrews 2:1–3 as my introductory verse, and as our text I chose the gospel passage Matthew 22:1 ff. dealing with our Lord's mercy and goodness, but also with His sternness and judgments. Once again I felt inspired to serve our Savior with body and soul, to dedicate the short remainder of my life entirely to Him, and to put all my strength to good use honoring Him. Our dear God blessed me also in my reading of the *Theologia Pastoralis* by Klosterberg, which edified me greatly.[1]

Tuesday, November 6. I asked one of the Salzburgers, a knowledgeable and hard-working man, why he and his neighbors planted the same fields every season and did not let them rest, as is the custom in Salzburg. He answered that they would like to do that if it were only possible; however, the nutrients in the fields would be used up more by crab grass and other high-growing weeds than if German and Indian crops were planted on them. Even the fields which are only used for growing grass have to be worked with a hoe several times if the hay is to be of good quality, in order to get rid of a kind of weed that looks like wild caraway and has hard, thick stems, and of another weed, an ugly kind of thistle. In Salzburg very good quality grass used to grow on fallow fields.

Thursday, November 8. Schrempf, the locksmith who moved to Carolina with his wife and family a few weeks ago came to visit us for a little while; and today he attended our service at church. He told me that he was full of remorse for moving, that he did not find the new place the way he had expected it to be, and that he wishes now that he had not sold his house and various other things. He is obligated for the next three years; after that, if he wants to return to us if we will have him back and provide him with another lot to build a house, which I will be glad to do. May God open the eyes of everyone so that they may recognize the spiritual and physical benefits they receive here. May the Lord endow them with obedient and grateful hearts!

Saturday, November 10. Mr. Whitefield has returned from Pennsylvania, travelling by the land route, and he had a letter for me from our dear pastor Brunnholz in Philadelphia, who had been sick with the measles for three weeks, which he spent in pastor Mühlenberg's care; but our Lord, who loves life, gave him his health back. He reports that the yellow fever, which the doctors consider highly contagious and which killed many people in Frederica last summer, also raged in Pennsylvania. The people there urgently need more preachers.

Friday, November 16. Since God has sent various illnesses and physical weakness to Brückner, the locksmith, he has been able to make good progress in the work that he has begun for his soul's salvation. He has a humble and patient nature, he is well content with whatever God chooses to give to him, and he is grateful for the dear cross he has to bear. Among the major blessings sent to him by our God he counts the fact that he was saved from spiritual blindness and bad company and that he was led to live in Ebenezer. He was dangerously ill a few weeks ago, and God has restored him to health again.

Saturday, November 17. There is a boat that goes between here and Charleston, and by this boat I had sent my reply to a letter recently from dear pastor Brunnholz which I had received. His letter was brief, but very pleasant; and its content encouraged us in part to praise God and in part to practice humble intercession. I want to quote the following from it:

> Twelve days ago I returned from pastor Mühlenberg's, where I had spent three weeks suffering from the measles. I am not yet completely recovered, but our God assists us in miraculous ways; His ways and works are holy, just and pure miracles. We are waiting for letters and preachers with all our hearts. We have much sickness here at present. The yellow fever which the doctors consider highly contagious is taking its toll from both rich and poor. Many people suffer from other fevers as well. This way our Lord is helping us to preach. Everything is for the best, Romans 8:28.

Sunday, November 18. Mrs. Riedelsberger, a young and pious woman, fell suddenly ill yesterday evening. She thought she would take her leave of her family and us. She sent word to me to come to see her and pray with her once more. Under such circumstances the true nature of a person's heart is revealed; from God's word and prayer she has gathered a beautiful treasure, which is more dear to her than the entire world. Such a treasure can give people a good deal of consolation when they feel frightened in the hour of need and death. I talked to her about the beautiful words of Christian faith: "I believe in the forgiveness of sins, the resurrection of the body (without sin), and in life everlasting."

Monday, November 19. Our dear God has blessed the medications given to the above-mentioned Mrs. Riedelsberger so that she has recovered and can attend to her duties once again. She is grateful to our dear Savior for the physical suffering and tribulations which He has sent to her so frequently since her conversion and which benefit her soul greatly. For some time she had had to miss our evening prayer meetings, as well as some of the Sunday church services, because of her husband's work. This has made God's word and public service all the more precious and dear to her as previously to our dear David. Now, as her husband's circumstances have changed, she is able to take part in this spiritual blessing regularly.

Tuesday, November 20. A wild grass, similar to bullrushes, grows here in fertile soil; it is called silkgrass and is as tough as undressed hemp. A woman from Salzburg showed me some pieces of yarn and thread which she had spun from this silkgrass. She boiled the long green grassblades, broke the leaves like flax, softened them by beating with a pestle in a wooden mortar of the kind as is used for rice, and then spun part of the fibers into thread. The grass grows in abundance here and can be propagated by its roots, but it is inferior to flax and hemp and it requires a lot of work to prepare it for the spinning. Shoemakers use a fine white thread for sewing, which is made from so-called Spanish silkgrass. If we knew how to prepare silkgrass properly then we could make this white thread probably as well as the Spaniards.

Thursday, November 22. Linen, clothing, blankets and the like are very expensive at present; and I therefore consider it a special sign of our heavenly Father's paternal care for us that He sent us the most welcome blessing of a good amount of money from Regensburg and other places in Germany as well as donations from other countries, which I received as a money order at the beginning of this month. A part of this money will be used to improve our beautiful mills by providing as much protection as possible from inundations and excessive amounts of water. In addition to that, we are in the process of building a dam of strong posts and clay for the little river above the mills, which had widened constantly in the past so that in the future we will have sufficient water for the mills when the water level is low. We are also building a schoolhouse near Zion Church; and a short time ago Zion Church itself was equipped with an attic and windows. I am happy that this ongoing construction has supplied several of our people with some extra money for winter clothes. May our merciful God continue to care for us!

Sunday, November 25. Mrs. Kogler has been quite depressed since her last illness, and she complains of her hard-heartedness, a lack of responsibility for her sins, and divine sorrow. She considers herself to be the most miserable person who is dearly in need of compassion. She can not believe that she was included in the Divine Order, right from the beginning, and she therefore refuses to appropriate any gospel verses. It is not easy to give her courage and to teach her the proper ways. I have tried to instruct her from God's word and to show to her that our dear God had started His work of grace in her and, further, that her complaints and tears about her hard, blind, and mean way of thinking were certainly signs of the penitence which she desired so much. However, God can not be commanded, I said, and He guides people's souls as He pleases and as is most beneficial to them. I asked her not stop her prayers and not to desert God's word because of the way things seemed to be. God would grant her to see the light of grace and consolation shining through the darkness. She is physically very weak, but she can still attend to her household duties.

Monday, November 26. Widow Zant, who is a genuine Israelite spiritually and lives in a manner that is appropriate for widows, had a little room built in which she, her two small children, and her maid will be able to keep warm during the wintertime. At her request it was dedicated this afternoon; we contemplated God's word, prayed, and sang. I quoted the consoling words: "Thou shalt guide me with thy counsel, and afterward receive me to glory." I finished up by reading aloud a short and very edifying treatise on Divine Providence and its effects on us for the dear people who were present. This treatise had been sent to us by a friend about a year ago from Memmingen, where it had been printed.

Wednesday, November 28. Praise be God! Today we finished the old church year, and we praised our merciful God in our Lord Jesus' name and thanked Him both in private and in public for his manifold blessings and for the way in which He averted harm from us. This week, in our prayer hours and weekly sermons we contemplated, as we should, the very edifying text from 2 Chronicles 7. We took this opportunity to remind ourselves of the Lord's everlasting grace and of the many blessings, both spiritual and physical, which He sent to us during this past church year. We also asked ourselves whether or not we had used His blessings well, whether or not we could, by His everlasting grace and through His good will, make up for whatever we had neglected to do, and strengthen our faith in His firm promises, which are made as everlasting by Christ's pledge as His everlasting grace. We thought of the words of Psalms 136 which describe His many miracles and wonderful deeds of the past and remind us that: "His mercy endureth for ever!" The Holy Ghost instructed us quite clearly as to how we should make good use of God's works and deeds which He has wrought as proof of His magnificence in both the Old Testament and the New Testament as well as in our times.

Unlike those of little faith who say that God's miracles have ceased or who say that whatever miracles God has worked in the past no longer concern us, unlike them, we on the other hand, should, can, and must attest to and affirm all that He has done for His church, from the beginning on, all that has gone beyond nature's order, and we must say: "His mercy endureth for ever!" Indeed, in the times when we are tested and God sends us tribulations, and when we suffer want of what we need, this will be a great consolation to us. Several writings, as well as passages from the Old and the New Testament, and the above mentioned first part of the seventh chapter of 2 Chronicles clearly instruct us in the proper kind of praise which we have to give to our Lord for His grace and mercy shown to us so far, if He is to be pleased by it and continue to show us His goodness.

Sunday, November 29. Today, on the first day of the new church year, seventy-five people went to Holy Communion (which we hold every six weeks), and our merciful God sent us His blessing from His holy word for the sermon given in the morning, for the sermon in the afternoon, and for our repetition hour, which we attend in summer as well as in winter. This coming church year my dear colleague will base his instruction in catechizing on the regular sermons for Sundays, since last church year he has worked the whole way through Luther's smaller catechism.

In the mornings, however, every year without change, as is the custom in our Evangelical church, we preach on the subject of the regular gospels for Sundays and holidays. Each time, in the exordium, we contemplate an important verse from the Old or the New Testament. Today, in this new church year, like the Israelites according to Joseph 24:24, we pledged ourselves to each other before the Lord and promised to serve the Lord, our God, and to obey His command for as long as He would grant us life. May He send us His spirit to seal this our pledge! May He protect us from the fickleness that afflicted the Israelites, and may He protect us also from behaving like the people who came after the Israelites, who lived in ignorance of the Lord and of His works which He had shown to Israel (and, in our time, to the Salzburgers and our community). There were three men from Purysburg present at our church service; one of them came to see me and gave me much joy by telling me of all the goodness which our dear God had bestowed upon him through the writings of our blessed Luther. He borrowed from me several edifying books which he discusses and shares with others in his area according to his simple talent.

Monday, November 30. Mr. Whitefield sent word that he would like to discuss several matters with me. I have not yet spoken with him because, since his return, he has spent only a few days in Savannah and at his orphanage and I did not want to travel there without the certainty of meeting him. He plans to return from Carolina and his plantation there and come to Savannah during the first few days of this week. However, the weather turned; it became cold and rainy, and this will most probably delay his trip to Savannah, as well as my trip there, for a few days. Through Mr. Lemke, he had requested me to write a short report on our community, our area, and our circumstances. He intends to use this report to our advantage (I presume he will give it to his friends in the northern colonies). I have put together such a report in English and will either give it to him myself or send it to him as soon as possible. May God bless this little undertaking also!

Mrs. Glaner, a pious woman, would have liked to take Holy Communion together with the other members of our community, but her physical weakness did not allow that. At her request, she received Holy Communion today in her house and, through God's word and prayer, she conducted herself in a proper Christian manner. Up to now, she, like many others, lacked the money for heating the house sufficiently in order to stay healthy; we expect that this problem will lessen, since now we can get inexpensive boards from the sawmill. If we only could buy glass for windows someplace cheaper than in Charleston, where it is very expensive. I have asked Mr. Whitefield to buy glass at reasonable prices for us in Pennsylvania or New England, where they make glass, but I do not know whether or not he had the opportunity to do so.

If we could only afford it, I would like very much to give away boards for barns or heating to all those of our people who are in need, not only to the widows. The mills do not return much profit in these poor times; also, we lacked the money and the experience to complete all the necessary construction work and to take care of all details properly. This we have to do now in little installments as our dear God sends us the means for our undertaking from Europe.

Last winter there was a big flood, and we saw how vulnerable our mills were. We had to prepare for similar problems this year, and we spent more than twenty pounds Sterling on various repairs; and for three weeks we carried out the work necessary to protect against high water. God be praised! He sent us the money and gave some of our workers here the strength and the opportunity to earn enough to buy winter clothing and other necessities by working on the mills which, in turn, benefits our entire community in many ways! We do not lack food; but clothing and bed linen, for both adults and children, are very hard to come by in this time of war.[2] Not many have sufficiently heated rooms and their health suffers in the winter cold. See Deuteronomy 10:18.

DECEMBER

Wednesday, December 2. Our schoolhouse at the plantations is not ready yet, and we and the children have to cope with the winter cold as well as we can. Steiner and Brandner, two Salzburgers, are letting us use their well-heated rooms for holding school until our schoolhouse is ready or the weather changes. Kocher is dedicated to teaching the children and I have added another pound to his salary of five pounds Sterling; he also receives various assistance for the running of his household.

N.N. repeatedly acted against his conscience while he was still in Germany working with other apprentices and assistants. He regrets this so much now that he becomes quite dejected at times. He told me several times, with tears in his eyes, that in Salzburg he had been ignorant not only of Divine matters, but also of meanness and sinning. Later, however, after leaving Salzburg, he had quickly learned how to be sinful, just as the other children were. He is seriously concerned with his salvation and he counts among the great blessings sent to him by our Lord the fact that he gave him quietude and has prolonged his period of grace.

Thursday, December 3. Balthasar Bacher's wife has been ill for some time now and quite unable to do any work. God is using this tribulation as a means of her conversion and her preparation for blessed eternity. She repents her former life with all her heart; in the past she led a very sinful life, both while still with her parents as well as later, when she was in service. Especially the misuse of Holy Communion causes her considerable grief.

Saturday, December 5. Last summer, Steiner and Brandner, the two Salzburgers, made a good quantity of peach brandy for themselves and other people. They used the only still we have at our disposal; it was given to our community by the most praiseworthy Society.[1] People from Old Ebenezer buy this brandy since rum is hard to come by and quite expensive. A man from Purysburg sells our brandy in Frederica, and we see in this trading another sign of God's paternal care for us. One gallon or four English quarts sell for four shillings Sterling. Some people used large iron pots instead of a copper distilling vat, and instead of the proper tubing they used gun barrels, but their brandy is said to have acquired an unpleasant flavor from this. In the past, unfortunately, because of the lack of a proper still, many hundreds of bushels of peaches just rotted away, partly while still on the trees and partly after having fallen from the trees.

It would be of great advantage to our people's diet if we could obtain from six to eight smaller distilling vats with a capacity of eight to ten gallons; we would pay for them either by having their cost deducted from the payments made to us or by a letter of credit. It would probably be best to get them from London, because it would be too difficult and maybe even illegal to get them from Germany. Simple copper containers of the kind people commonly use for making brandy would serve us just fine. The large vat mentioned above, which was sent to us by the Society, also has a large brass spigot at the bottom, which, however, is not necessary for just the simple process of distilling. Also, cooling vats need not be sent, our people can easily make those, but we do need for each copper container the copper tubing, through which the brandy will run, well tinned on the inside.

Those of our people who are not very strong physically would be able to add to their income by making brandy; beautiful and juicy peaches grow here in abundance. Trees have to be planted, but more care is not necessary, other than harvesting the fruit after three years. We have also enough water and wood close by. There are also plenty of wild grapes growing on vines in the woods. Those can be harvested by the bushel, and one of our people made a strong brandy from those, using gun barrels. I was told that almost every farmer has his own distilling vat in Virginia and that the people there use brandy to supplement their diet.

Monday, December 7. People in this and the neighboring colony find it very difficult to obtain enough food and to make a good living, and they think of various ways to earn some money.

A certain man from Purysburg, who seems to have fallen into poverty as a consequence of keeping black slaves, borrowed our large boat in order to ferry various kinds of food to Frederica. An undertaking such as this is a gamble, however. Flour is in high demand in Savannah, and our flour from Indian corn is starting to fetch good prices, which is a welcome benefit to our people since everything has gotten so much more expensive than it used to be. Some are starting to send butter to market, which is an improvement also; it used to be that our Salzburgers melted their butter and turned it into lard, but nobody wished to buy that.

Thursday, December 10. Two weeks ago Mr. Whitefield sent word that he had to discuss some things with me. Since I thought that he had returned from Carolina last week, I traveled to Savannah last Monday and arrived safely back here again today. He is still a true friend of our esteemed Fathers in London, of Germany, and of our community here and of its elders. If he only were rid of the large debts he incurred on behalf of the orphanage, then he would be able to do much more for us than is presently in his power to do. This time he gave us two old horses which can still be worked and which I intend to use for the benefit of our widows. He also gave me nine shillings Sterling in cash for the widows, with which I purchased winter bonnets for them, making up the difference out of my own pocket. He liked my little treatise on the spiritual and physical circumstances of our community which I had written, on his request, and sent to him last week. He will use it to our Ebenezer's advantage.

Mr. Whitefield has not been well for some time, but he still keeps active. He preaches frequently, very energetically, and emotionally; and he uses up considerable strength in doing what he does and it would be a miracle if he were able to last long at this pace. His plans for next spring are to go to England and from there to Halle and Augsburg; and he intends to meet our esteemed Fathers there, for whom he has the highest regard. He was very pleased with Doctor Francke's answer to his last letter, and he is looking forward to writing to him again. This time I enjoyed several spiritual and physical benefits at the orphanage.

For our poor, Mr. Whitefield purchased a quantity of heavy

material for winter clothes in Pennsylvania; however, the boat which was to transport it to Charleston has been captured by the Spanish and so this dear and much needed gift is lost to us. Mr. Whitefield also paid the bills for the purchases which Pastor Brunnholz had made on behalf of our farmers, and he is giving us this sum of money, which comes to more than five pounds Sterling. May God reward him as well as all our other benefactors for their gifts and bring them to us safely across land and sea! The boat which was captured also carried more than one hundred pounds Sterling worth of merchandise for Mr. Whitefield's orphanage, and it would be a great tribulation for him and us if this also were lost. For the windows of the school at the plantations which is being built now he gave me fifty large panes of glass as a gift.

Saturday, December 12. Our dear God has shown much mercy to our locksmith, Brückner, in his illness, which lasted for quite a while this time. Brückner is genuinely grateful to his benefactor for this tribulation, and he wishes to devote the rest of his life entirely to His glory. He is poor and wants to make an honest living from his trade. We are going to lend him as much money as he needs for the purchase of some iron and tools. All of our hard-working people here in Ebenezer, and their farms and households, will benefit from this, with God's blessing.

Sunday, December 13. Young Lackner is hard pressed in these hard times; he has a household to take care of, and a wife and two small children. Both are true Christians, quiet and content; and they believe patiently that, if they continue to work hard and remain steadfast. our Lord will come to their aid during the span of their lives which He allotted to them. Among other things I am pleased that our dear people here prefer to suffer want in physical matters rather than to incur debts. If they have to borrow, out of most dire need, then they are eager to repay their debts as soon as possible, and therefore merchants in Savannah are willing to give them credit. Our merciful God, who is called a God of patience, of consolation, and of hope, Romans 15, does not desert us in our present tribulations without sending us instruction and consolation. Today we contemplated the gospel of the Third Sunday of Advent, which deals with the tribulations sent to God's friends and children; specifically, 1) the variety of tribulations, and 2) the great benefit of tribulations. For our introductory verses we had Judith 8:19–29.

Tuesday, December 15. This morning all our people gathered in Zion Church. We started and ended with song and prayer. Two main points were discussed: firstly, pending the approval of our community and the Lord Trustees, Mr. Mayer, our surgeon, has agreed to take over some of my duties in the future and to represent the best interest of our dear people here by attending to the legal and non-local business on their behalf. I have very important reasons for charging another with these worldly matters, if our entire community is willing to consent. The people were convinced by my arguments, which I had mentioned in the past and repeated today, and they are glad that we have a competent and trustworthy man among us, whom we already know, and who is capable of assuming this office. All agreed to accept his authority and to supply him with wood and grain until his salary from the Lord Trustees starts to arrive. He will also get a horse.

The second point of our conference concerned the improvement of our mills through the industry and communal work of our people here. God does not give everything all at once to us, but one thing at a time in order to increase our praise of Him, our joy, and the strengthening of our faith. He has recently shown us how a ditch of approximately one thousand feet in length and eight feet in width could provide much additional water from the Savannah River to our mills. Through this and with God's merciful guidance and blessing, the mills could eventually be put into a position not only to cover the mills' operating costs but also to repay gradually the debts incurred when building them and consequently be of benefit to our community.

The members of our community were encouraged to build the aforementioned ditch by working together and contributing their labor because I had to spend fourteen pounds twelve shillings Sterling for continuing the work on Zion Church (its interior is not yet completed), twenty-three pounds nineteen shillings in cash on the mill dam and the mill channels (and this very practical work was finished on December 12), and I expect to pay another five pounds for the building of a supporting dike at the mill stream a few hundred feet above the mill dam to control the very dangerous and destructive surplus water. Furthermore we will need more money for the school we are in the progress of building and for the many other expenses of our community. If God granted me some means, I would gladly make some contribution.

If our plan works out and we succeed in channelling more water to the mill when we need to, then we would have the additional benefit that the European crops such as wheat, rye, etc. could be milled soon after the summer harvest, which would be a great advantage and encouragement for our farmers. At that time of year the waterlevel in the mill stream is at its lowest and the mills have to stand still without additional water. Otherwise, worms, little flies, and bugs infest the crops very quickly and ruin them. The flour, on the other hand, keeps very well. Our people seem to be willing to undertake this work, but we will probably have to wait until next spring or summer, if we live so long, before getting started because of the cold weather and the high waterlevel expected soon.

The aforementioned incorrect runoff of millwater will be dammed in as soon as possible with posts and clay. This was done already some years before but not properly and not with the necessary caution; therefore the water broke through the dam, and the mill river was widened considerably as a consequence. From the very beginning, our community lacked people experienced in matters of building and construction and Captain Avery died prematurely.[2] If this had not been the case then we would have been able to save a good deal of money. May God continue to show us His goodness! Our help stands in His great name. He will come to our aid, Amen!

Wednesday, December 16. Today, in the afternoon, we had a short thunderstorm and a long lasting downpour. Usually cold weather or high water in the Savannah River follows and, as a consequence, inundations. I praise our dear God for helping us so far that our mills, the damm, and the channels have been rebuilt and properly repaired.

No sooner had the pious Mrs. Glaner recovered somewhat

than she was stricken with yet another weakness, and I and others expect her to leave this world soon. She talks in an edifying manner and shows all signs of being gifted with the noble treasures of her heart. She usually finds consolation and encouragement in the great patience and edifying conduct of her late pious foster child, Paul Klocker. She complains only about the lack of obedience in her heart, and she can not praise God enough for His mercy towards her and her husband in their solitude. She is eager to hear God's word and she applies everything she sees or hears to the best advantage of her spiritual life, as befits the children of God.

Thursday, December 17. Yesterday evening the sky cleared, and a strong northern wind brought a hard frost. This afternoon, when I went to see the widow Zant, she invited me right away into her warm little house, which our dear God had given to her sooner than I or she could ever have suspected. We spoke about the good verse for next Sunday's lesson: "Be careful for nothing; but pray and thank God in every thing by prayer and supplication . . . ," but not only in good days and with the enjoyment of blessings but also in tribulation, misfortune, and all sorts of unpleasant situations. These last words impressed me especially as this pious widow told me of a mishap that befell her a few days ago. According to her, the way she thought of it and described it, things could have turned out much worse if our merciful God had not intervened. Christians therefore have good cause to pray and to thank God in all things.

Another widow told me that two years ago her late husband had asked her to visit the widow Christ[3] and to bring her a present and this verse and that it has consoled her herself as well as that other widow. She recalled this verse today when she had to deal with her troubles. Our nine widows are well pleased with their winter bonnets, for which Mr. Whitefield contributed nine shillings, and they praise God for this gift. In their cut and make the bonnets are like those which were sent to us in great quantity some years ago from Salzburg.

Sunday, December 20. Our merciful God is continuing His work on the knitter Schäffler's soul in order to bring him to genuine conversion through His word, and through physical tribulations such as poverty and sickness, but also through various benefactions. Schäffler greatly fears God's wrath, and he is not yet ready to die because he feels he is not properly prepared for the important change from time into eternity and needs to do more penance and strengthen his faith. He is very ignorant and his way of thinking lacks order; I have high hopes however, that with God's help he might become a new man and then recognize gratefully (like many among us) that our merciful Savior had beckoned him, led him into the wilderness, and talked to him kindly. Our Salzburgers did not leave their home for the sake of good living; under the merciful guidance of our miraculous God they landed in this quiet corner of the world in order to strive first and foremost for God's kingdom and His justice. As a reward, they will receive as many physical benefits as God deems necessary and beneficial.

Monday, December 22. Balthasar Bacher's wife /Anna Maria/ seems to have come very close to leaving this world. By sending her lingering women's complaints God impressed upon her most emphatically the reminder of her perdition and the sins of her youth, including the most offending of sins, namely, the neglect and repudiation of Christ out of a lack of faith. This is causing her much unrest and great sadness, and she regards the symptoms of her sickness to be a specific punishment for her sins in the past, since she remembered from one of our dear Senior Urlsperger's sermons the verse: "As a man sinneth, so shall he be punished." Today, among other things, she told me that she had sinned against Divine guidance by being discontent and by complaining even after arriving in Ebenezer, although our merciful God had intended nothing but her true salvation all along. She is now turning towards Him, praying and beseeching, like a little worm in the wounds of Jesus.

Tuesday, December 23. Kocher, our schoolmaster, who is an experienced weaver, is going to attempt to work with our spun flax and to weave some heavy material for sacks. We still have enough lightweight material for the kind of bags we use for wheat, rye, and rice flour. Spelt or dinkel is also in great demand by some of our people and, for a while, I had hoped to obtain several bushels from our friends in Pennsylvania, but we did not succeed in that, and the planting season is over now. It is hoped that such crops will grow as well as rice here and keep better than wheat when stored in the kernel so that it would be possible to postpone threshing into the fall or winter instead of doing this hard work in the heat of summer.

Wednesday, December 24. Several months ago, through the letters of our most esteemed Fathers and benefactors, our merciful God had given me the hope that He would allow them to share with me some of their temporal goods in order to serve Him and to benefit my two small sons at the same time. I immediately started them in their private lessons with Mr. Thilo, in addition to their regular schooling. Among other things, they are being instructed in vocal music so that, while they are still young, their voices can be trained properly for singing their Creator's praise and pleasing those around them. Both have the necessary talent and willingness. Recently they learned an aria for two soprano voices and sang them in church after our prayer hour, supported by my voice, their mother's, and that of Mr. Thilo, who is a good basso. God used this meager example of our skills for edifying several members of our community and awakened in our younger people such an interest for religious music that they, too, wish to be instructed by Mr. Thilo in return for a small honorarium; and they are taking lessons several evenings each week. I intend to assist those who are short of funds. In our meetings we sing many old, as well as new and otherwise unknown, melodies; and from time to time we learn additional songs from our beautiful and complete hymnal from Halle.

Thursday, Friday, December 25 and December 26. We have celebrated Christmas for the past two days, in blessed remembrance of the precious incarnation and birth of Christ which is such a great source of consolation for us sinners. We prepared ourselves for some hours in Jerusalem Church and Zion Church by contemplating in sequence several instructive and comforting verses: 1 Kings 9; 1–3 dealing with the merciful apparition of the God of Israel before Solomon and the granting of his prayers. Our merciful God sent us not only the weather we had wished for but peace as well; and we derived much edification and blessing from His word, prayer, and beautiful

Christmas songs. May His illustrious name be praised!

Saturday, December 28. Mrs. Balthasar Bacher, who is still sick, lost even more strength during the holidays. Her soul, however, partook amply of our Savior's gentleness and kindness. When I came to visit her today I inquired after her state of mind and she said: "Our Lord Jesus has taken me to His bosom. I found justification and peace, and I am not asking for anything more but to loosen my earthly bonds and go to Him for all eternity." Although she was very weak, she talked to me of various matters and told me that Jesus has pledged to her His repeated assurance of His grace and the hope for life eternal. She was filled with the praise of God and showed herself to be humble in spirit. She also wishes that God may reward her pious neighbor, Mrs. Maurer (whom God has brought to a fine understanding of Christianity by sending her several difficult tribulations) a thousandfold for her edifying company, support, and prayer, which she enjoyed and which benefitted her soul especially during the holidays.

Other pious women visited her also and added to her spiritual comfort. She commended into her Heavenly Father's care her two young children and her husband, and she is at peace. She thinks constantly of Jesus, His love, and blessed eternity. She is too weak to take any nourishment; and He is her food and her drink, and He refreshes her spirit. In order to strengthen and increase her desire for blessed eternity we read aloud for her the twenty-first chapter of the Revelations of St. John 21 and the precious song: *Alle Menschen müssen sterben.* When I made a remark on the song: *Der Bräutigam wird bald rufen* and mentioned the blessed in Heaven, she remembered the late Mr. Gronau and assured me of her remorse over saddening him so frequently. She asked me also to speak with two pious women in our community and to ask them to forgive her for all the things she had done to spite them in the past.

One of the women who had met her in Augsburg had once asked her (the sick Mrs. Bacher) if she not also kept company with certain people who were known for their loose living. At the time she had denied it and, by lying, had become guilty of sinning against her own conscience and against God, who ab-

hors all sins. She is also greatly agitated and full of sorrow because she had taken part in dancing, a godless activity, and because of the lies which she had told to her elders in Augsburg
when her evil way of living had been examined. Since God
opened her eyes, however, and she has become very fond of our
solitude, where we are protected from public nuisances, God be
praised! I asked her whether I should write to Augsburg on her
behalf? But she did not think that necessary. She does not know
whether or not her old parents are still alive but she does not
believes that anything good could be written about her or her
life; and, besides, after God has taken her into Heaven, nothing
else would matter anyhow.

While we talked she quoted the most beautiful verses from
Holy Scripture and she talked so coherently and lucidly of divine truths and with such respect that it is a pleasure to listen to
her. I was especially touched when she fainted (she frequently
does now) as the song: *Herr Jesu Christ, mein Lebenslicht* was read
to her; she lay like dead, her hands folded on her breast as in
prayer. After a little while she started to speak the following
words very clearly, but without the least movement of her head
or or any part of her body: "He on the cross is my love," etc. and
"Oh world, see here thy life on the trunk of the cross," etc. and
"And even if a struggle is appointed, it does not matter. Alas, I
have already seen such a great splendor, now," etc. and "He will
give me life eternal up there, my heart should forever . . ." etc.[4]

Between the verses of these songs she made a pause, lay quite
still, and did not move. Then she started to pray in such a forceful, coherent, and impressive manner as I would not have expected of her back in the days before her sickness; she prayed
for herself, her husband, her children, me, and our community.
She repeated her wish that the dear people of Ebenezer should
not give their pastor any cause for worry as she herself had done
in the past; rather, they should act according to the word which
was being preached to them so faithfully so that they would become blessed people. She showed a great need for my company
although she seemed to be in a state removed from others.
When her husband put his hands on hers she asked who was
there? Then she said to him: "Look, Balthasar! Look! Take com-

fort in the Lord. He will bestow unto thee" etc. and: "My heart is filled with our Lord Jesus. To be sure, Mrs. N.N. said I should accompany her, but I chose another way, namely, to my Lord Jesus" etc.

Her husband told me that she frequently talked about such edifying matters although she was very weak and often close to fainting; and she had no more interest in any worldly matters.

Monday, December 30. Mrs. Kogler is still anxious and lacking in consolation. She is unable to find the strength one would wish her to find in God's word or prayer. A short time ago she had a right heavenly refreshment while on her sickbed, but after that her soul grew so dark that she considers herself the most miserable sinner and cannot find in herself even the smallest sign of repentance. All verses which affirm that grace is awaiting her, too, despite her condition she rejects as if they had nothing to do with her, for instance: "I will look, even to him that is poor and of contrite spirit," etc. On the other hand, she had nothing to say to disprove my well-meaning consolation: "Thou hast ascended on high, thou hast led captivity captive. Thou hast received gifts for men; yea, for the rebellious also, that the Lord God might dwell among them," etc. Whenever I speak with her I beg her not to cease to to pray frequently and to listen to God's word even if it seems to her to be of no use. It would be enough for a beginning for her to prove her obedience towards God by applying the means of salvation. God wants to help us with the means prescribed by Him but whenever He pleases and when He deems it to be in our best interest.

Tuesday, December 31. I will close the diary of this year with the song which we recently started to use for closing our evening prayer hours. On holidays we sing to the same melody for two sopranos and one basso also the beautiful song "*Sey willkommen, sey willkommen, Jesulein! mein Freund*" etc. which we found in the hymnal we received from our dear Wernigerode.

1. Good night, you idle fears! Leave my heart free, today I fear not for tomorrow, since God is ever true. He nourishes me late and early, without my care and trouble. My joy in this tranquility is what my Father wills.

2. I shall struggle for the best, for eternity, and shall live in

justice and in Christ during my span of grace. If this is so, then I shall easily find what redounds to my profit. See how calm a true Christian is in God.

3. Well then! My whole life, what I have and am, I will pledge to God: it is to my profit, my soul flies upward towards the place of joy. Jesus! help me to it; otherwise I shall find no rest.[5]

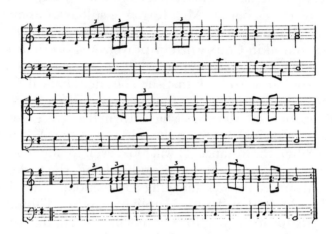

Appendix

SONGS SUNG BY
THE SALZBURGERS
IN 1747

Hymns followed by F-T and volume and song (not page!) number are reproduced in Albert Friedrich Fischer—W. Tumpel, Das deutsche evangelische Kirchenlied des 17. Jahrhunderts) (Gütersloh, 1916, reprinted Hildesheim 1964). Authors of all identified hymns are listed in (AF) Albert Friedrich Fischer, Kirchenlieder-Lexikon) (Gotha, 1878, reprint Hildesheim 1967).

Alle Menschen müssen sterben . . . (All men must die), by Johann Georg Albinus. p. 139

Als Gottes Lamm und Löwe, entschlafen und verschieden) . . . (When God's Lamb and Lion slept and passed away), by Paul Gerhardt. p. 41

Der Bräutigam wird bald rufen, kommt all ihr Hochzeitgäste . . . (The Bridegroom will soon call, come all ye wedding guests), by Johann Walther. p. 139

Fort, fort zu Himmel zu, unidentified. p. 118

Gott Lob, ein Schritt zur Ewigkeit ist abermals vollendet) . . . (Praise God, another step towards eternity has been completed), by August Hermann Francke. p. 86

Herr Jesu Christ, meins Lebens Licht . . . (Lord Jesus Christ, Light of my Life), by Martin Behm. p. 140

Herr! will ich als Pilgrim wallen? . . . (Lord, will I wander as a pilgrim?), unidentified. p. 119

Ich will einsam und gemeinsam . . . (I shall go alone with Thee), from a Dutch hymn by Jodocus von Lodenstein. p. 120

Ihr armen Sünder, kommt zu Hause . . . (Ye poor sinners, come home), by Laurentius Laurenti. p. 48

Jerusalem, mein Vaterland, wenn werde ich dich einmal er-blicken? . . . (Jerusalem, my Fatherland, when shall I view thee?), unidentified. p. 118

Mein holder Freund ist mein . . . (My dear Friend is mine), by Ulrich Bogsilaus von Bonin. p. 118

Mein Schöpfer bilde mich, dein Werk, nach deinem . . . (My Creator, build me, Thy work, according to Thy...), anonymous, in Freylinghausen's *Geistreiches Gesangbuch.* p. 118

Meine Seel, komm in die Wunden Christi ein . . . (My soul, come into the wounds of Christ), anonymous, in Freylinghausen's *Geistreiches Gesangbuch.* p. 114

Sey getreu in deinem Leiden . . . (Be loyal in thy suffering), by Benjamin Prätorius. p. 36

Sey willkommen, sey willkommen, Jesulein, mein Freund, anonymous. p. 141

Zu dir erheb ich meine Sinnen, anonymous, in Freylinghausen's *Geistreiches Gesangbuch.* p. 117

Notes
∼ for the Year 1747 ∼

JANUARY

1. *In nomine Jesu Amen*, In the name of Jesus, Amen.
2. During Oglethorpe's absence, Maj. William Horton was the senior officer at Frederica.
3. Boltzius spoke highly of Dr. Thilo in his reports, but less so in his private letters, which mentioned frequent occurrences of insanity.
4. (Johann) Ludwig Meyer, a barber surgeon who came with the fourth Salzburger transport, helped Boltzius in many secular duties.
5. "emphatically."
6. In 1747 the "last Germans" were those aboard the *Judith*, Walter Quarme captain, which arrived on 22 Jan. 46.
7. The "order of salvation" was the theological steps of confession, repentance, and absolution by which one was saved.
8. Mrs. Anna Kurtz was the widow of Matthias Kurtz, a Salzburger from Dürrenberg, who had emigrated to Cadzant and later to London before being taken to Ebenezer by Heinrich Melchior Muhlenberg in 1742.
9. "Every word that proceedeth from the mouth of God."
10. John Wesley had refused to give Holy Communion to Boltzius because the latter had not received the "laying on of hands" in the Apostolic Succession.
11. At this time in Georgia the word "Frenchman" often designated a French Swiss, particularly if he were from Purysburg.
12. The Kieffers of Purysburg had often been rowed to Ebenezer by black slaves, who even attended church.

FEBRUARY

1. Mrs. Driesler was the widow of the late German pastor Johann Ulrich Driesler at Frederica, who had died after only four years of service.
2. Ruprech Kalcher and his wife Margaretha, nee Gunther, were a selfless and saintly couple who had managed the orphanage.
3. Johannes Arndt, *Vier Bücher vom Wahren Christenthum*, the most popular devotional work among colonial Germans.
4. Friedrich Curtius (Kurtz), a swindler, who cheated Bichler and other Salzburgers in a lumber operation.
5. "Legalistic" meant based on the law of the Old Testament, rather than on the grace of the New. A legalistic person was penitent only through fear of punishment, not through love of Jesus.

6. Because they are "legalistic" (see note above), they cannot believe they can be justified by faith.

7. Theophilus Grossgebauer, *Drey Geistreiche Schriften, I Wächter-Stimme aus dem verwüsteten Zion*. Leipzig 1710.

8. Every year the Salzburgers celebrated a memorial and thanksgiving day on the anniversary of their safe arrival in Georgia.

9. For years Boltzius assumed that Theobald Kieffer, Jr., was older than Jacob, but he finally realized his error.

10. *Beten, Wachten, Kämpfen.*

11. "She" naturally refers to the wife of the man N.

12. Rottenberger's brother was among the large group of Salzburger exiles who found refuge in East Prussia.

13. The Salzburgers sold only boards made from heartwood and retained the slabs, or outside boards, for their own use.

14. Jacob Metzger of Purysburg had sent his son to Charleston to take his two youngest children from their mother, who was begging on the streets. On their return, their boat capsized and his three children were drowned. He later moved to Ebenezer, where his children became prominent inhabitants.

15. Ambrosius Wirth, *Christliche Anweisung zu GOtt wohlgefälligen Beichten und Abendmahlgehen.*

16. Johann Friedrich Starck, *GOttgeheiligtes Herz und Leben eines wahren Christen.*

M A R C H

1. "The Lord hath helped so far" was one interpretation of "Ebenezer."

2. The Salzburger Matthias Zettler came as a youth with the second Salzburger transport.

3. Many of the Salzburgers had resided at Memmingen, not far from Augsburg, after their expulsion and before their migration to Ebenezer.

4. Whooping cough was the cause of many infant deaths.

5. Sola Bills were bills of exchange issued by the Trustees and negotiable only when signed.

6. This daughter is never named.

7. In the first years of the colony there was a crane on the bluff manned by German indentured servants, but it had been discontinued. The bluff was some forty feet high, very steep, and sandy, making drayage very difficult.

8. See Feb., note 15.

9. Christian Scriver, *Seelenschatz.*

10. This is an example of the Pietists' faith in theodicy. Since God is omniscient, omnipotent, and all-loving, anything He does is for our good, even if human understanding cannot comprehend the fact.

11. Although George II was the head of the Anglican Church, he was a Lutheran and maintained a Lutheran court chapel.

A P R I L

1. C**s was Friedrich Curtius, or Kurtz, who posed as the son of a Lutheran minister with prominent connections in Philadelphia. He organized a big-time

timber operation and then absconded with the cash and left the Salzburgers with heavy debts.

2. Lucius Junius Moderatus Columella, *Scriptores rei rusticae*, a classical anthology of agricultural writings.

3. "Be loyal in your suffering."

4. *Trägheit*, "indolence," meant indolence in prayer.

5. Abraham Kyburg, *Historien- Kinder- Beth- und Bilderbibel mit eingedruckten Kupferstichen. Drei Theile*. Augsburg 1736–42.

6. Schauer's Balm was a panacea manufactured in Augsburg by Johann Caspar Schauer.

7. This is not in the 3rd Psalm but in 1 Timothy 5:3.

8. By *Arbeiter* Boltzius surely means a minister, or laborer of the Lord.

9. See March, note 10.

10. Despite his admonitions, even Boltzius had lost some of his parishioners, including Andreas Grimmiger, Stephan Riedelsperger, Rosina and Johann Spielbiegler, Ruprecht Zittrauer, Andreas Zwiffler, and many more.

11. The Trustees had tried to prevent large land ownership by restricting grants to fifty acres tail-male. They seem to have been influenced by the social theories of James Harrington.

12. Of all the many children born during the first two years in Old Ebenezer, only three survived infancy.

MAY

1. Either Boltzius failed to give the amount the Trustees paid, or else the typesetters deleted it.

2. Johann Joachim Zübli, son of David Züblin of Purysburg, was then preaching to the Reformed Swiss and Germans in and around Savannah despite his extreme youth.

4. For Arndt, see Feb., note 3. Heinrich Bogatzky, *Schatz-Kästlein der Kinder Gottes*. Halle, many printings.

5. The District of North Georgia was governed by a council of a President and five Assistants. At the moment the president was Col. William Stephens.

6. Perhaps because the Cockneys often dropped their "h"s, the Germans thought they were doing so with the name Abercorn, which sounded to them as *Hafer* (oats) and *Korn* (corn). Now, thirteen years after first stopping off at Abercorn, Boltzius had learned its true name, that of Georgia's benefactors, Lord and Lady Abercorn.

7. Schinmeiers *Schatzkästlein*, not to be confused with Bogatzky's work. See May, note 4.

8. Senior Urlsperger. Samuel Urlsperger was the Senior of the Lutheran Ministry in Augsburg.

9. Johann Anastasius Freylinghausen, *Compendium, oder kurzer Begriff der ganzen christlichen Lehre*. Halle 1726.

10. This was probably Johann Adam Treutlen, later the first elected governor of Georgia.

11. Thomas Stephens, the disloyal son of Col. William Stephens, had persuaded several inhabitants of Ebenezer to side with the Malcontents, the disaffected party in Savannah that wished to combat the Trustees' plans.

12. With or without a German pastor, the Germans would have left Frederica as the regiment was decreased, since they lived entirely from it. Actually, they did not go away gradually, but mostly in one decisive emigration.

13. She uses the word *Lehrer*, which invariably meant ministers. Teachers were *Schulmeister*.

JUNE

1. See Feb., note 5.

2. Now Boltzius is using the name Kurtz instead of Curtius. See April, note 1.

3. Apparently a Latin version of his *Compendium* mentioned in May, note 9.

4. Boltzius used the superlative even in distinguishing between two things.

5. For Treutlen's origin, see George F. Jones, "John Adam Treutlen's Origin and Rise to Prominence," in *Forty Years of Diversity*, ed. Harvey W. Jackson and Phinizy Spalding. Athens, Ga.: U. of Ga. Press, 1984, pp. 217–232.

6. Matthias Kurtz was actually from Dürrenberg; but, since the Protestants from there were expelled simultaneously with the Salzburgers, they were associated in the public mind.

7. The British treaties with the Indians had stipulated that the whites would occupy only the tidal lands, but this stipulation was honored mostly in the breach. Ebenezer itself was some miles above Purysburg, which was built on the highest reach of the tides.

8. See note 3, above.

9. See note 4, above.

10. See March, note 3.

11. The "Newlanders," or recruiters for ships' captains and colonial authorities, often forged optimistic and enthusiastic letters, purportedly from recent settlers in America.

12. Col. Stephens and other officials complained that the settlers who had been settled around Savannah at the Trustees' expense would leave the farm to their wives and children and work on the fortifications for wages, thus defeating the Trustees' purpose.

13. Christian Gottlieb Priber, who was trying to unite the Red Men against European encroachment, was kidnapped by Creek Indians and sold to Oglethorpe, who imprisoned him at Frederica, where he died.

14. See June, note 3.

15. This was probably Treutlen. See May, note 10, and June, note 5.

JULY

1. One might expect to find Deists in Charleston, but hardly Arians and Socinians.

2. Sinners.

3. These children were suffering from pica or "clay-eating," the result of a dietary deficiency. Eating inedible food was the result, not cause, of the ailment.

4. Boltzius, using the Roman numbering, numbers these two commandments as the fourth and fifth, but this translation uses the Greek system found in English literature. Children who succumbed to their desire to eat dirt were

violating the fifth by disobeying their parents and their ministers. They were also violating the sixth commandment by killing themselves.

5. The Francke Foundation of Halle was sending missionaries to India under the auspicies of the Danish crown.

6. As the German word *Baumwolle* (tree-wool) suggests, cotton grew on trees as well as on bushes.

7. Only forty-six years later Eli Whitney solved this problem only a few miles from Ebenezer.

AUGUST

1. Boltzius must be in error here, for there are no records of a Peter Grung. There was an Abraham Grünig or Grüning, who arrived with the Moravians on the *Simonds*, Captain Cornish, on 17 Feb. 36 along with the third Salzburger transport. He dwelled for a while at Old Ebenezer and then went into military service at Frederica, before being promoted to lieutenant on the campaign against Cartegena.

2. Weissiger had returned with the second Salzburger transport after collecting money in Germany for churches in Pennsylvania.

3. In 1740 the British attempted, but failed, to take Cartagena, a fortified city in Columbia.

4. See Feb., note 4.

5. Samuel Urlsperger, *Schriftmässiger Unterricht für Kranke und Sterbende.*

6. See Feb., note 4 and April, note 1.

7. Boltzius says *leihet* (lends) instead of *ehret* (honors). This would appear to have been a typographical error except that a few lines further on he speaks of "lending to the Lord." The word *leihen*, which now means "to lend," still had its medieval meaning of to grant or to enfief.

8. The Protestant Body was a kind of caucus to protect the interests of the Protestant minority at the new permanent diet at Regensburg.

9. *Ich gäbe dir wol tausend Welten, die treue Liebe zu vergelten*, from a hymn.

10. *Vernunft kann das nicht fassen; Sie spricht, es ist nun alles verloren; da doch das Kreuz hat neu gebohren, die deiner Hülf erwarten. . . . Hilf nur, das wir nicht wanken; Vernunft wider den Glauben ficht, aufs künftige will sie trauen nicht, da du wirst selber trösten.*

SEPTEMBER

1. See May, note 4.

2. These dear brothers were Heinrich Melchior Muhlenberg, Peter Brunnholtz, Johann Friedrich Handschuh, and Johann Helfrich Schaum. Boltzius' extensive correspondence with these Pietists in Philadelphia can be found in Kurt Aland, *Die Korrespondenz Heinrich Melchior Muhlenbergs*, Vol. I, Berlin-New York, 1986.

3. *Die glauchische Hauskirchordnung, oder christlicher Unterricht.* Halle 1699.

OCTOBER

1. Boltzius and Gronau had been ordained in Wernigerode, an East German city, on their way to Rotterdam to join the Salzburgers.

2. The Red Bluff, on which Ebenezer was built, was discovered by people from Old Ebenezer searching for acorns for their swine.

NOVEMBER

1. Klosterberg, *Theologia pastoralis.*
2. War of the Austrian Succession.

DECEMBER

1. The Society for Promoting Christian Knowledge, the missionary society in London that paid the wages of the ministers and schoolmaster at Ebenezer and helped in many other ways.

2. The skillful surveyor and engineer Joseph Avery rebuilt the mills and then returned to Savannah to recuperate, but he died there.

3. The widow Christ, first name not given, had married the convert Gottfried Christ. Her father was Jacob Metzger of Purysburg.

4. *der am Kreuz ist meine Liebe, etc., etc. Und ist auch gleich ein Kampf wohl ausgericht, das machts noch nicht; Ach, ich habe schon erblicket die so grosse Herrlichkeit, itzo, etc. Ewig Leben wird er geben mir dort oben, ewig so mein Herz, etc.,* fragments of different hymns.

5. Modern notation provided by The Rev. Raymond E. Davis, Jr. who had the transcription made (in the same key) by Dr. Robert L. Harris, Assistant Professor of Music, Fine Arts Department, Armstrong State College (a division of the University of Georgia), Savannah, Georgia. The original notation was as follows:

Index
for the Year 1747

Walther, Johann, hymnist 143
Watchman's Voice, see *Wächterstimme*.
Watson, Joseph, alderman in Savannah, writes diary 76, 78
Weaving, being undertaken 64, 95, 137
Weissenbacher, Jakob, fine and honorable German, drowns 82; July, note 2
Weissiger, Daniel, German from Pa. 99; Aug., note 2
Wernigerode, city in East Germany 119, 141; Oct., note 1
Wesley, John, founder of Methodism, former preacher at Savannah, 6
Wheat, see Crops.
Wheelwright in Ebenezer 44
White Bluff, same as Vernonburg
Whitefield, George, English evangelist, returns to Bethesda 15, has cattle, wheat, and rice 15, letter from 25, 91; supplies flax 96, returns from Pa. 123, summons Boltzius 128, 132, donates bonnets 136, not well 128
Whooping cough; March, note 6
Wirth, Ambrosius, pietist author 18, 28, 40, see *Christliche Anweisung*
Wolves, roam forest 10
Wool, a supply in Ebenezer 95
Worms in corn 80

Zant, Sibille, nee Bacher, wid Piltz, wid Bartholomäus, a pious woman 22, has mulberry trees 27, receives help 107, a true Israelite 126, 136
Zettler, Elisabetha Catharina, nee Kieffer, w Matthias, awakened in Christianity 14, endures tribulations 23
Zettler (Zedler, Zetler), Matthias, Salz, shoemaker, endures tribulations 23
Ziegenhagen, Friedrich Michael, royal chaplain, "Reverend Father" of the Georgia Salzburgers, mentioned 26, 84, letters to 80, 92
Zimmerebner, Margaretha, nee Berenberger, Salz, w Ruprecht, recognizes God 24
Zimmerebner, Ruprecht, Salz, to aid orphanage, a righteous man 24
Zion Church, church on plantations, being repaired 86, mentioned 21, 23, 27, 39, 43, 53, 59, 65, 86, 92, 102, 119, 126, 134, 138
Zittrauer, Anna, w Ruprecht 85
Zittrauer, Paulus, Salz, carpenter 99
Zittrauer, Ruprecht, Salz who deserted Ebenezer 84
Zübli (Zubly), Johann Joachim, Swiss minister, welcomes Boltzius 48; March, note 3s

Detailed Reports on the

Salzburger Emigrants

Who Settled in America . . .

Edited by Samuel Urlsperger

VOLUME TWELVE, 1748

Contents

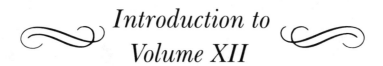

Introduction to Volume XII

The year 1748 was an uneventful one for Ebenezer, where life and work continued as in the past several years. Progress continued in the silk and lumber business, and the crops were fair despite early pessimism caused by worms, rust, and mildew. There was abundance of fruit, enough for man and beast and for distilling into brandy. Donations continued coming from Germany to stimulate the local economy.

The lack of hired hands still made life difficult for those farmers who had lost all or most of their children. Deaths greatly surpassed births in the entries given, but these were somewhat offset by new additions to the community from Purysburg and Savannah. "Clay-eating," or pica, continued to be the greatest scourge and carried away many people, mostly children; but malaria still played its part in weakening people for more mortal diseases. Although there were many rumors of Indian wars, Ebenezer was left in peace.

While "external matters" such as providing for food, clothing, and shelter for his congregation took much of Boltzius' time, he still provided all the spiritual guidance and discipline it required, and he never had to appeal to the civil authorities for aid in keeping order. His stand against slavery was not yet causing repercussions in Savannah.

At this time I wish to express my thanks to the Rev. Raymond Davis for valuable advice, both theological and musicological, concerning this and previous volumes.

I.N.I.A.
Daily Reports
Of the Year 1748

JANUARY

Friday, the 1st of January 1748. On this first day of the new year our merciful God has given us much blessing through His holy word and through prayers that were offered several times in public with the congregation, young and old, before His merciful throne. May He accept today's prayers, intercessions, and thanksgivings with pleasure and all others that will be brought before His merciful throne this year in the name of our Lord Jesus Christ, for the sake of Christ's merit and intercession. May He abundantly shower us ministers and our listeners as well as our dearest benefactors, close-by and far-away, with His blessing for the glorification of His great name, the expansion of His kingdom of mercy, and for their and our well-being and salvation! May He reward all our worthiest known and unknown benefactors everywhere for the many good deeds they have done again this past year in so many ways through heartfelt prayers, good counsel and alms, which we rightfully appreciate.

Further, may He make them able and willing, with God's good hand leading them, to come to the help of our congregation in this difficult, distressing time by pleading to God, interceding with people, with good advice and deeds! And may He also give us peace and quiet in this country during these perilous times of war; and may He let it be, through the Holy Spirit, our most noble practice to get to know the name of our Lord as a strong and invincible fortress and, as upright people, to take refuge in it. In this way, we will be powerfully and miraculously protected! Should this be the last year of our pilgrimage on earth, may our beloved Immanuel, who has also been created by God to save us, deliver us from all evil through a blessed death and help us to enter His Heavenly Kingdom; Glory to Him from eternity to eternity. Amen!

Saturday, the 2nd of January. Last night, following the public prayer hour, I had the pleasure of receiving a short letter from a boy servant in our village, who since the time of his public confirmation, before taking his first Lord's supper, has led an irreproachable and edifying life and already has felt the blessing and care of our Heavenly Father in a clearly visible and welcome manner.[1] He lacked, it seems to me, time and paper: otherwise he surely would have revealed even more the present state of his soul. Meanwhile, what he wrote suffices. It will give me the opportunity to keep it in mind in my dealings with him as well as in preaching the word, because several among us are likely to be afflicted by his spiritual sickness.

Monday, the 4th of January. A pious woman told the sick B. that during the holidays we jointly sang several songs which pleased and edified those present. She mentioned with much sadness that, by misusing her voice in Augsburg for secular and shameful songs by day and night, she had greatly sinned against her Creator. She remembers these great sins and they weigh on her conscience almost as often as the moon shines; because that, in particular, was the time when such things and sins had taken place. She said that, in addition, God had to provide the light for such misbehavior. She added that the ministers were preaching themselves almost to death but that only a few worry about it: one should not ask where so much misfortune and distress is coming from.

Thursday, the 7th of January. Today, we unexpectedly had the dead body of a little seven-year-old boy, who is Schweiger's eldest son. He did what several children, who are already dead, had done before him: that is, he secretly had eaten earth, ashes, clay, etc.;[2] that made him very pale and sick, and he had now died unexpectedly with a great burning in his chest. If there is something that makes me very sad, it is that we have prematurely lost to death so many fine children because they ate such unnatural substances; and yet one does not know how to help. Had the dear members of our community kept all of their children from the early years after their arrival at Old and New Ebenezer, the eldest would already be thirteen to fourteen years old and hence great help to their worn-out parents who cannot find any servants here. This Schweiger has already had seven children in this country; only a three year-old son, also sickly, is left. May God take pity on this misery!

Saturday, the 9th of January. At the beginning of this new year, our dear God has shown a new miracle of His goodness and almightiness in the case of shoemaker Zodler[3] and his journey-man; they have reason to thank Him for it with their hearts, mouths, and conduct for the rest of their lives. They both were at Purysburg; and, when they left in a small boat, they arranged it in such way that they would stay in the woods because of the deer and bears. Because it was dark and cold, they started burn-ing a thick pine tree whose top had broken off but was still standing firmly, hoping that they might attract deer and bears. It seems that they had looked at the tree earlier and had found the tree to be stable; then they lay down, with their heads touch-ing each other, and went to sleep. Within a very short time, the burning tree fell across the lower part of the journeyman's body; and, since he was screaming wildly under this burden and the fire, the master woke up and, with a feeling of extraordinary strength, was able to push the heavy burning tree off the body of this poor man. The master's hand was slightly injured by the fire, and he was so frightened that he became feverish; however, the journeyman was more seriously injured, and he spit blood. However, he is now on his way to recovery and his life seems to be out of danger. If the tree had fallen higher or lower, one of them, if not both, would have been dead. Thanks to God for His extraordinary mercy!

Monday, the 11th of January. Glaner's dear wife, whose health continues to be weak, regretted with much sadness being unable to attend the public church service during the holy days. She said that in her healthy days she usually had not made good use of the opportunity for edification, and hence she had not given credit to God for such a blessing. However, she had to admit in praise of God that he had shown her soul much mercy in what she was told and read from the sermons and that there was hardly a word that had not been of benefit and use to her. She is

bringing up an orphaned girl who lives with her; and she complains that she is secretly eating raw rice and grain, also wheat,
and has lost a lot of strength because of it. However, after dis-
covering this unusual behavior and keeping her away from it by
much love, earnestness, and diligent supervision, she is regain-
ing her strength and color.[4]

Glaner's wife remembers that, some time ago, she, too, had
such an inappropriate appetite and that her strength had markedly weakened. However, she fought it with fervent and constant
prayers, and God soon delivered her from it. This experience of
hers was completely in line with what I reminded my listeners of
yesterday during the sermon. Based on the gospel, we spoke, on
the first Sunday after Christ's epiphany, about the God-pleasing
behavior of the parents and the Jesus child, for all parents and
children to follow. Our parents were particularly admonished to
observe this point, the eagerness of their worries about the children. The very misery they see in their children is to lead them
to Jesus, to believe in Him and pray. Before the sermon we had
read the fifteenth chapter of the Book of Genesis, and on this
topic I particularly stressed the two last verses. In it, it says that
the Lord promises to be our healer and that He will spare us
from unusual illnesses and distressing incidents. The Lord's
word through his Apostle that "the prayer of faith shall save the
sick," is far-reaching. "The prayer of the righteous can accomplish much if it is serious."

Tuesday, the 12th of January. Our Jerusalem Church has not
been in existence long; yet, when the thresholds were examined,
they were found to be already half rotten, although they were
one and one-half feet from the ground and resting on dug-in
pinewood. The walls consist of thick rough-hewn and smoothed
wood, six inches thick. Since there is reason to believe that they,
too, will gradually be attacked by the rot, we have decided to
cover them from the ground up to the windows with good thin
boards. Above that, the rain cannot hit them so hard because of
the overhanging roof. Then the outside walls will be painted
with turpentine and the inside with good paint. The underside
of the double overhang in front of the two church-doors, which
are to keep out the rain, must be repaired in their entirety. That

would prevent the collapse with a minimum of expenditures. It is also known in Pennsylvania that in America wood rots very easily. This is why our esteemed Pastor Muhlenberg had to decide to build the churches there with stone. However, we here, with our difficult beginnings, did not have the money to do likewise. We are also planning to protect our Zion Church on the plantations from the rot as soon as this is feasible.

Wednesday, the 13th of January. Kogler's dear wife continues to be in a very distressing and inconsolable state, and none of the Evangelical ideas taken from the word of God have the effect we wholeheartedly wish for. It may be because the hour the Lord has chosen to console her soul has not yet come. Great efforts are being made to persuade her not to abandon the means of salvation, they being the word of God and prayer, because she believes that nothing will help her anymore and that she will only sin by doing so. She applies to herself those quotations and expressions in the sermons that refer to the conditions of the godless and hypocrites, and it is very difficult to tell her otherwise. We are visiting her as often as we can; we talk to her about God's word and pray with and for her. May Jesus Christ, the dear Shepherd, who has come to seek and to redeem what is lost, take care of the timid little sheep and tell her, "Look unto me and be ye saved."

Thursday, the 14th of January. A distinguished and learned German gentleman, who lives in Carolina, sent me yesterday the following letter by way of Savannah.[5] I was all the more impressed by its contents since recently, following a specific circumstance in the available biblical history, I had to speak about the comforting teachings of eternal justification in accordance with what our theologians taught us in a pure and comforting way from God's word and the symbolic books. The first portion of the letter relating to this matter reads,

> I was told that your Worship has Dr. Lange's book on universal mercy.[6] Although I like this comforting teaching, it cannot help me with various difficulties. However, I believe that this book may give me complete satisfaction. For this reason, I am asking you to do me the favor of lending it to me for a while. I will not only return it to you with thanks but plan to use it to serve others.

Although I am a member of the Reformed Church, I do love the Lutherans (the lovers of peace) as much as the members of the Reformed Church. Because the Lutheran teaching about justification seems to me much more comforting, I am spreading it in our community as widely as possible. Therefore, I would like to have, against payment, Heinrich Schubart's sermons about the Gospel and epistles.[7] I wrote to Hamburg in this matter but have not received a reply.

In the postscript, he also requests some short edifying treatises by the late Professor /August Hermann/ Francke and other pious ministers, for which he is willing to pay or which he will return.

I have assembled the *Book of Universal Mercy,* some continuations of the reports from East India and a number of edifying treatises and will send them to him at the first opportunity.[8] In my letter, I have offered to send him more if God's word as reported in these books is well received in the souls of the readers and listeners. I no longer have Dr. Schubart's books of sermons. I gave part of them to Pastor Muhlenberg,[9] and others I lent to Savannah; when the man moved away, he took them along against my will. I also gave the book of prayers to a German congregation in Charleston at the request of their reader. We like to make the most of good books in this country.

Saturday, the 16th of January. The harnesses used for plowing the fields, which Mr. Whitefield purchased for us in Pennsylvania, have arrived in good condition.[10] That has pleased our congregation greatly. We need more of them, and soon arrangements will be made with a man in our community to see whether he can make such things from hides sent from London. We need a saddler who can also make all kinds of harnesses as urgently as we need a plow and wheel-maker or a cart-maker.

The merchant in Savannah has purchased German scythes from Pennsylvania for our community; although they are very expensive, namely, 3, 4 and 6 pence, also one shilling apiece, they are very good. They had urged me for a long time to get the scythes for them from Germany, but I did not want to burden our benefactors with such matters.

Sunday, the 17th of January. We had a very mild winter. For several days it was as warm here as it is usually in March, and the peach trees have started budding. The water in the river is still very high, probably as a result of the melted snow since we have not had any rain for quite some time.[11] With such good weather, God is giving us the peace we desire and much edification.

N.N. administered the rod to two men from Old Ebenezer for misbehavior that is quite customary in this country; and by doing so, he has put himself at the same level as the world. For that reason, I had to admonish him from God's word and warn him of harm. Although he pretended not to hold it against me, I easily see from his behavior and words how angry and annoyed he was in his heart about this friendly chastisement. However, God was soon after him with the rod and properly reinforced the admonition I had given in accordance with the Scriptures. For he came down with a high fever, but by Saturday he had sufficiently recovered and was able to attend church yesterday. Thus our gracious God made him aware of his old and new sins with such emphasis that he became so frightened as to call for me to confess with much fear and tears his wretched and dangerous condition.

He had been, he said, unfaithful to God several times: feeling personally attacked in the sermons, he became enraged against me and my office, committed falsehood against me and other people, and burdened his conscience in many other ways. He thought he had sinned against the Holy Spirit and that, because of that, there was no longer any mercy for him. Several times he mentioned the words: "I truly fear that God's mercy, which he has mocked at all times, will hang heavily upon him." The two verses, "Thou hast ascended on high, etc., hast received gifts for men, yea for the rebellious, etc." Also: "I will look to the poor, etc., and even to him who trembleth at my word," have somewhat comforted his mind. Then in my prayer I presented his condition to our Lord Jesus Christ, our Healer and Savior, asking Him for mercy.

In this country there is a lot of confusion about money in trading and in our dealings: we see hardly any English gold and silver money (since the law prohibits in strict terms the export of such coins from England), and copper coins do not stay in this country for very long either, since the captains of vessels from New York and Pennsylvania buy them up because their value there is almost twice what it is here and in England. The trustees' "sola bills," or notes, are one pound Sterling, some also five pounds, which, however, disappear as soon as they get here. Because the gentlemen in Savannah do business only by going into debt and because they pay the people who are entitled to something for their work, crops, etc., with a written order or note, which the merchants accept instead of money, these issued orders or notes are paid with the trustees' so-called "sola bills" and sent to London instead of drafts. Hence none of their money stays in this country.

General Oglethorpe has had struck some small coins for his regiment, such as one shilling, half and whole crowns at two shillings six pence, and five shillings, also printed and signed paper notes. However, these tore very easily and were gradually withdrawn from circulation so that they are hardly ever seen anymore. During this time of war much Spanish silver money, called pistrins or pieces of eight or Spanish thalers, is coming to Carolina and to this colony; but the fact that its value there is different from what it is here causes losses and obstacles in buying and selling. In our Georgia, the value of a pistrin is one shilling Sterling, but in Carolina it is two pence, that is, four kreutzers less; and it is the same way with the pieces of eight and other small Spanish silver coins.

Today I received a letter from a friend in Savannah informing me that the merchants in Savannah and Frederica will soon no longer accept the Spanish money at a value that is higher than in Carolina because the drafts are taken to Charleston and thereby much silver money—to be sure at the value prevailing there—is brought to this colony and, at the merchants' loss, spent at the value prevailing here. We have no other money in our place except Spanish silver coins, and spending them here unexpectedly would cause a lot of harm in our poor community. Because, in one pound, they would lose forty pence or three shillings four

pence, or almost one-and-a-half florins. If they wished to exchange their small, hard-earned reserves, that would be impossible because there is no other money in the country. Little or no
paper money from Carolina gets here. Even if it were in circulation here, we would not be any better off because it does not always have the same value. Sometimes one pound Sterling there
is equal in value to six, six-and-a-half, or seven-and-a-half, and
sometimes even eight pounds. No matter whether its value goes
down or up, it is always at the expense of the poor. I cannot understand why the money in a king's country cannot have the
same value, regardless of whether it is made of silver, paper, or
leather.

Wednesday, the 20th of January. A woman, who is often sick
and therefore unable to work, was treated somewhat harshly by
her husband, who found it difficult to keep house because of ill
health, and she had to do much work that went beyond her capacity. However, our merciful God heard her sighs; and on the
Sunday after Christmas He addressed His word to her husband
in such a way that he has been more gentle and friendly toward
her since. The opening words that penetrated his heart particularly deeply at the time were taken from Phillipians 2:14,15,
"Do all things without murmurings and disputing, etc." Our listeners, adults and children alike, value the opening words very
highly throughout the entire year; they learn them by heart and
derive much benefit from them. Because of this, we are a bit
more generous in interpreting and applying them than we usually are with exordia.

Friday, the 22nd of January. Last night, Balthasar Bacher's
wife succumbed after much struggle and peacefully entered the
joy of her Lord. When I visited her yesterday morning, she was
in great pain, which she was no longer able to express in words
but only through pitiful sounds. Also, she no longer had the use
of her hearing. One of her last words was for her husband to
extinguish the light, since Jesus was now her light. Despite her
pain, she never showed the slightest indication of impatience
during the fifteen weeks of her illness, which, thanks to her Savior's grace, seemed like hours. The time did not appear long to
her because she always busied herself with her dearest Savior

who meant everything to her. She did not complain about anything but her sins and that she had given her pastors reasons to
sigh. Therefore she felt that she not only deserved this long and
serious illness but also any punishment by God.

Worldly matters, including those concerning her husband
and her two young children, were no longer in her heart, and
her heart was entirely full of Jesus and His grace. Hence she did
not want to hear and talk about anything else. Yes, that was probably the reason why, when she was completely out of herself, she
did not mix into her very edifying words and prayers the
slightest worldly or disorderly thoughts. No matter how weak
she was, whenever good friends wanted to read, pray, and sing
with her, she was not weak but very eager for the edification. She
deplored with the greatest of regret the great blindness and
wrong thoughts among many of her acquaintances in A.[12] and
was worried that she might encounter in Heaven few of those
who stayed with such thoughts and false comfort. She would
have liked it very much for her little sister to be with her in this
loneliness. Her burial was held today with great blessing.

Sunday, the 24th of January. Last night, shortly before going
to bed, (Psalms 127:2), I received an unexpected letter from Mr.
Verelst in London, which I welcomed very much for several reasons: first, he wrote that Mr. Harris, a pious merchant from Savannah who is well-disposed toward us, had duly delivered my
letters to him and the honorable Lord Trustees and, by doing so,
caused much joy. He hoped to get the small box with our spun
silk from the ship the day he was writing his letter to me. Second,
this friend and benefactor acknowledges in fine language "that
we and our flock are quite evidently under the protection and
blessing of our Almighty God." He wishes us everything good
and (in his words) joyfully wants to be a tool to show us all kinds
of friendship and acts of kindness to the best of his ability, etc.

Tuesday, the 26th of January. I am delighted that more and
more congregation members are inclined every year to plant a
good number of mulberry trees.[13] They are also gaining more
and more experience in speeding up their growth through necessary industry and caution. Other people in the country would
deter them with words and examples if they would heed them.

This they have done too frequently in previous years to their disadvantage; and, for that reason, they are now planting only what they should have planted, to their great advantage, a long time ago when every year they had all possible seeds and saplings furnished them. The mulberry trees that other people in this colony may have planted have been allowed to die or have been neglected, while those useful trees here, in town and on the plantations, grow and multiply year after year. This reminds me of the Holy Spirit's noteworthy words: "David waxed stronger and stronger, and the house of Saul waxed weaker and weaker." The noteworthy story of these two kings and their houses, to which these words refer, can teach us a great deal.

On the mill plantation we have the best land and the best opportunity to put in a large garden because we have there a lot of wooden planks which would rot or be burnt since they are not worth being carted off and hence are in very low demand even if we were to give them away for free. And, because fence posts made out of white oak and pine are available nearby, I have made arrangements to fence in one acre of land with the aforementioned planks, for which only wooden nails are needed. In this large garden we are now planting 126 young mulberry trees, each between four and eight feet high (this is how high they grow here in two years), in straight lines so we can plough between them. The garden, which is close to the mill, has been set up in a way that permits its gradual enlargement. The noise from the mills will keep the deer from damaging the young mulberry trees as they tend to do when the trees are a little farther away from the houses. Also, unlike the town, we have sufficient dung; and, since our soil is much richer than in and around town, I hope we will be able to produce in several years a good quantity of silk at the mill. These trees are planted primarily for widows, orphans, and frail and aged people. With God's continued blessing, we want to build a spacious and clean house to make and spin silk. This will be done at low cost because, with the planks close by, we do not have to spend any money on hauling them. May our merciful God also crown with his blessing my plan and weak effort which is in His honor and for the good of our congregation!

Thursday, the 28th of January. We have some fine young men in our community who have come to us with their parents or have gradually moved here. Because some of them are too weak for farming or are not really interested in it, and because we are concerned that they may move elsewhere for good earnings and fall prey to disorderly people, I help them to learn a good craft through advising and admonishing them or through money. Some have already been placed with the sawmiller, cartwright, plowmaker, locksmith and shoemaker. Tools are very expensive here and often are not even available. If the Lord Trustees and our other benefactors could send them to me from Europe, then this might help to do more good among our young men. This would also benefit our congregation in that the young craftsmen would step into the shoes of the departing old workers. As mentioned earlier, we lack several needed craftsmen. Thomas Bichler, who has started to make Salzburg-type saddles and harnesses from treated sheepskins sent to us, works as a saddler in some fashion. He has done very well.

Friday, the 29th of January. Some Englishmen, who moved to our colony from Virginia and North and South Carolina and have settled at the Ogeechee River and travel back and forth, have started to buy from our people their supply of grains, beans, flour, rice and meat (although the latter in a small quantity) and to haul it off in their horse-drawn carts. This is new proof of God's gracious providence for us and is considered a good omen that God will gradually permit beneficial trade among us. With God's blessing, our mills earned more this winter than in all previous years combined. In the beginning, some people in the neighborhood did to our mills what they did when the orphanage was first set up: they ridiculed it and would not predict its continued existence. Whenever these same people come to the mill now, they behave quietly and honorably, are friendly, and admire the good installation and reinforcements.

Even strange impartial people, who know about those things, praise our accomplishments and are amazed at the rice which can be stamped so white and beautiful—large quantity within a short time, without extraordinary efforts by the miller. The miller is able to grind and, at the same time, stamp and sift the rice in the two mills that are in two special houses situated at a distance of about one hundred feet from each other. This is why a bushel of rice costs little, namely, only three pennies. Nobody among us knows about barley-stamping; for that reason it cost us a lot of effort without really leading to anything. I believe that, when the time comes that God resolves to give us a barley stamping mill as well, things will develop nicely and wonderfully, just as the pleasant experience we had in other instances. I am hoping for such gracious help, at the right time, in connection with the planned ditch a little more than one thousand feet long, which would channel a large quantity of water directly from the Savannah river to the mill river.

We hope to get the water for the mills at least two feet higher so that they can be operated, either fully or with only the lower millrace, for most of the year for the great benefit of those who live here and also for strangers. If the people from other places knew that throughout the year they would never come in vain to have their grain ground, they would also come to us from faraway places; as, some days ago, a boat loaded with grain came from a plantation at the Ogeechee river to the mill and, within a few hours, was able to leave again loaded with flour.[14] Our help comes from the Lord who created Heaven and earth. On a recent Sunday the words of Zachariah 1:3 served us for edification: "Turn ye unto me, saith the Lord of Hosts, and I will turn me to you, saith the Lord of Hosts."

Saturday, the 30th of January. Some time ago, a young Indian was kindly received in my house, something he apparently considered an honor and an act of friendship. He therefore returned to my house yesterday with another six young Indians and a young woman. Except for the woman, they had decorated themselves in their own fashion as best as possible. They had painted their faces with vermilion and braided green twigs of from pine and spruce trees into their hair. They brought me a piece of beef as a gift and in return received rice, bread, and beer. One of them knew some English and said, "This man stayed with you at one time and has come to see you." He then asked for brandy for everybody and, because he could not get that, for ten bottles of beer. Ultimately, he was satisfied with three bottles since we only boil some from syrup and Indian corn for our pressing needs. They promised to bring more meat, but I told them that this piece already sufficed. I would have preferred some bear oil for our sawmill, which has been rare for some time. They asked for permission to camp close to town and I allowed them to do so on the condition that they be careful with fire and not light any fence. We don't like these guests in our community, and they come seldom because they do not get any rum or brandy here. When they are here, we like to show them every possible love, wishing that we could contribute something to save their souls. At this time, no efforts are being made in this country to assist these poor people in learning about the Christian religion.

Sunday, the 31st of January. The Christian preparation of Bacher's late wife for a blessed end and her edifying behavior during her drawn-out illness have assured her of a blessed memory among some of our listeners, especially women; and I again got some special proof of that yesterday. Her husband as well has a healing impression of her last hours and intends to prepare himself to follow her through God's spirit, by way of His word. He also hopes sincerely that our merciful God will bring his late wife's aged parents and two sisters in Augsburg into the order of salvation since she lived in this world and left it for a better life. He wants to have a letter written to them: whether our wondrous God would bless the news of their daughter's blessed end and prior true conversion in order to awaken and convert them. He has two children of minor age of whom our good Father in Heaven has taken care so that they will be raised by Christian people. The godparents will care for them to the best of their ability because he is poor and wants to earn some money as a carpenter journeyman in addition to farming his plantation.

Somewhere on our plantations the Indians got some brandy and got drunk from it. As a result they carried on last night, roaming about and screaming as drunken whites in Europe and in this colony, who claim to be Christians, usually do. Although they have not insulted anybody, we consider such heathen excesses terrible because, through God's gracious care, we are used to the pleasant stillness of our solitude by day and by night. This morning some of the fellows visited us and, in their own way, politely said goodbye. It is quite possible that they left or set up their camp close to our plantations. The one who knew some English told me that they got drunk on peach brandy which they got on a plantation, pointing his hand towards it.[15] He asked me for a written note that he would get more, but I turned him down. We will try to find out who gave them the brandy. Thank God, they didn't disturb us this Sunday in our prayers!

M A R C H[1]

Tuesday, the 1st of March. For important reasons concerning my work with the German population and the good of our community, I had to spend five days in Savannah. Although I left there today, I did not get beyond Abercorn because of the torrential river which makes it almost impossible above Savannah to distinguish between low and high tide.[2] On the following Tuesday, at daybreak, we continued our trip on the two boats and arrived happy and healthy at the mills about noontime. We are always very glad to finish traveling and to again see our dear Ebenezer as a quiet Zoar.[3] Our dear God has shown me many good deeds in Savannah, and among those I include the good physical and emotional strength I have despite my many travels and external discomfort, and the diligent and eager acceptance of God's oft-repeated word which I felt this time among the Lutherans and Reformed on Sundays and workdays.[4] However, a number of things, of which I became aware in the course of my work and which rank among the greater annoyances, saddened me a great deal and I discussed them with the Council.[5]

Sunday, the 6th of March. The young N. had already asked me before my most recent trip to come and see her soon; and yesterday I had the time and opportunity to do so. She told me how wondrously the Lord led her some time ago through much inward and outward suffering, and how He let her see afterwards that everything was well meant and for her salvation. Her anguish and internal anxiety, because of her sins and the anger she deserved for them, had at times been so great that she was

unable to pray or find much comfort in God's word. Her constant weak sighing consisted of the few words, "Think upon me,
my God, for good!"Also, she kept thinking the beautiful words,
"Thou shalt guide me with thy counsel and afterwards receive
me to glory."and "We have been healed through His wounds."
Had she found in the Holy Scriptures the example of a soul who
went to Jesus and was rejected by Him, she would have died in
her misery. The teaching of His universal mercy provided her
with great comfort in her temptations.[6] God finally accepted her
sighs, eased her conscience by assuring her of His mercy in
Christ and freed her husband's heart from the ropes of some
harmful entanglements and, earlier than she expected, drew it
towards Himself, so that also outwardly she feels great relief.
She told me about some scruples, from which I freed her with
God's word. She values Christ, His word, and His cross very
highly and talks from good experience.

Monday, the 7th of March. Fourteen years ago, about this
time, our merciful God brought me, my late colleague, Gronau,
and the first transport of Salzburgers safely across the ocean and
to land. The three other transports followed us in the subsequent years. In grateful memory of God's mighty and gracious
guidance, as well as His protection and care for heart and soul,
we usually hold a solemn memorial and thanksgiving in early
spring of each year so as to remind the congregation in our sermons of God's good deeds and of their duty and debt to God,
our benefactors, and themselves. We also take the opportunity
to encourage one another by singing and praying, to God's
glory. On Monday after Reminiscere Sunday we celebrated, to
our great joy, this year's memorial and thanksgiving in good and
welcome outer peace and Christian unity. The weather was good
and the public church service was well attended. The exordium
of the morning sermon was from Job 25:5: "Until my end com-
eth, etc." and the text of Psalm 125:4 and 5. In the afternoon, my
dear colleague's text was Psalm 9:10 and 11, and for the exordium Genesis 28:15. After the morning sermon we sang the
beautiful song in its entirety in all voices, *Hoffnung macht doch
nicht zu Schanden,* etc.

Tuesday, the 8th of March. Yesterday's memorial and thanksgiving was a blessed festival for our dear listeners, as I heard today among other things. Specifically, our faithful God has once again awakened our sawmiller, Kogler, vigorously; and I wholeheartedly wish that for him, as with dear Job, it will become a true and lasting piety. Our morning text from Psalm 125 dealt with the happiness of believers and the unhappiness of nonbelievers, and the various very beautiful names, honorary titles, and descriptions of the believers in this psalm do not merely show us clearly who the true God-pleasing people are, but also how happy they are already on earth, and even more so up above. And it was of great comfort to us and our small group that the psalm reads, also to our benefit: first, they will not fall but remain in all eternity; second, our Lord takes care of his people; third, he makes joyful the good and pious hearts; fourth, peace is over Israel!

This last point reminds me in my meditations of a letter from dear Mr. S.U.,[7] which he wrote us in late 1744 and in which he refers our congregation to the important words of Galatians 6:15 and 16 with his warmest admonitions, warnings, and appeals; and I read them this important passage again. God's words, which were read in the morning and in the afternoon, re-energized and strengthened in our belief and hope those of use whose hearts are easily discouraged. We sang among others the following songs: *Wunderlich ist Gottes Schicken, wunderbarlich ist sein Rath, etc.* We have experienced that and will continue to experience it to our blessing if we persist in our belief and hope like Abraham, Job, David, and all pious people. We are very impressed by how God crowned Job's true and consistent piety with spiritual and physical blessings contrary to what all men thought and hoped. God can boundlessly do anything we ask for or understand. That he has proven to us many times; why should we not trust Him in the future? The beautiful song that we sang in all its verses, *Hoffnung macht doch nicht zu Schanden, etc.*, had an edifying effect on our dear listeners. Despite their poverty they have offered to collect money so that I can purchase a small organ, or positive,[8] for our Jerusalem Church. Our good people do not know how expensive these instruments are, especially in this country, but I have promised to do everything possible without asking for their contribution since, although they have the best intentions, they have very little money.

Thursday, the 10th of March. We had a long winter this year. Parts of January were as warm as it is usually in the spring. This is why our field seeds such as rye, barley, and peas grew fast and, in many instances, the peach, mulberry and other fruit-bearing trees started budding. However, the severe and long-lasting frost in February not only killed the rye, peas, and barley that had come up, but also severely damaged the trees I mentioned, and we can expect few peaches this year. The young long branches of our mulberry trees, filled with sap by the long warm January, are entirely gone. On the good branches, the leaves are only now beginning to come out, and we are worried that we won't have as much silk this year as last year.

Some of the young silkworms, I am told, came out several weeks ago, and more and more are coming out every day. Yet most are probably going to perish because, as we believe, there is not enough food for them, i.e., mulberry leaves. Whatever young orange trees we had in our community, they are all dead; and all of Col. Stephens's and Mr. Whitefield's big orange trees, which already had borne much fruit, not only froze to death but were split apart by the severe frost and very cold wind. Hardly any green is left in the gardens since we had the very hard frost; even the cabbage and turnips are completely gone. Likewise, the young grass in the woods is dead and the cold weather has thus far kept the new grass from growing. That is bad for those with cattle who had been unable to store enough hay; especially since they are also short of turnips and cabbage, which serve as fodder. We have never had such a winter.

Saturday, the 12th of March. With his feelings greatly moved, the sawmiller /Kogler/ told me that some days ago our merciful God protected his house from a great tragedy. His young daughter, together with her sister, had returned from school around noontime; and, because their usual way home from school to the mill is rather bad as a result of the rain, she went through the fields and across the little millbridge and fell into the canal which carries the water onto the sawmill wheel. To rescue her, and to our joy, God's wondrous and wise care had seen to it that, a short time earlier, her father had been called for lunch; he immediately put down his work and left. At any other time, it probably would have taken quite a while for him to follow the call to come and eat. Now, although the mill is closed, the little tributary, which channels the water from the canal to the river after the mill has been closed down, was open, and it was in that very area that the little girl fell into the water. Had God not mercifully prevented it, as new evidence of His loving kindness, she could have been pulled with great force through the above-mentioned canal opening into the depth of the river, and nothing could have saved her, even if the wheel had missed her. The millmaster was in the process of sharpening his stones and hence had stopped the water wheel, and soon he heard the elder girl screaming. He ran out and rescued the child. The father, upon hearing the screaming from his house door, believed his little girl to be already dead. But, when he got her back alive, he was filled with indescribable joy, while the mother was so frightened that she fell sick. We thanked our merciful Father in Heaven on our knees in his house for rescuing the girl, and I told the two girls to repeat and reflect on the first verses of Psalm 103 and by doing so to follow dear David. We are planning to build a small bridge soon so that there will no longer be any need for these children to use this dangerous path.

Sunday, the 13th of March. Glaner's dear wife is again confined to bed. She is getting weaker and weaker, and the time of her farewell isn't far off. At night she had a dream in which she saw herself in great danger because of bad spirits; but, when she screamed, she experienced Jesus Christ's mighty help in abundant and wondrous measure. She did not know how to give Her Savior sufficient praise.

Tuesday, the 15th of March. I will not say or write anything more about a certain matter but leave everything to our wise and faithful God who provides all help on earth. He has never been remiss in anything in His regime; nay, no matter what He does and lets happen, it ends well.[9] My comfort now is in our Lord's words from Psalm 132, upon which I am going to build my sermon on the Gospel on Laetare Sunday: "I will abundantly bless her provision, I will satisfy her poor with bread."

Wednesday, the 16th of March. I was informed this morning that the eldest small daughter of Balthasar Bacher's late wife is dangerously ill, and that made me go to Bacher's plantation and pray with him over this child. I found him kneeling and weeping in front of the child's bed and joined him in his prayers; and while we were praying the child died, sooner than anticipated. Her last word was that she wanted to be with her mother. During and after her mother's burial on the twenty-second of January of this year, she said several times that, if her mother would wait in the churchyard just a little while, she would follow her soon; that has now happened this morning. Early this month she became four years of age. She had eaten almost from her very early childhood such harmful things as dirt, clay, coal , etc., as many other children do, and it was impossible to make her stop.[10] Soon these children acquire the color of death and their face and other parts of their body become swollen; and because they hardly ever stop eating such unnatural food, no medicine helps. I would very much like to know the reason for this strange appetite among children and adults in this country. It is quite common for grown children and other persons to eat raw rice and Indian corn and then turn very pale and weak. Perhaps the reason is some kind of disease I do not know and fever. Some time ago, I asked our medico, Mr. Thilo, to report the *casus* and *status*[11] of these dirt and rice eaters to the highly experienced Dr. and Prof. Junker,[12] who is his teacher, and to ask for his advice.

Friday, the 18th of March. The honorable merchant in Savannah, Mr. Habersham, writes me that he received from his correspondent in London a letter dated the twenty-six of October of last year, in which he informs me that he received from his partner, Mr. Harris, a variety of goods on the ship *Hopewell* through Capt. Kitching. However, it seems that this ship, like another one before, was involved in an accident at sea or taken by the enemy. These young and righteous merchants, our sincere friends, have had twice the misfortune of losing on the way over the goods sent to them from London. Who knows what happened to the letters from our Fathers[13] and friends. Since last August we haven't heard anything from Europe except what Mr. Verelst wrote me in a short letter of the nineteenth of September of last year about the box of linen and the letter delivered by Mr. Harris, which I received the twenty-third of January of this year and answered soon. The merchant writes about the twofold loss of his goods as follows, "It seems it will be very hard for us to bear this loss and misfortune; yet God knows best what is best for us."

Saturday, the 19th of March. Hanns Maurer's wife is an upright Christian. She carried her long cross with great patience and recognized with humility and gratitude that these are the right ways in which her Savior wants to protect her, or better free her, from sin and to lead her to Christian sincerity. Not too long ago, as she told me today, she was exposed to serious temptation[14] and saw herself without any hope for mercy and very close to hell's abyss. Everything became a sin to her, and she was unable to pray or receive any comfort from God's word. Her husband has little or no experience with Christianity and hence could only help by reading to her from a good book; but that, too, became a burden to her and almost unbearable. On the third day, our dear Lord gave her a light in the darkness by enabling her through Jesus Christ to take some faith in Him and comfort that her prayers would be heard. Under these painful circumstances she truly longed for me to instruct and comfort her; but she lives on the plantation and did not want to trouble me because of the long way. However, I did not like that.

Monday, the 21st of March. For lack of rain, it has been quite dry here for quite a while. But today our dear God has blessed us with very fruitful soaking rain that lasted until evening. He now plagues us very much with wolves and worms that cause a lot of harm in our gardens and fields. However, I do hope He does not do so in anger but grace and to our best. We now receive our instruction from the Bible story in 2 Chronicles 7 on how to behave in all trials and punishments according to God's will. May God make us faithful! God's words there sound very impressive and are worth being deliberated diligently at this time.as we are also now doing in our prayer sessions and weekly sermons. They read, "If I shut up heaven that there be no rain, or if I command the locusts to devour the land, or if I send pestilence among my people; If my people, which are called by my name, shall humble themselves, and pray and seek my face, and turn from their wicked ways; then I will hear from heaven, and will forgive their sin, and will heal their land."

Tuesday, the 22nd of March. For quite some time I have been taking dear Court Chaplain Ziegenhagen's impressive song on the three main articles of the Christian doctrine as the basis for teaching the catechism to some grown children on our plantations. I find it very convenient to instruct the children in the most important parts of Christian doctrine, *quoad Credenda & Agenda*,[15] in an easy, understandable and enjoyable way. I started today with the third article and spent a very useful hour on the words "The Holy Spirit refreshes the heart, punishes sin, and causes remorse and pain," by not only telling them, according to their instruction, much of what they must know about the person and function of the Holy Spirit, but also about the deep corruption of the human heart, what it is and how we can be helped to overcome it through God's word in the Old and New Testament.

At the end of the lesson and prayer a boy stayed behind and told me, shaking and with tears, "Alas, I have committed a great sin, and I fear that God will no longer accept me in grace." I asked what kind of sin it was and he answered that until now he had secretly eaten raw Indian corn and that, by doing so, he had greatly harmed his health. I explained to him that this sin was serious and damnable under the sixth commandment, that he had known and also had been told by me and his master that, by eating such things, he would harm his health and life.[16] Still, I encouraged his weak soul with the comforting assurance in the gospel that Christ would not reject him because he deeply regretted this and his other sins and would not repeat them.

Wednesday, the 23rd of March. Some years ago the widow Granewetter developed a fever during her late husband's first illness and such feebleness of her mind that she, as half-mad people tend to do, understood everything in a wrong and strange way and had all kinds of peculiar ideas. She now seems to be very close again to this sad paroxysm. She visited me yesterday, told me about her terrible and suspicious illusions and asked for my intercession and instruction and comfort from God's word. Her heart is honest and she is seriously concerned about saving her own soul and the souls of her family. However, mentally and physically she is in such a bad state that she herself does not know how she is and what she should say about herself. I talked with her in her own way, also urged her to make use of the doctor and follow his advice, which she did at once. I told him of the widow's condition as I saw it. I visited her again today, but didn't find her any better. However, the fact that I did come to see her gave her some edification and comfort. I have asked her neighbors to treat her with love and kindness and to help her to the best of their ability.

Friday, the 25th of March. This evening our large boat, which had carried fifty bushels of Indian corn flour and meat to Savannah to be sold there, brought me a letter from our friend, Mr. Habersham. In it he tells me among other things that the Council there has issued a written order to all constables in the country to pick up and arrest all Negroes in this colony, who may number about four hundred.[17] Because of the Spaniards' inability, they felt very safe in this colony despite the ongoing war. But now they had to experience that two boats full of Spaniards, under the command of an Englishman or Irishman, had come to the plantations between Savannah and Frederica and heavily fired at some people. This unexpected horror may have forced the gentlemen to issue such an unexpected order to arrest the Negroes.

Saturday, the 26th of March. Our dear God seems to have blessed the blood-letting administered to Mrs. Granewetter, but most of it was probably accomplished through Christ's and the intercession of the believers who knew about her condition. I found her today in good order and she remembered very well that her mind and head had not been all right. She does not suffer from any physical hardships, and we are also trying to help her in every possible way.

Sunday, the 27th of March. This year we have had cold weather for a long time, especially at night. As a result the leaves of our mulberry trees, all of which the frost had killed in February, could not quite come out. The people in our community are very eager to produce a lot of silk, which they need very urgently in their present poverty. However, in view of the lack of leaves, there probably is not much they can do. The severe frost last February destroyed many branches as well as young trees that had already been full of sap as a result of the warm weather. In addition to this punishment by God, there is another one, namely, an unbelievable number of caterpillar-type worms which do very great damage to our wheat, barley, and oats. They also eat down to the ground the Indian corn sprouts and whatever young plants we have in our gardens. It would be even worse except for the birds, particularly the starlings, which fly over the fields in large numbers and eat the worms. Also we see a lot of woodpeckers, which look like parrots and are also called parrots here,[18] in the fields and gardens searching for food wherever they can find it. Our comfort is: "God is faithful, who will not suffer you to be tempted above that ye are able; but will, etc."

The peach trees here are usually very hardy and not easily damaged by frost; but even they appear to have suffered quite a blow. The peach trees that bloom late and bear ripe fruit early, namely, as early as July, appear to be bearing some fruit after all. The remainder, on the other hand, have nothing but leaves. A woman from Salzburg thanked me in friendly words for the New Testament I gave to her young son. When he brought the dear book home, father and child enjoyed it very much, and, because the boy's name is John, the father, with simplicity and an eager heart, opened the book in the mother's presence at a page where there was a passage from Saint John, as a lasting reminder for both parents and children. When, on opening the book, the beautiful and comforting words: "I am the resurrection and the life: he that believeth in me," etc., (John 11:25–26), were the first to catch their eyes, a quotation which mother and child soon joyfully learned by heart; and our dear God gives her great comfort and joy with these, our Savior's dear words.

Wednesday, the 30th of March. Steiner's wife is now confined to bed, and it seems that she will hardly ever be able to rise again from that bed. Her honest husband's greatest worry in her healthy days was to save her soul, and this is now his primary concern. He complained that she does not quite wish to accept the comfort for poor sinners who are willing to repent because she is too much of a sinner. But it seems to me now that she is not only frightened by her sins and is learning to exaggerate them; but she is also beginning, through the effect of the Holy Spirit, to derive comfort and take joy in Jesus Christ and His dear merits. When I came to visit her today, she had the beautiful passage on her mind: "Can a woman forget her suckling child. . .yea, they may forget, yet will I not forget thee, etc." She has a pious husband and three well-behaved young sons.

Mr. Habersham, the merchant from Savannah, informed me that merchant Woodroffe, who was traveling from Savannah to London, and other passengers on Captain Cowie's ship had fallen into the hands of the enemy on their way over, and that all our letters and diaries sent through him were lost. He had accepted for delivery several large parcels containing copies from April and May, original letters from July, August, and early September and an English and German diary, as well as a list of the earnings and expenditures of our community. The originals of the lost copies arrived safely with Mr. Harris; and the parcel from the tenth of October of last year, sent after Mr. Woodroffe's departure, contains the copies of the currently lost original letters, except for the diaries in German and English, which had not been copied. Perhaps our dear Lord saw to it that the previously mentioned parcel arrived safely, which would give us great joy. We thought the other day that it has also been a long time since we received any letters from our Fathers and friends in Europe, but we are praying for them in hopes that our merciful God may keep them in good health and alive, to our benefit and that of His church.

Thursday, the 31st of March. Hanns Maurer's wife sent for me and told me with tears in her eyes that her current sad condition is expressed in the hymn *Immanuel, des Güte nicht zu zählen, etc.*

She sees and feels nothing but sin and unbelief and cannot accept anything from God's word that would comfort her. She remembers many things from the past that cause her much trouble and worry and badly affect her poor sick body. Whether our merciful Lord will bless the words of encouragement I have taken from His word and the prayer I said with her (as I hope he will in His loving care) remains to be seen. She is an honest soul and carries her great cross with patience. In widow Granewetter's case the paroxysm keeps changing; and, whenever she has a feverish heat, her mind is so feeble that she does not know what she is saying and doing. She never stays in bed and always says edifying things; however, at times she says things which indicate that she is not all right in her head. With her eldest son being only about four years old, she is carrying a heavy burden.

APRIL

Friday, the 1st of April. The sick boy /Georg Adam Leinebacher/ who works for Brandner, asked his mistress several times to put in a word with me and help his sister /Salma/ who is a servant in an Englishman's household in Savannah, to move to our village.[1] When asked whether he wanted her to be with him in his sickness for only a few days, he replied that this wouldn't be of any use to him; she is as ignorant as he is, he said; and the reason why he would like to see her in our parish was the good instruction which she, like him, could have here to save her soul and, if she were indeed to come here, he would be happy enough to give her his cow and calf. He is truly sorry for not having followed the religious instruction (as he called it) and was hopeful that his sister would apply it more faithfully. However, I can attest to his having been attentive and diligent at all times and ahead of other children in my catechism lessons, in school, on the plantations, and during my sermons. He willingly learned the catechism and the passages from the Bible and expanded his knowledge of God's truth well.

Saturday, the 2nd of April. I found very few children in school on the plantations; some are sick and others have to help their family in the fields or with the silkworms. Because of the frozen branches, consistently cold nights, and the continuous dry weather since this spring, there has been a great shortage of good mulberry tree leaves to feed the silkworms, and the people have had a lot more trouble than usually with this otherwise pleasant and useful work to raise their worms to the point where the silk could be spun or processed. The Spanish type of mulberry trees and those growing naturally in the low and rich areas of the forest have not suffered any damage at all from the frost because they tend to bud later than the common white mulberry trees. They now serve their owners well. I was told at school about the epileptic seizures of Eischberger's small son. Hence I visited him and found him to have recovered rather well. He is, like his late sister, a pious child and longs to be in the near future with Jesus Christ and his sister, whom he remembers frequently.

Sunday, the 3rd of April. A very pious Salzburger told me that, although our good Lord provides him meagerly with food for his body, he must work beyond his capacity year in and year out because he does not have a servant. This, he said, weakens his health and also has an harmful effect on his Christianity, since he is unable to pray, read, and repeat with his family as diligently as he would like to and is necessary. When he gets up at the brink of dawn, his tender children and sickly wife are still asleep so that he has to pray by himself, only briefly prays with them during breakfast and reads one page of the *Treasure Chest*.[2] In the evening, after finishing work, he is so tired that he falls asleep as soon as he sits down. He is already fifty years of age and has worked hard in Salzburg and in the Empire. Since his children are still young and he cannot get any servants, he is worried that his life will soon be over. He said that unless God's word, which he listens to and reads with diligence, gives him courage and strengthens him in his belief that there is hope where there is no hope, he would torture himself with worries and lose his strength even more. This distress makes him and others pray.

Monday, the 4th of April. The Salzburger Brandner's sick serving boy asked me to visit him once more before his death. He said he would like to talk to me about his sister /Salma/, who is a servant to an Englishman in Savannah and whom he would like to have in our community because of the instruction we provide.

This morning I found him physically weak but mentally alert and in good spirits. He said among other things that our dear Savior had heard his prayer and freed him from his sins and pains and that he therefore had slept very quietly last night. He said he knows that he had sinned a great deal; in particular, he had very often gone to instruction with an unwilling heart, and whenever he had learned something good there from the Holy Scriptures, Satan had taken it from him soon after. But he is quite sure that everything was forgiven to him and that he was in God's grace; he is completely wrapped up in his dear Savior; his heart is filled with Him and, whenever he starts talking of Him, he does not know when to stop. He is fully devoted to His will whatever He might want to do with him, die or live; but he would like it best if he could soon be with Him. He also asked me whether he could attend tomorrow's class; he would not be able to walk but somebody would carry him. His mistress told me that he loves God's word immensely and talks about it until late into the night. He also recited in my presence the most beautiful passages from the Bible, with very pious gestures. This boy is by nature somewhat simple and he was very ignorant when he came to us.[3] However, he was always very attentive in school and church, and studied the required passages in the Holy Scriptures with great eagerness and diligence. In time this provided him with a good knowledge of the Christian doctrine. This boy is a living example of what the Holy Spirit can do with His word in souls that do not resist Him wilfully and maliciously.

Tuesday, the 5th of April. Granwetter's widow, thank God, has now completely recovered. She is well aware that she has not been in good health; still, she cannot remember her actual misunderstandings in both her words and work which sometimes were stronger and sometimes weaker. Neither is it necessary for us to tell her about it. Once, on a Sunday, while we were singing, she started talking and walking about in front of the pulpit with her two children; she believed, that very hour, the Day of Judgment had arrived and she was responsible for so many people being unprepared. However, the fever's heat may have frightened her heart to such a degree that she left the church in a hurry before we had finished the song and the sermon had

started. Several understanding people led her to the orphanage
and took care of her. By afternoon the paroxysm had passed and
she sat quite orderly at the church door, and after the service she
went quietly home with our people. I have diligently visited her
in her home, as my dear colleague has done to the extent that his
very limited time permitted it. The neighbors as well have
helped her day and night, as needed, to the best of their ability.

Thursday, the 7th of April. The young N., our N.'s wife, is
developing under the cross through the Gospel into an honest
dear soul who forgets what is behind her and reaches for what is
ahead of her. God makes her remember, gradually and one after
the other, all that was part of her past sinful life (because her
feeble mind and weak body would be unable to endure it all at
the same time), especially that, while in the Empire, she had
handled in an unfaithful way God's grace which she already had
received in Salzburg,[4] that she had demonstrated physical un-
faithfulness towards her employers and conformed to the world.
She would die in her misery unless our beloved Savior strengthened her with His word. She heard what we were singing, "*When
I am praying and singing in my need, my heart becomes of good cheer.*"[5]
She asked for my comfort and intercession in very moving and
oft-repeated words. She is now ineffably happy that Jesus is also
drawing her husband with ropes of love towards Himself so as to
make him a great comfort and useful tool in her weaknesses and
temptations. Previously her suffering was twice as severe and
manifold, since he could not accept her outward and inward
cross or his own trials.

Friday, the 8th of April. Today we celebrated, as we do every
year among ourselves, the commemoration of our dearest Savior's death as the Day of Atonement of the New Testament; and
seventy-two persons received the Holy Sacrament. Some Evangelical Lutheran people from Carolina were also here and attended the Holy Sacrament, and some of them are planning to
stay here over the Easter holidays. May our Lord abundantly
bless His holy word, which was preached to them yesterday and
today, in them and in us all so that it may be, and stay with us, as
an odor of life to life. Also, early this week a Lutheran man
/Straube/ with his Reformed wife and six children moved to our

community from Vernonburg near Savannah and rented locksmith Brückner's plantation and house for a year. They arrived
here in great poverty and, out of Christian compassion, are receiving from us some assistance for their first essentials. They
make good promise, and the future will tell us whether they are
honest and serious. Although the man has frequently attended
our services in Savannah, he has not been, as our people know, a
friend of us Ebenezers. Many hate us for no reason and because
they are envious.

Sunday and Monday, the 10th and 11th of April. During these
two days we celebrated Easter in good health, peace, and edification. On Easter Monday the pious serving boy /Georg Lein-
bacher/ of the righteous Salzburger, Brandner, died in peace.
Among those he associated with, he left a blessed and uplifting
memory. He deeply appreciated and was grateful for the spiritual and physical good he received from Brandner and his wife
in his days of good health and of sickness, and would have liked
to leave him his few possessions, had he wanted to accept them.
But now his sister /Salma/, who works as a servant on a plantation
near Savannah, is getting them, and I am going to write to her
master to report to him her brother's last words and will, since it
had always been his heart's desire that she come to our community because of the good instruction. She is thirteen years old
and the deceased boy was twelve years old; their parents died in
Spain where they arrived as prisoners.[6]

The only cause for the boy's illness, which started a long time
ago and gradually had grown worse, was probably the fact that
he ate raw rice and Indian corn. He admitted the other day that
he had learned it from the German people in Savannah and
done it here up to his most recent serious illness and that afterwards his conscience had caused him great pain. It is very deplorable and causes me great sadness to see that many of our
children lose their life at a tender age because they eat dirt, coal,
rice, and corn. Some small and some older children, even some
adults, have the color of death and earth on their faces which is
caused by such unusual and unnatural eating habits. People who
used to suffer from this strange appetite told me that the lust
and yearning for raw corn, rice, etc., are bigger than in pregnant

women and that it almost goes beyond natural strength to overcome them. You can see it in children who can hardly ever break
such habits, once they have acquired them. Jesus, our Prince and
Savior, have pity on us in this misery!

Tuesday, the 12th of April. Yesterday, after the forenoon service, had indicated that this forenoon, instead of the usual
weekly sermon, we would inaugurate our new school on the
plantations.[7] Because the burial of the pious boy who died yesterday was taking place at the same time, my inauguration sermon about the gracious and very friendly behavior vis-a-vis the
two disciples in yesterday's gospel, was also a funeral sermon. It
showed both adults and children that what our beloved Savior
had done to the two disciples as their good Shepherd, He had
also done to the dead school and serving boy, that in fact He
would do the very same to anyone of us, if only we would follow
in their footsteps, as the gospel teaches us and as we could see
from the beautiful example of the boy. Also, we made the disciples' prayer into our own prayer with regard to our new school:
"Stay with us, our Lord, for evening is about to settle in," etc. To
His glory I can attest that He gave me a particularly strong feeling of His gracious presence during this solemn occasion. I have
no doubt that He has also heard our joint prayer for our honorable benefactors who contributed their share to our school.

Wednesday, the 13th of April. Glaner's sick wife is wholeheartedly longing for, and looking forward to, her approaching salvation from all evil. Although her confinement to bed has been
long and hard, she is very content with the way God is guiding
her; she does not complain about anything but is constantly full
of praise for our Lord. She indicated several times what her funeral text should be, Psalm 102:18. "Our Lord turns to the
prayer of the lonely ones and does not spurn their prayer."
These comforting words had already touched her heart and edified her several years ago when they were discussed in public.
She was of the opinion that I had contributed something to her
journey from Germany to Ebenezer and wanted to thank me for
this good deed: because, in healthy and sick days, she always
considered it a great blessing and thanked our Lord and the
people for bringing her to this quiet place and so close to God's

word. She was sorry that she did not give enough thanks to her late brother, Veit Lemmenhofer, for his love, which made him call her by letter to Ebenezer. She and her pious husband know, of course, that God's word and the gospel are offered purely and abundantly in many places in Germany, but they are also aware of the obstacles to being good and the temptation to being bad, which helps them in their heartfelt intercession.

Tuesday, the 14th of April. Early this year, at his request, I lent Dr. Lange's treatise on universal grace[8] to a Christian and learned gentleman in Carolina, who had been an official in his home country; and gave him some other edifying small treatises. Yesterday I received a letter of thanks from him, together with the treatise he had borrowed. He wants to buy it and other useful writings, if I can help him to do so. I would like to quote something from his letter. Among other things, he writes,

> I could hardly read enough in the book on universal grace. The author treated the matter of universal grace very convincingly and clearly so that the only thing one can say is Amen: no book has pleased me more. There were still some difficult verses (in my mind) to which I had taken exception; however, now not the slightest doubt is left. Thus I now share completely his (Dr. Lange's) view with respect to predestination and the doctrine of universal grace.[9] To be sure, I had defended them in my home country and could hardly tolerate the dogma and still do not like it—namely, that one should not pray for all people since the clear verses of the Holy Scriptures distinctly teach us to do so.
>
> Indeed, if there were such an unconditional predestination, as we are taught, it would in many instances be useless to pray. Because those who had been chosen would have no need for it; and, to the rejected, it would be of no use because the former would, of necessity, be blessed and the others could only be damned. It is true that this objectionable doctrine is being applied less and less, and there are clergymen among the Reformed, who take Christianity seriously, who know no limit to Jesus's love and are well aware that Jesus would not have told us to love our enemies and to pray for them if He himself had not done so, etc.

After writing in his letter something about preachers who eagerly teach their religious beliefs without giving them much thought and who arouse the blind zeal of the common people, he talks about the experiences he had in his home country with his Reformed countrymen. He writes, for instance, that

> somebody had told him and others during a Sunday meeting that the Lutherans, too, were in error with respect to justification; and, when asked what that error was, nobody dared answer. I then explained to them what the Reformed and Lutherans believe but did not say which of them was the Reformed doctrine. Then, when they, without exception, decided it was the Lutheran teaching, I told them that they themselves believed the errors for which they had criticized the Lutherans. At the same time, I referred them to Arndt's *Christianity,* a blessed book which, together with others, is found in most Reformed homes. I now hope that the doctrine of universal grace will receive more and more credence. The worst is that some clergymen, in their blind religious zeal, are restraining the common people.

At his request, I sent him again some very edifying treatises and sermons, including four sermons by our dear Pastor Schubert,[10] whom he likes very much. I informed him to his great joy that, some years ago, one of his fellow countrymen /Krüsy/ had become a member of our community, that he thoroughly enjoyed God's truth as presented here, and that he prepared himself for a blessed death. On his deathbed he asked me to provide spiritual and physical care to his only son /Adrian/. He is a child of good hope.[11]

Saturday, the 16th of April. Our skilful Rottenberger fathered three children by his first wife who, however, do not give their father any joy, but cause him much grief. His youngest little girl is unable to walk or talk although she is already four years old; she seems to be quite foolish.[12] The middle boy, seven years of age, was skillful by nature and very alert, but he ate such unnatural and awful stuff and could not be dissuaded from eating it that, gradually, he became very sick. Some days ago, just after his father had left for Savannah with a boat loaded with flour, he unexpectedly died. Complaints about children eating all kinds of unnatural substances continue to be heard: and the parents cannot possibly keep their children with them all the time. Also this would be harmful to their health and they would not be able

to attend school. For that reason I have mentioned at various occasions this highly disturbing matter in my diary hoping that it
might be used by our pious Fathers and friends for heartfelt intercession and perhaps serve them for discussion with experienced medical doctors and provide us good advice.[13]

Sunday, the 17th of April. Late last evening our big boat returned from Savannah and unexpectedly brought a package
from Mr. Albinus addressed to me.[14] Although it did not contain
any letters from our dear Fathers, it was enough to please us
thoroughly and to redound to the praise the Lord when we
heard that, as Mr. Albinus reported, they are well and alive and
that our merciful Father in Heaven keeps using them as His
blessed tools to provide us, our homes, and our dear congregation with spiritual and physical help during this distressing time.
I see this with joy and to God's praise, from the list of monetary
contributions sent to us from Augsburg and Halle and from the
box containing a considerable supply of medicines and beautiful
books. May He think upon them for our good and for Christ's
sake!

Mr. Albinus' letter was dated August of last year. In it he reports that, at that time, none of last year's letters and diaries
from Ebenezer had arrived in London and he suspected that the
package was lost at sea early last year. These are dangerous
times; may God help us through them! He will certainly and
willingly do so if we faithfully observe through His grace what
we contemplate in our evening prayers and weekly sermons
from the Second Book of Chronicles 7:14. They undoubtedly
are important words; and it is highly worthwhile that we consider them, especially in these distressing times. In the package
just received there was also the copy of a letter from Prussian
archpriest Schumann to dearest Dr. Francke as well as some letters from several pious Salzburgers to ours, which I like wholeheartedly and which, I hope, will serve to our listeners' great edification. On the day of His magnificent epiphany, our dear
Savior will abundantly reward the dear archpriest for the spiritual and physical good he has done to the dear Salzburgers in
his and our congregation, as these letters indicate again.[15]

Monday, the 18th of April. A good friend from Savannah wrote me that Major Horton had inquired about me during his visit last week to Savannah; and when he heard of my concern that he might not be entirely satisfied with me (although I did not know the reason for my error), he immediately sat down and wrote me a very friendly letter from Savannah.

Tuesday, the 19th of April. After a long wait our merciful God blessed us with a good rainfall that still came in time. This spring we have not yet had a thunderstorm although thunderstorms are quite common in this climate. If it had rained and if a thunderstorm had shaken the soil (this helps to enhance fertility),[16] our big and small mulberry trees, which had been seriously affected by the late frost and the subsequent severe drought, would have grown more leaves. The dear members of our community could have produced a good deal of silk, for which they have shown considerable enthusiasm for quite some time. They used the few leaves they had very sparingly, and our merciful God (who is the source of all good in our physical life as well) blessed their industry in a way that amazes and pleases me. Also, this year we are going to produce more silk than we had reason to expect for the reasons mentioned earlier.

It is a great inconvenience and it discourages some people because they believe that they may not be permitted to keep their silk here but have to send it to Savannah for spinning. Most of them have only a few pounds. Also, the worms do not spin their cocoons at the same time: some do it earlier, others later, depending on when they leave their eggs and whether they receive good or bad care, including warm weather, food, etc. We hardly ever have the opportunity to go to Savannah; hence the worms bite their way through the cocoons, to the disadvantage of the poor people, before the latter have an opportunity to send them down there. Col. Stephens does not permit us to keep more than fifty pounds here in order to practice spinning.[17] However, since the good people for lack of an opportunity to go to Savannah have already brought a larger quantity to my house and are planning to bring more, I believed it would be hard and against the Lord Trustees' intent if I sent them away. Those who are able to wait are prepared to wait until the 22th of April when I or my dear colleague will travel to Savannah on official matters.

Three of our young women took delight in spinning the silk produced here, hoping that this would meet with our Lord Trustees' pleasure, especially since they gained considerable experience through practicing during the past two years, particularly last year. I also saw to it that the walls and other things needed for spinning were improved so that such work can be done in a cleaner and more convenient way this year. The only thing is that the Lord Trustees have not written to the Council in Savannah; otherwise we undoubtedly would already have permission to spin our silk here. Neither would we have needed the cauldron and the machine they sent us at great expense. A friend from Savannah wrote me some days ago that, just recently, the Spanish capers had again captured two ships off the coast of Charleston, which had arrived from England, while the people stood at the shore watching.

Wednesday, the 20th of April. Although the often-mentioned late and very severe frost caused noticeable damage to our European agricultural crops,[18] which— unlike those in Germany— are not covered by snow here, and although the long-lasting dry weather, great heat, and strong winds have greatly hampered their growth, our wheat and rye look well, to our amazement; and we hope that we will get some barley and peas as well. Last month the unusually large number of worms threatened to ruin our crops completely, but it pleased God (for, according to the Second Book of Chronicles 7:13, He commands the locusts to devour the land and, according to Verse 14, He promises to heal it) that a large number of starlings and other small birds came to the fields and gradually ate all the worms. Thanks be to God for His merciful regime!

Friday, the 22nd of April. To be sure, Glaner's dear wife is very weak physically, yet she becomes very cheerful whenever somebody talks, reads, or sings to her from God's word about her dearest Savior, whose sweet love she cannot praise enough. Christian friends visit her, and she considers that to be a dear good deed and she eagerly remembers their comforting words. She is dying with pleasure and with joy which, according to the

Holy Scriptures, is like going to rest and a journey to peace. On hearing of my official trip to Savannah and afraid that she might pass away in the meantime, she bade me a warm-hearted good-bye, asked my forgiveness if ever she had offended me, and thanked for all good deeds.

Sunday, the 24th of April. This Sunday, Misericordia Domini, I performed my official duties with the Germans in Savannah and preached God's word extensively on both Friday and Saturday evenings as well as on Sunday, and their attendance was good. Eighteen persons came to the Lord's Supper. This time, since the English minister was not home, we had the church to ourselves and did not have to hurry with our church service as we must if the English attend church at 10 o'clock in the morning and at 3 o'clock in the afternoon. They are still in the process of building the English church; meanwhile, they and we make do with the courthouse or townhall, which lend themselves easily for church services.[19]

Monday, the 25th of April. We left Savannah in good and still weather last night and arrived safely at home about noon. Among other things, I brought back the welcome news that Col. Stephens, upon my repeated written requests, had given us permission to spin in our community the rest of the silk we produce here. This caused great joy among our women who make and spin silk. It not only prevents the inconvenience discussed earlier but it also increases (in addition to many other things) the benefit of not having to send any half-spun silk down to Savannah, to the disadvantage of our Lord Trustees and of those who produce it. For, until now, whenever a boat traveled down there, some people took off and sent away some silk which the worms had not yet completely spun. As a result the silkballs stayed light and soft. This time, we sent down one hundred and five pounds of silk in balls; the rest is going to be spun here through hard work, and a good start was already made last week. According to the ordinance issued by our Lord Trustees, the silk consists of fifteen to twenty threads, hence is strong yet soft.

The other pleasant news I brought back was for a pious Salzburger who, nearly 12 days ago, had been unlucky with thirty bushels of Indian corn he was supposed to carry from Savannah to Old Ebenezer. The evening before he had put that much in a big boat and then had left it safe in an otherwise secure location on the river bank near Savannah. He had found and left everything in good order at 10 o'clock at night. However, on his return at dawn, the broad and rigid boat had turned over and the entire corn had fallen into the water. Everybody thought he might have to pay for it; however, I heard from Col. Stephens, to whom he had sent a petition, that he will receive it as a gift.

The third good news I heard and read about and which concerned our small group was the favorable attitude of Col. Heron, the current commandant of Frederica, who requested in a letter to Col. Stephens that he inform me that, in these dangerous times when the Indians want to stir up new trouble, he is planning to send a corporal and six men from his regiment to our village. If I so desire, they will watch at night so that hostile Indians will not attack us. He will select and send people who will not cause us any trouble. The Cherokee Indians are making peace with the Creek Indians, and it looks as if they want to start something against the English. They recently killed an Indian trader, an Englishman who had dealt with the Indians, and in the case of another person, they took away all his belongings, leaving him almost naked and bare, and led him to God knows where.

After painting him with certain war-signs, they dispatched a boy to the governor of Carolina telling him that this is what the Cherokee Indians are sending him, which is the equivalent of a declaration of war. May God watch for and over us! The reason why the Indians are angry may very well be the miserable treatment some of them had to accept from the Carolinians. They all consider themselves gentlemen and are very haughty; if beaten, offended, etc., they seek revenge at the earliest opportunity. 2) Since many ships that are supposed to carry goods to Charleston get lost at sea, the Indians cannot be supplied with trade goods which they are accustomed to. They accept no reasons and do not believe that there is no merchandise for the Indians. 3) Currently they are very often cheated in their trade in terms of goods and weight. To them, the price of goods must neither increase nor fall but always remain the same. Otherwise they start trouble. To compensate themselves for their loss, the merchants who buy goods from Europe at high prices commit many forgeries and intrigues which other merchants betray to the Indians (because one person envies the next). 4) The primary reason is the local sins that are common among both the wealthy and the poor people.

The Cherokee Indians would not be able to inflict much damage on this and our neighboring colony, unless the Creek Indians, who live between the inhabitants of both colonies and the Cherokees, would make common cause with them. But Col. Stephens told me that the Cherokee Indians are also very restless and that they want to drive out the people who are settled on the Ogeechy River. They consider this and other land to be theirs, and they are planning on getting large gifts, for which that miserable man Bosomworth (erstwhile Anglican minister in Savannah and Frederica, who later married a half-Indian woman, became an Indian trader, and has been living among them for quite some time) is agitating. He is an irresponsible man; and there is concern that, unless stopped, he may eventually cause great tragedy.[20]

Old Thomas Bacher died on Saturday after a brief illness and was buried yesterday following the afternoon sermon. On his sickbed he was sincerely sorry that he had not observed his Christianity with the faithfulness and seriousness that God's word demands and for which he had the opportunity. He hungered and thirsted for his Savior and probably was content as it is clearly promised in Matthew 5:6. He proved to be patient and Christian on his sickbed although he was unable to talk much because of his constant feverish heat and weak condition. He leaves behind a very pious and understanding widow who is a very well-liked midwife in our village. His two only daughters, well-mannered and of good hope, are well married to Christian and understanding Salzburgers.[21]

Tuesday, the 26th of April. The widow Granewetter did not suffer any damage from her latest heavy cross; rather she experienced great benefit and blessing. She had markedly grown by recognizing God and her nothingness and by believing in, and trusting, her dear Savior; and she is filled with religious joy and good hope although she has two small children (she just weaned the youngest) and a difficult household on her plantation. The latter is very fertile and well located, and her husband left it to her well-equipped. However, unless she can hire a farmworker, she will not be able to keep it in good condition for any length of time. The buildings as well as the fences are gradually deteriorating, and strong people are needed for farming. For that reason, she wanted me to write to dear Mr. S.U.[22] in her behalf and to ask him whether it would be possible for her brother, Johann Georg Sturmer, could be sent to her, or, in case he is weak or has married, a pious, industrious, knowledgeable farmworker. She believes with certainty that God has not granted her such a good plantation in vain and that He will surely send her help in His time so that it can be cultivated and maintained. All our exhausted Salzburgers greatly need loyal servants; and for this reason I wrote some time ago to the Lord Trustees and Mr. S.U. May God give us peace and His blessing!

Wednesday, the 27th of April. An Englishman who lives at Mount Pleasant (between Old Ebenezer and Palachocolas) came with his wife and three Englishmen at about noon to our place to have his child, which was born on 22 February of this month, baptized. I did it gladly.

Thursday, the 28th of April. The pious Mrs. Thomas Bacher received a deep impression from her old husband's departure from this world; and it is her sincere resolution to spend the short remaining period of her life in the service and praise of her Lord and thus preparing for a joyful and blessed departure. She is a quiet soul and knows how to apply her beloved solitude well. She has no worries about material things because she knows that the Lord is caring for her and has cared for her abundantly so far. She does not consider herself poor (which she actually is); and I had difficulty in persuading her to accept a small monetary gift, which our dear God sent this time from East Prussia. Some pious Salzburgers in the parish of the righteous and diligent Archpriest Schumann have sent some edifying letters to their kinsman Stephan Rottenberger and to others of their compatriots at our place; and they donated to the poor among their brothers and sisters here three Reichsthaler, or ten shillings one and ha'penny, from what the Lord has let fall to them. I passed this dear gift on to two sincerely pious widows and to a poor woman who is a true Israelite without guile.

Our merciful God is still continuing to look out for the needy condition of our Salzburger community in these difficult and dangerous times of war.[23] This time, news has come from our worthy Mr. Albinus that in Halle and Augsburg a beautiful monetary blessing has flowed together to make good our lack. Also, some worthy benefactors have contributed something for the salary of Mr. Thilo, the instructor in my house.[24] We are wishing and petitioning God for all divine blessing as a recompense for these as well as our worthy benefactors.

MAY

Sunday, the 1st of May. Our faithful and merciful God has given us much healing instruction and comfort at this difficult time and in our current trials from both today's chapter of the Holy Scriptures, Dominica Jubilate, and the opening verse, Micah 7:8. Just as the entire seventh chapter of Micah can easily be applied to the current situation in this country (as it would be easy for me to prove, if necessary and appropriate), we look at the opening words and some other comforting verses in that chapter as if they were in the Bible primarily for our sake. We are, as it were, a thorn in the eye of those many people who rejoice in the serious adversities that were placed upon us according to God's counsel and will, as did those during David's times: See, see, we enjoy seeing that. We now must be humble and trust in God: "Rejoice not against me, mine enemy, that I fall, I shall arise," etc., etc.

Notwithstanding all trials, our gracious and almighty God has given us His help and blessing in many instances so that we trust in our belief and say: "We will arise; the godless will see it and it will annoy him; he will gnash his teeth and forgive, because whatever the godless want, it is lost." Some of the poor people in this country believe our Lord Trustees use our arrival as an excuse for not permitting Negroes or Moorish slaves; that is why they hate and envy us, and they can hardly bear anything good being written to our Lord Trustees about our community and people. They blame me for reporting nothing but good and wonderful things about Ebenezer in my letters to the Lord Trustees while withholding our shortcomings and difficult circumstances, although it is quite clear that in my diary or letters I forget neither the good deeds nor the trials.

Tuesday, the 3rd of May. Now not only can Steiner's wife merely believe the gracious forgiveness of her sins, but our merciful Lord has also given her a sweet example of it in her heart. She found it difficult to free herself from her natural and distrustful character. She was not content with repenting: she always wanted to be aware of, and feel, her sins as she knew other people, who converted to God, had been aware of, and felt, them. She also considered her prayers to be too poor and inferior, especially since she was unable to express herself in words like other pious souls; and for that reason she believed that she and her prayers would please our dear God even less than they pleased her. Thinking of Christ's great joy in calling all sinners to his side, in rejecting nobody, and in accepting graciously the most simple-minded prayer, even if it consisted of only a few words, has drawn her frail heart to our Lord Jesus Christ; and, through the Holy Spirit, it is filled with trust in His name. This morning our dear Lord granted her a sweet and peaceful sleep which she had to do without during her painful female illness. For that reason the verse "Remember that Jesus Christ . . . was raised from the dead," etc., was very sweet and it stuck in her mind and she woke up with it to her joy. The illness has ravished her body very much.

Thursday, the 5th of May. Yesterday afternoon our dear God delivered Glaner's dear wife earlier than she and her husband had expected. He had come to see me yesterday morning to tell me with tears in his eyes that she was having great pain and was growing increasingly weaker. Therefore he would let her go home if our Lord would take her to Him. He got some candles from the orphanage assuming that he would have to sit up with her for several more nights and burn the candles. She was content and happy to die and was buried with much blessing this

afternoon. Many people, particularly women, from the plantations attended the burial; most probably because of the love and
esteem they felt towards this dear soul whose body we interred
today in its eternal resting place. For she was known in the entire
congregation as an honest and reliable Christian.

Some time ago she had variously mentioned to me her burial
text from Psalm 102:3,18; and I spoke about it with joy and blessing and to the great edification of my listeners. In doing so I
have truthfully stressed the great treasure of grace which our
gracious God put into our earthen vessel and which was amply
demonstrated in her lifetime, in her suffering and death, to the
glory of God and the edification of our fellowmen. She was a
very humble woman, patient and tested by temptations, and also
a devoted Christian who spent her long-time weaknesses and
subsequent real illness by constant communication with God and
by talking about and to her Savior, and by interceding for her
fellowmen. Her body and soul now rest in peace.

Monday, the 9th of May. The hard work which our inhabitants
displayed this year in manufacturing silk amazes and pleases me
very much. Those with a Christian heart and enlightened eyes
must recognize that our hard work met with God's marked blessing, which makes it possible to produce much from little. Although, as mentioned earlier, very severe frost partly destroyed,
or partly badly damaged, our mulberry trees, we had more silk
this year than last. At that time we produced four hundred
pounds, compared to this year's fourhundred and thirty-seven
pounds, apart from a small quantity from some trees which
started later and whose harvest, therefore, is not yet available.

Somewhat more than one hundred and fifty pounds were sent
to Savannah for spinning, but most of it is being spun here by
three fine, skillful, and respectable women; and progress is
good. The Trustees' trees yielded only thirty-four pounds of
silk. Our dear inhabitants are short of many things at this distressing time, and it is still another indication of God's special
concern that the silk is providing our community with some
money once again. If only the price of linen and other things for
making clothes were lower, our hard-working inhabitants would
soon be able, with God's blessing, to earn their food and simple

livelihood, especially if some provision and preparation in this well-located country were made for trading so that industrious people would be able to earn some money outside of farming.

Thursday, the 12th of May. It pleases our dear God to put many a cross and sorrow on our honest Steiner and his wife. However, they do not complain; they pray more and praise God. She has been dangerously sick for many weeks, and he, too, is in poor health because of the heavy workload, for which there is nobody to help him. If only this pious, sensible, and industrious man were able to get a faithful servant, he and his household would be in good condition. His help lies with God who created heaven and earth.

Friday, the 13th of May. When Maurer's sickly wife heard that we are going to celebrate Holy Communion on Ascension Day, she asked me to visit her to find out whether she, too, might approach this, our Lord's, distinguished table. Although she wholeheartily wishes to do so, she considers herself completely unworthy of such a great favor because of a great wound that weighs on her conscience. So far her weakness has kept her from leaving the house and from going to church (something it would be hard for her not to do under normal circumstances). Should this weakness continue, Holy Communion will be administered to her in her home at the same time the congregation receives theirs.

Wednesday, the 18th of May. Ever since we started harvesting our crops, we have had rain, which has been very good for other crops. Although our wheat recovered after being severely damaged by caterpillars, most of it became infected by so-called mildew, so that even those who planted it late in the season will have a poor wheat crop. Rye, on the other hand, turned out well everywhere, except that the late frost made it very thin. The same happened to barley. I understand that the people in Purysburg and in other places grow some type of wheat that fails to turn out well every year. A man in our colony has a beautiful field of Sicilian wheat, which looks very nice. I have also noticed that our people do not yet know the proper time for planting: they usually sow wheat too late, and barley and peas too early. Because they have no hired hands, they are not in control of what they want to do and, therefore, cannot do it the way they want to do it.

Friday, the 20th of May. This morning Maurer's sickly wife received Holy Communion at her home with heartfelt eagerness and true poverty of the spirit. I talked to her about the short verse: "And I, if I be lifted up from the earth, will draw all men unto me," which we covered yesterday in the exordium and which our dear Savior blessed in her and my soul. By using the rod of softness as well as the rod of woe on this soul, He is trying to draw her fully into Himself so that her spirit may become one with His. Hence she is truly happy with the good guidance she receives from her Shepherd and knows that her sins will be forgiven and that she has a merciful God in Heaven. Such souls, in whom our gracious Father in Heaven has attained His purpose, recognize the benefits He bestows upon them in this solitude despite all trials and tribulations, especially in a spiritual way, and they humbly praise Him for them.

The others as well are faithfully told of the good our merciful God has done for them and their children and of the benefits they enjoy which many others in America do not have, in order to protect them from ingratitude and disobedience and in order to give them no excuse on the day of judgment. With this in mind I read to my listeners a passage from a beautiful letter I received from Pastor Brunnholz and explained to them, on the basis of a sad example, the misfortune people suffer if they do not stay with their profession and disregard warnings. The passage was this: "Jacob Zübli gave up his school again last summer because he wanted to learn how to paint; but he died after being sick for only a few hours. Later his wife gave birth to a daughter: and, since I did not want to give her special consideration and my Germantown congregation was unable to support her, and since she was never very eager to work and I had chastised her for it, she is now becoming a Tumbler with her two children."[1]

Saturday, the 21st of May. Mr. Mayer came back from Savannah with the news that there had been a big commotion yesterday on Ascension Day in Savannah and that all soldiers had been called together by the drum to take their arms. An Englishman's

wife with her children, Negroes, and a white family on their island below Savannah towards the ocean noticed two vessels full
of Spaniards. Thereupon she fearfully ran into town and caused
a commotion. The vessels left as a result of the fuss. Some Englishmen, who had been imprisoned and were returning from
St. Augustine, stated that a very evil Englishman or Irishman,
who had been jailed in Charleston, set fire to it and deserted to
the Spaniards and wished to serve the Spaniards in St. Augustine as their leader to attack the most remote plantations in
Carolina and Georgia. He was extremely well informed about
the two colonies and their rivers and landing spots. The governor in St. Augustine is reported to be a good friend of the English and to have sent several gifts to Major Horton. I was also
told that the Spanish would like to leave us alone, if only we
would leave them alone: however, two experiences in a row have
shown how misplaced it would be to trust the Spanish. Much is
being said to make simple-minded people believe that it does not
mean anything, although so many Negroes were brought to this
colony at a time when England is engaged in a war with two po-
tentates.[2]

Monday, the 23rd of May. The German family consisting of
the father, the mother, and six unreared children, who moved
from Vernonburg to our community approximately two months
ago, behaves in a Christian-like manner among us; they love
God's word, the Holy Scriptures, and the good opportunity for
edification.[3] They also work hard on their land and, during the
current barley, wheat, and rye harvest, for other people for
wages. Nobody among us is as poor as these people were when
they came to us; but they felt in a noticeable way God's fatherly
care for themselves and for their almost-naked children when
they received many gifts of clothing and household utensils.

Tuesday, the 24th of May. A Salzburger told me that he received the certain news that his former neighbor and godfather,
Ruprecht Zittrauer, had died in Charleston and had left behind
a very poor widow with three children.[4] He is godfather to
the two eldest children and will try to get permission to raise and
supervise these two children, away from their badly-behaved
mother and her ruin. I will gladly assist in this matter in every

possible way. This wretched man left Ebenezer because he was
lazy and because his lazy wife talked him into it, and they moved
about the country for a while. Then he worked in a small for-
tification south of Savannah. Finally he moved to Carolina and
became a slave-driver. I do not know why he left here, but one
thing is certain: in the end he became a soldier in Charleston
and he died a miserable death there.

She was used to being idle and to go begging in the Dürrenberg area[5] and, if permitted, would probably still do so in
Charleston. Several disorderly people left Georgia for Carolina to beg there, which led our adversaries to claim that everybody in this colony would become a beggar unless our Lord
Trustees permit Negroes. Poor Zittrauer was not only lazy but
had also taken to drink, and his wife had faithfully helped him
in doing so. People like them do not get ahead anywhere in the
world. I pray to God that He let the sad news of Zittrauer's decline serve our people and others as a warning against ingratitude and disobedience. We are indeed very fortunate!

Thursday, the 26th of May. Hanns Flerl's wife, who takes her
Christianity very seriously, had some unnecessary worries and
doubts about her state of grace, from which God's words freed
her, in part, some days ago during our weekly sermon and, in
part, today without my knowledge. They are good souls, who
are seriously concerned about their salvation, always careful not
to subject themselves to the the law and to seek there what they
can only find in Christ, namely, peace of their souls.[6] He keeps
calling in the Holy Scriptures: "Hearken diligently unto me and
eat ye that which is good, and let your soul delight itself in fat-
ness." Even though they read good books which call for active
Christianity, these souls must be diligently reminded lest they
lose sight of the Gospel and Christianity, because it says in
Hebrews 5, "And being made perfect, he became the author of
eternal salvation unto all them that obey him." (and not for
Moses and the moralists); compare Matthew 17:15.[7]

Flerl's wife also said that she knew about the struggle but not
how to overcome it, which makes it necessary for us not only to
completely subdue and extirpate our spiritual enemies, but also
to feel a true aversion to their sense and will, and not to give in to

their lures and temptations, as I explained to her from the example of the pious, chaste Joseph and from the verse in the Galatians 5:17.

During the conversation she also talked about the guidance with which God had provided her when they started to expel the Salzburgers. She was born in the state of Bavaria and brought up in ignorance by her seriously erring mother and some relatives. However, when God recognized that He could save her soul, He saw to it that among the twelve journeymen of a papal masterbuilder from Salzburg who worked on a church in Bavaria, there was a Lutheran journeyman, called "the Lutheran," about whose religion strange things were said. Because he got room and board at the house of her cousin, for whom she worked, she was very much aware of his Christian behavior. And, since she noticed great peace, nonconformance to the world, and diligent prayer and intercession as well as sympathy and tears when he saw the bound Evangelical Salzburgers being led past him, she had the deep desire to talk to this man secretly about his and her religious faith.

One evening God arranged for her cousin to be busy with the soldiers who were accompanying the Salzburgers on their way across Bavaria, while the servants were in the tavern. She grasped this opportunity to make this knowledgeable man, who was experienced in Christianity, teach her the Evangelical truth for three hours; upon her request, he also sent her a good book, namely the *Schaitberger,* in a small well-secured barrel.[8] In it, they eagerly read for three consecutive weeks at night about the Evangelical truth and her previous misunderstandings. Because the people concluded from her overall behavior, especially her absence from monthly confession, observance of brotherhood meetings, participation in pilgrimages, and telling a rosary, that she might have suspicious books, they waylaid her, took the book away from her, and threatened her with jail and death unless she stayed away from this heresy. At the priest's instigation, her mother, in particular, behaved very badly.

Finally God gave her the courage to leave, although she knew neither the way nor the area. A woman potter, also a secret Lutheran, referred her to her very close kinswoman in Austria;

but there she was advised in confidence that she was to go to Salzburg rather than to pretend, in violation of her conscience, because here they searched very much after Evangelical people and books. Since the journeyman bricklayer had given her instructions on how to get to the Goldeck jurisdiction and, there, to a Lutheran family, she traveled there without a passport, like a poor abandoned sheep, in the name of God, who was her leader and guide, and she was well received. However, because the Evangelical people were being expelled at that time, she was summoned to appear before the authorities and was threatened that, if she stayed with these Evangelical people, she would enjoy neither God's care nor any favor from the people in the Empire, but would die a horrible death. Nevertheless, she said that she would go with them regardless of what might happen to her. She preferred all misery and even death itself to renouncing God, her Savior, and the Evangelical truth. She did not start with good days, but with misery and death, as the bricklayer had told her earlier while assuring her of God's help.

Friday, the 27th of May. Our inhabitants are convinced that the Sicilian wheat mentioned earlier would do best in our climate, and they wanted very much to get seed. When I was about to write to the trader and planter who had brought such wheat from Portugal, he unexpectedly arrived in our community to look at our mills and to buy boards to be loaded on his ship to the West Indies. He promised me eight bushels of the beautiful wheat, which caused much joy among our people. This knowledgeable and wealthy merchant is having two windmills built for him in Carolina, namely, one grinding mill and one sawmill; but he is currently encountering many obstacles in building them. He wanted me to encourage the people in our community to plant European crops[9] and to make silk and indigo as well as to prepare pitch and tar. On the other hand, he thought it might be better if they would stop planting Indian corn and beans, which require much work during the hottest season, yet yield little. One acre does not produce more than about 2 pounds Sterling, while one acre of indigo would bring between 10 and 12 pounds Sterling. In previous years I had offered seeds; but since I do not have a servant to test them myself and since one cannot hire

dayworkers even for cash when they are most needed, nobody can be persuaded to get involved in something he has never seen.

It appeared recently that our inhabitants would have a bad wheat crop. However, after a fertile rain, the wheat has recovered so well that we now have reason to thank our Lord. Where it was planted too late, it was rust that caused the largest damage; but otherwise most people have had a good harvest of all European crops, with the exception of barley and peas, which were damaged too severely by the late frost. It is like a miracle that real iron rust forms on wheat, and sometimes on rye, destroying the stems to such an extent that no juice is able to rise to the ears. Barley, too, is at times affected by rust, but the grains are free from damage. I understand that this rust is due to heavy night dew; and, if two men are unable to shake it off with a long cord, it is as if the hot sun had boiled it and glued or baked it onto the stems. However, it is amazing that in some fields wheat and rye were seriously damaged, and in others little or none at all. However, the rust had also damaged some stems of the little Sicilian wheat planted here. It seems to me that early planting is the best way to preserve it. The indigo bushes or plants have no enemy at all, since, in contrast to corn and beans, neither deer, bears, squirrels, wildcats,[10] nor worms feed on them. This is not to mention such other great advantages in storing and transporting the processed indigo.

Sunday, the 29th of May. Today our merciful God has given us another holy Whitsunday, which we will celebrate today and tomorrow as customary. It is very hot, but we have cool places of worship. Yesterday I felt the beginning of a fever, but it now seems to be over so that I and my dear colleague will be able to preach our Lord's word unhindered.

Monday, the 30th of May. On this Whitmonday a corporal and seven common soldiers under his command came to our community. The commandant of Frederica, Col. Heron, sent them by water upon receiving my letter so that they can keep a watchful eye on the current dangerous movements of the Indians, who are said to have already committed all kinds of violence in the areas north of Savannah Town in Carolina.[11] In response to the colonel's offer to send us an eight-man guard, I wrote that, if he should consider it necessary for our preservation and protection, we would gratefully accept his care, especially since he assured me that he would select only people from his regiment who would not cause us any trouble. I know that God deals with people only through means, and we would tempt God if we would not make use of the means to protect us since they come from God, just as it would be some kind of false worship to trust in the means and not in God.

Who knows what benefit one or the other soldier will derive from coming to our place. Their instructions with regard to their behavior towards me and our community are very explicit, and they know that the colonel will severely punish any excess. His letter to me was written in a very friendly tone, and at the end it says, "We all here would be extreamly obliged to you, Sir, could you recommend to us a good clergyman. It is a terrible thing, that so many people, as we have here, should be without a spiritual Guide." (Thus recognizes and writes a soldier, who is a colonel.) There are always complaints about Frederica and that it is so disorderly and godless there, but no thought has ever been given to provide the community with an honest minister. Some of them have caused more damage than good.[12] Everybody respected and admired the late minister Driesler, although he was unable to serve them with his office because of his inadequate command of the English language.[13]

Tuesday, the 31st of May. We produced 464 pounds and several ounces of silk balls this year, that is, 64 pounds more than a year ago, although the late frost inflicted severe damage on the white mulberry trees and destroyed some of them completely. Most of it was again spun on our machine for practice, and everybody who sees it and is able to pass judgment praises the uniformity of its threads.

JULY

Tuesday, the 12th of July. I am shocked that the cabinet maker in Savannah who, on orders of the Council in Savannah, built for our village a very simple machine for silk spinning, said that his labor (without the iron structure) alone came to 3 pounds 10 shillings and that the rest would cost 1 pound. The Lord Trustees gave us a big cauldron to spin the silk and sent it to us eleven months ago. In her scorn of our silk produced and spun here this year, the new silk spinner in Savannah (an English widow) does no better than the Italian woman who was dismissed.[1] This is why we will not send her any more silk from our place for spinning in the future. According to some knowledgeable men who looked at it, the silk spun this year in our community is better than last year's which the Lord Trustees praised very highly in their secretary's letter of the 10th of March.

At their request, I kept a diary in the English language for our Lord Trustees but, for special reasons, have not made any entries since last August.[2] But now the Lord Trustees have given a clear indication of their pleasure and of the usefulness of the small information and observations contained in my English letters about how to improve this colony and how to meet their good intentions. And because I expect, with God's blessing, some benefit for our community from doing so and because I am indebted to our Lord Trustees in many ways, I have decided in God's name to continue the diary in English, although I have not made any entries for almost a year. Since it is short and does not require any elaborate words, it will not take much of my time; this is also what our friend in Savannah and my dear colleague have advised me to do. What dear Mr. Albinus wrote to me on the second of November was very comforting to me: "As for your fear that your well-meant suggestions might be printed, you can put your mind at ease. It will not happen for now; however, if one or the other matter must be published, our court chaplain will see to it that it will not hurt you or your office."

Thursday, the 14th of July. Soon after returning home last night, I was told that a suspicious young man, who is trying to cross the Savannah River to Carolina, had secretly come to our community. My investigation showed him to be a Spaniard who had lived in Carolina and in this colony for several years and that his intentions were not good. I had him guarded by the soldiers over night in order to obtain more information from him this morning, and I also asked some men from Old Ebenezer to come here. But, since the soldiers believed him to be more honest than he really was, he escaped under an apparent pretext this morning, leaving behind his flintlock and a few other things. He seemed to be a desperate lad, sufficiently cunning, wicked, and daring to inflict damage wherever God permits him to do so. If he is not spying, he is planning to do, or has already done, something bad, as I detect from the dissolute way of his speech and today's escape.

Friday, the 15th of July. Our dear friend, Mr. Habersham in Savannah, unexpectedly lost his gifted and beloved little daughter to death, which caused much grief to both parents and other friends. My visit, which was quite unexpected, and the comfort I provided were appreciated and useful. Within a few days the little girl had been healthy, sick, and dead. Red dysentery with high fever is making the rounds in Savannah, a disease that put an early end to the girl's life.

This summer we had very heavy thunderstorms in the Savannah area, and some days ago tremendous lightning struck next to a mother and her four children in a way that the mother was like dead and ashen-faced and the children turned dumb and senseless from it. The mother reportedly feels a little better now. At that time our shoemaker Zettler, together with some other people from our community, had traveled to this area toward the ocean, partly for professional reasons and partly because of his health. And no sooner had they returned, when lightning struck. Prior to that Savannah had experienced a heavy rain storm that was so fierce that we believed our boat would go down in the ocean, but they did not know about this storm.

Saturday, the 16th of July. Yesterday in the late afternoon, Rottenberger's deathly sick daughter sent me her greetings twice. Since I was busy with many other things and since I had not seen the evening coming, I did not get around to pay my planned visit. On visiting her today, I found her unconscious and in the throes of death. Yesterday, at the time of our evening prayer, she had undergone a tremendous change. Although she no longer was in command of her senses, she was praying the most beautiful verses, the Lord's Prayer, etc., but no longer understood the questions we asked and what we told her. Our dear Savior has done much to her soul during this illness: she has become a completely different girl. God's words and prayer were her constant solace. I prayed for her today and blessed her on leaving the world, and this is probably going to be soon.

In the late afternoon Rottenberger informed me that his daughter Susanna passed away gently and peacefully and that her Savior, whom she had loved dearly and for whose presence she had been waiting with joy, had taken her home. While she gravely sinned when she ate raw beans and, by doing so, damaged her health, she was sure of Christ's forgiveness.[3] Dr. Graham, who cares for the sick in and around Savannah, told me during a recent visit here that he knew of many children in Savannah, Vernonburg, and even in his homeland of Scotland who were eating dirt and all kinds of other unclean and harmful substances, and he expressed the view that worms were the cause of this unusual and unnatural appetite and that it would pass as soon as the worms disappeared.

Sunday, the 17th of July. After our afternoon service today, the little girl who died yesterday was buried with blessings and to our edification. Before carrying the body outside, we sang in the church: *Meinen Jesum lass ich nicht*, etc.; and, while it was being lowered in the cemetary: *Alle Menschen müssen sterben*, etc., two songs our dear God has blessed especially in her during her illness, since she had felt the desire to die, although previously she had not liked to hear about it. Since on the sixth Sunday after Trinity, in the morning as well as in the afternoon, the congregation had heard God's word abundantly from the Holy Scriptures and from the regular epistle, as well as from the two exordium verses from Proverbs 11:18–21, and 1 John: 6,7,[4] I briefly told the adults and children during the burial only two things about the late Susanna, 1) something they already knew, namely, that, like many other children, she had been foolish and naughty in her healthy days and that she had harmed her health and shortened her life by her unusual eating habits; and 2) something nobody knew, namely, that Jesus, our good Shepherd, looked for her long enough to find her, made her realize and feel her sins and also made her believe in His name, assured her of His forgiveness of her sins, and made her to eagerly look forward to an early and blessed end, and that she showed unmistakable signs, which I recently mentioned, of this. Most of it appears in several places of this diary. The tears my listeners showed that this simple sermon penetrated their heart.

Monday, the 18th of July. Our merciful God does not let us take care for our children in vain; but now and then He gives us with their souls some visible blessing, about which I reported on or the other detail yesterday and in the past. Yesterday, in the late afternoon, after sunset, a serving boy in our community, who has very wicked, worldly parents in Savannah, sent me the following note:

> Greetings, dear Pastor! Please forgive me for writing again. I do not dare communicate with you verbally and probably would be unable to do so. Because as soon as I see you, my heart bleeds in my body so that I cannot express myself. I often wonder whether it would be possible that even I, a poor worm, could be saved and become one of God's children; but my heart tells me that this is impossible; even if God took all people to Heaven, he would banish me to Hell. For without faith it is impossible to please God. Yes, God wants to give us faith, but one must pray for it. And one cannot pray because one's prayer, and everything one does, is a sin. So who is going to take pity on me! I will be lost in all eternity unless God takes pity on me poor soul in time. I now hope and ask you to pray for me as well.

I asked him to see me at noon today. I instructed him from the Holy Scriptures, prayed with him and gave him, as a present, dear Bogatzky's wonderful book, called the *Paupers' Book*,[5] which describes very well and clearly the Evangelical order of salvation and the privileges of forgiven sinners. I underlined for the frightened boy the points relating to Evangelical instruction, which also answered his letter, and marked the pertinent passages on the page with a *nota bene* so that he will read them soon and often. If he has more time, he will read the whole book. Not too long ago, on a trip to Savannah, I also used it to help an elderly Reformed widow who had listened to God's word with blessing in our community several times. She told me of her doubts and temptations,[6] which undoubtedly would have been so much greater, had she believed her church's dogma of the *absolutum decretum*.[7] I happened to have the booklet on me, which I lent to her.

Tuesday, the 19th of July. Among many other alms, our dear God gave us a pair of good shoes for an orphaned girl, which brought much happiness to a truly pious, industrious, and hopeful girl, who has neither father nor mother and helps our pious widow Zant, formerly Pilz, around the house. I hope that the dear unknown benefactress will achieve, through God's blessing, the purpose for which she sent us the gift. She added a brief, very edifying note, which deserves to be copied by me here as a constant remembrance andfor the edification of others:

> Immanuel! May God live in all pious homes.
> And should there be sorrow and misery here and there,
> May God be our counsel and deed, which gives us peace.
> So, at all times it means "Here is Immanuel."

"Dearly Beloved Souls! May Jesus be your shield and your all! This small gift, a pair of shoes, is for an orphaned girl whom I wish and ask to love Jesus and to pray to God that his dear Son be loved more ardently by my poor soul. May Jesus be your shield and your all, Amen."

This gift with the inspiring note came from Hanover. And thus our wonderful God has blessed us from a number of other places with good deeds and written admonition to be patient in our sufferings and steadfast in good, trust in God, and praise of His name. Among them, in particular, are two women of high standing, whose name I am not at liberty to divulge, but whom I respect greatly as the apples of God's eye. Their forceful letters to the congregation and to me have refreshed, strengthened, and encouraged me greatly and that is why I would like to quote something from them here:

> Therefore, you dear people of Ebenezer, do not tire even though, outwardly, you may have to suffer a great deal and live through much hardship and sorrow. Because we know that, although the human body is wasting away, the soul is being rejuvenated day after day. For our hardship, which is temporary, etc. Oh, so be

joyfully patient before our dear God because the Lord will not abandon His people, now or ever, etc.

I humbly thank our good God for giving me the opportunity through N. and N. to collect some little things (although it is much linen or cloth, and money, which we ask our dear God to take under His powerful protection during the journey!). So, accept with gratitude these little alms from our Lord, through whom we receive everything and whose grace and kindness will preserve everything. May our Lord let you enjoy it with His blessings and in peace, and may He continue to protect and shield you in the future!

May He bless your bodies and souls, here and in all eternity. May He show you on your bodies and souls what is meant by: 'Blessed be the poor,' etc. He provides shelter to strangers, He takes care of the orphans, fulfils widows' prayers, etc. So let us now join in praising God: we will sing a thousand times our praise, glory, and gratitude, etc., to God, our Lord.

Another very dear, distinguished friend of our Ebenezer congregation, whose name I do not know, wrote on the 21st of November in a very edifying letter, sent from a place I do not know, that two years ago, in God's strange ways, she received news from Ebenezer which our gracious God had blessed to edify her soul and which had turned her soul to Christian love and a favorable disposition towards me and my congregation. She humbly worships the wondrous love, wisdom and omnipotence of God who proved his magnificence in establishing and supporting the dear Ebenezers. She prays with all her heart that God's grace may continue to be with us, that He may protect us from spiritual and bodily harm, strengthen and maintain the good in Jesus's true disciples, and let us have a good odor among the heathens here that they, too, may come to recognize the truth. She then adds the following sincere wish:

May Jesus Christ, our true arch-shepherd, spread his wings of mercy over them, strengthen, fortify, and establish them so that together we may finally accomplish the goal of our faith, namely, to save our souls. I will not forget in my unworthy prayers to think of them before God; and, if there is anything that may contribute to their bodily welfare, I will gladly do it. But may Jesus fill you, my dear Sir, more and more with comfort and strength of soul and body. May He bless ever more your (and your colleague's) dear work in time and eternity! God is faithful; what He promises He will do.

In conclusion it reads, "I commend you to Jehovah's protection, in Jesus's blood and wounds, which is the true fortress, and ask for your and your dearest congregation's intercession."

Wednesday, the 20th of June. The only reason why a shoemaker from Vernonburg near Savannah made the long trip to see me this morning was to ask me to lend him and his wife for some more time the late Arndt's *True Christianity*,[8] printed in large letters, i.e., the book for which their married daughter asked me for some time. I heard that her lifestyle was contrary to the Bible and this book: hence I preferred to lend it to somebody to whom it would be more useful. But, since the man had come such a long way for the book, I let his wife have the book with legible letters for a little more time, and I lent her daughter another one. We received some copies of Arndt's *Christianity* from both Halle and Hanover, and they will serve some eager people well.

Our boat returned from Savannah with the sad news that the youngest daughter of our friend, Mr. Habersham, was buried last Monday, the 18th of the month. Hence, within an eight-day period, he had two deaths in his house. That, of course, caused him and his weak wife much grief. May God give them new courage and comfort! Although he does not have enough words to express his grief, he informs me that God has given him and his truly pious wife the grace to behave like Christians and to completely accept God's will, which can only be good.

Thursday, the 21st of July. Bacher's widow fell seriously sick at the end of last week; however, she is feeling better now. During her illness, our gracious God blessed the Scriptures of His son, the Savior of poor lost sinners, in such a beautiful way that she could consider herself nothing else but just and blessed in Him and felt in herself the foretaste of eternal life and a great longing for a blessed death. She looks upon her illness as a great blessing.

She asked that I sing with her the beautiful and popular pil-
grims' song, *So bin ich nun nicht mehr ein fremder Gast,* etc., and I
was pleased to do so.

Friday, the 22nd of July. /Stephan/ Rottenberger's wife /Catha-
rina/ exerted herself excessively during the late Susanna's
lengthy illness and caught a cold last night. As a result she came
down with quite dangerous symptoms. While I was with her, she
could neither see nor hear; but I prayed with those present for
her and her husband, who so far has had nothing but grief.
Apart from housekeeping work, which was too heavy, the young
wife has had in the past all kinds of serious, although unnecessary problems of the mind which were more harmful to her
body than the work. Also, so far the weather has been extremely
unsettled: one moment it was hot, the next cool, then it was dry,
then wet. Unless people do not take good care of themselves under these conditions, they will soon catch a fever or another illness. In this country women have much trouble with menstrual
difficulties, and that is the reason why many have suffered very
sad symptons and why they brought about their early death.
This is actually a healthy country, but to stay healthy, one has to
eat a good diet and be careful in view of the often rapidly
changing weather.[9]

Saturday, the 23rd of July. Yesterday during my weekly sermon and evening prayer service I indicated that today we would
distribute the alms we received fourteen days ago in good condition, while we would sing, pray, and read some letters. Towards
this end, adults and children were invited to come to Jerusalem
Church at two o'clock. After young and old had assembled in the
church, as signaled, we sang the inspiring hymn, *Sey Lob und Ehr
dem höchsten Gut,* etc., from which dear R.R Mrs. W. in St.[10] recommended a number of verses for edification. I then read, with
a clear voice and the necessary application, both the beautiful
letter of our dear benefactress and what two others had lovingly
written to me and the congregation (from which I had copied an
excerpt in this diary some days ago); and finally I added an exceedingly inspiring hymn on the 107th Psalm, which a pious and
learned R.R. in the charitable St. had composed about
Ebenezer.[11] We then knelt down, thanked our merciful Father,

in the name of Jesus Christ, for all His past and current good deeds for the spirit and the flesh. We prayed for our known and unknown dear benefactors in Augsburg, Halle, Stuttgart, Hanover, and other towns inside and outside the German Empire. Also, we humbly told Him of our and the country's needs, and then said a devout Amen.

After this religious exercise had ended, the grownups went to my house and received their alms with thanks. On the other hand the children who had not yet celebrated Holy Communion were led or carried to my colleague's house to be edified by him from the words of Psalm 8:3 to God's praise and to pray with him. Then everybody was handed a fine gift. We had 136 adults and 87 children, and all were pleased with their nice presents. In addition to their gifts, the small children also received edifying small books for themselves and their parents. Only Jacob Mohr was excluded from receiving a gift pending his recovery. He is a stranger[12] and has not yet adapted to our ways, from which his soul and body could benefit. I told him that I would give him not only his present, but some more for good behavior as soon as he accepted an orderly profession and lived an orderly life in the best interest of his soul and body. He seemed to recognize that I meant well and therefore did not mind the procedure.

Our children will copy the previously mentioned, very inspiring song about the 107th Psalm many times over and it will be made so well known in the congregation that when, through God's grace, the gifts collected in Stuttgart arrive here in good condition, we can sing it together in praise of God and for our joint edification. Above all, with God's help it will be our main song for our annual memorial and thanksgiving festival. Also, it has a very cheerful and pleasing melody which we know very well from the first part of Freylinghausen's *Songbook*,[13] page 964, *Der lieben Sonnen Licht und Pracht,* etc. We are particularly impressed by the example of the highly respected Lady R.R. and a very dear distinguished benefactor in Hanover. They are not ashamed of the Ebenezer poor: not only have they given us many good things from their own belongings, but they have also commended us to others and gathered for us much blessing.

Since they are not ashamed of Christ's poor followers and actively prove their true belief through love, Christ, their leader, will not be ashamed of them either when they meet, but will say, "Inasmuch as ye have done it unto one of the least of these my brethren, ye have done it unto me."

A family of four was inadvertently forgotten during the distribution of gifts, but they will be included, God willing, in the future. In the meantime we did what we could. Another family, who think themselves superior to other people, have shown that they have a very low opinion of our public divine service and the meetings we had today in church, that is, they make themselves unworthy of this gift. For it says: *Absens carens.*[14] Small children at their mothers' breasts did not get any gifts this time. Similarly, my family and those of Mr. Lemke and Mr. Mayer, who participated in these gifts, were not included in the above-mentioned number; otherwise the number of our inhabitants would have been larger.

Sunday, the 24th of July. Today, in the late afternoon, we had much rain and thunder, and that is why we did not hold our public Sunday prayer hour in church. Last year God let us have, presumably from blessed Wernigerode,[15] a number of small elongated songbooks with new selected hymns that were distributed among people who live in town and attend our regular evening prayer hours. But every family could get only one. We now received several more of these beautiful hymnbooks from dear Hanover, and now every husband, and probably also some children, has a book so that we can make better use of the inspiring songs in our evening prayer sessions. Ordinarily we use for our edification on Sundays and workdays the beautiful Freylinghausen hymn book, especially the extract.

Tuesday, the 26th of July. By taking effective medicines and with God's blessing, Rottenberger's wife has gradually become so much better that she is now able to get out of bed. Here again, God has abundantly done beyond what we prayed for or understand. I pray that she will accept God's sparing and helping her for a true penitence.

Wednesday, the 27th of July. Some time ago I and the children in our plantation school contemplated the impressive song which court preacher Ziegenhagen composed about the three main Articles of the Christian dogma: "I believe in God, our Father, etc., means . . ." By so doing, I told them catechistically the truths of the entire Christian teachings in a simple and clear way and reinforced them on the basis of the added biblical verses. In our community we value repetition greatly, and that is why we assign only small homework in the church and in school and spend several weeks on one chapter, story, or song, etc. This time, they sent us among other beautiful tracts, a very small one, entitled: *The Doctrine of Atonement and Forgiveness of Sins, in Short Phrases.*[16] Since we received several copies of this wonderful booklet, which is written in clear language for simple people, I can give a copy to each child who knows how to read so that it can memorize one sentence per week, together with the added biblical verse, and teach it to their small brothers and sisters by reciting it to them. Otherwise we do not think much of learning books and long questions by heart (except for Luther's *Catechism*, biblical verses, powerful prayers, and songs): but it is easy to learn such a useful book.

Thursday, the 28th of July. This morning I received a letter, dated the 18th, from the scribe of Col. Heron, the commandant of Frederica. In it he informs me on behalf of the Colonel that:

1) according to information from Charleston, war with the Indians seems unavoidable. And, since he holds me and the well-being of our industrious people in high regard, he assures me that he will do everything possible to protect us from these savages. He says that, if I deem it necessary, he will send us an officer and soldiers (in addition to those we already have) for our protection because (as his letter states) he shares the feelings of all those who wish this colony well: it would be a pity if such industrious and useful people would be not be taken care of.

2) The commandant had been informed that a party of Spaniards was advancing to the St. Johns River (towards Frederica), and he marched there with part of his regiment to repel them.

3) He wants to know whether we received fine linen from Germany to be sold here.[17] He assures me that, if our people want to bring it or any other surplus goods to the Frederica market, they can easily sell it there and get good money for it.

Sunday, the 31st of July. I was asked in a recent letter from Europe to report in my diary on the kind of, and changes in, our weather and to comment on any peculiar aspect of our climate and congregation so that the readers can make up their own minds, as it were, *uno intuitu*[18] and compare our conditions with those in Germany. Since I feel obligated to thank our dear benefactors for their love by returning our love and services in every possible way, I will gladly comply with this request and add these points at the end of each month to the extent that my limited ability and insight permit me to do so and with the humble request to take my will for my deed and to excuse mistakes.

1) This second summer month, July, is usually one of the hottest. However, this year the weather has been as temperate and cool as it usually is in the fall. On the one hand, this is because of the morning, evening, and midnight winds and, on the other hand, of the nearly always overcast sky and frequent rainstorms, which are often accompanied by heavy thunder and lightning. However, the rain was so unevenly distributed that, while it was more than sufficient in town and enough for the grain and grass to grow in the surrounding plantations, the plantations farther out, from Zion Church to beyond the mills, from east towards south, had to do without. Nevertheless, they did have a long, thorough rainstorm on the 24th of July, i.e., five days before the full moon. Although it was cool during the day and at night and very pleasant for sleeping at night, our people on the plantations complained about the uncomfortable heat at night.

Often rainstorms cover half of the sky from morning till late afternoon, and from evening to early morning. The Indians, too, must have had a lot of rain in the northwest (where the Savannah river, like all big rivers in Georgia and in neighboring Carolina, originate and from where they flow into the ocean in a south-easterly direction) because this summer the Savannah river was higher than during the same time in previous years. At full moon (the 28th of July) and two days before it, we had dry weather and warm days. On the 28th of July, after sunset, the sky was covered with clouds, and at midnight we heard thundering towards the west. Gradually the thunderstorm and lightning moved toward us and stayed with us throughout the night. It did not rain and the moon was shining. The following evening we heard another thunderstorm farther north, but it did not come to us. The wind seems to blow in an easterly direction and the weather seems to stay dry; and that is very good for haymaking. I have not mentioned the frequency with which the winds changed this month and other interesting aspects of our weather; however, I will do so in the near future if, God willing, I have the opportunity. For that purpose, I am planning to install a painted iron weathercock on my roof overlooking all our tall mulberry trees. I wish I had a real thermometer; we have nothing like that here.

2) The swallows, which tend to arrive at our homes in early March, left early this month. Many nest under the roof and around the firewall of my home, and the people in our community have set up tall poles by their houses. To the top or tip of these poles they fasten a type of wild gourd whose skin gets very hard and which they use like pots to scoop water.[19] In these pumpkins, the swallows build their nests and raise their young. They protect our young chickens, geese, and ducks from the many hawks.[20] As soon as a hawk comes near, the swallows dive toward them and pursues them as far as possible. Late this month some swallows returned to settle again in our house; we have no idea where they have been meanwhile and where they will go.

3) A common complaint of our people is about the big and small woodpeckers, also known here as tree choppers because they use their sharp beeks for pecking worms from dead trees. Just about this time of the year our people are also very unhappy about the black starlings that frequently descend on our ripening Indian corn, forcing the shucks open, which firmly protect the big beautiful ears, permitting the rain to accumulate on them. The corn then begins to rot and is invaded by worms. Ravens and crows inflict the same damage. And so do bears and squirrels, of which we have many in both black and gray (the former in pine forests and the latter in oak forests): bears at night, squirrels during the day.[21] However, deer feed on Indian bean leaves and pods; and on some plantations there is nothing people can do to get rid of them regardless of whether they try to

frighten them off or to disperse them by planting strawmen and other types of scarecrows (*terriculamentis*). Others use drums, and they are more successful than the others.

4) This is about the time of the year when the Spaniards and Indians like to attack and wage war against white people (when the Indian corn matures), and that is what is happening again now. This is why we are usually worried about such things around this time of the year. Whenever we hear of an Indian war at any other time, we do not believe it. Invariably the Indians stick to this time: although I do not know why, it is easy to guess.

We have here (as in other English colonies in North America) large forests with all kinds of big, tall, and dense trees, such as two types of pines, Scots pines, many kinds of oaks, several types of walnut trees, beech trees (which, however, bear no fruit), cypresses, poplars, laurels, some kind of small chestnut trees, and wild cherries. The latter two do not grow into big trees and measure no more than six inches in diameter. We also have wild grapevines, an arm or a thigh thick, which climb their way up the highest trees. Many cedars grow along the coast and also in some places northwest of us along the Savannah river. With enough help, we could manufacture pitch, tar, turpentine, and potash, although the potash would be only for our own consumption, and we would not be able to send any of it to Europe; to do so would interfere with European trade of this commodity with Russia. The saying is, "The daughters," i.e., the American colonies, "must do nothing to harm their mother," i.e., the trade of Old England. The same applies to the manufacture of glass: it must not be sent to England, but must be consumed in America. We have here in abundance of clay (white and red); if only somebody would only start making pots, earthenware, and bricks. We have plenty of wood and water here. It is a shame that so much wood is cut on the plantations and then left rotting. We collect here the ashes of hard wood for making soap, and many people produce their own soap.[22]

6) An old Indian woman whom we have known for over fourteen years heard that my wife suffers from frequent fevers; and, because she likes her, she picked a black, soothing, strong-smelling root in the woods and brought it to her, instructing her to eat

a small piece of it whenever she had fever and saying that this would make her sweat or sleep. We could not quite understand what she said. Thank God, we do not need such unknown things since we get very nice well-prepared medicines from England and Halle. Nevertheless, I wish the Indian woman had stayed over at our house until the next morning. She should have shown me the root with its leaves in the woods as well as some other roots and herbs that the Indians use for medicines. Some people make a great ado about their knowledge of herbs and roots, and that may be justified. There is no doubt that we have here in the woods a large number of plants which our wise and gracious Creator has given us to keep us humans healthy in this climate. I would very much like to collect something for our benefit and that of our friends, provided God gives us the time and strength to do so.

7) This month several crops our community likes, among them sugar melons and water melons, will be ripe for harvesting. Water melons are healthier than sugar melons; both often attain the astonishing weight of 12-18 pounds and taste very good. The water melons derive their name from their refreshing cooling water and their very many seeds, and they multiply almost by the millions since they also grow very well and abundantly in poor soil. At this time of the year, we usually also have many grapes and blueberries in the woods. However, the late frost has destroyed these and many other blossoms, and the few that did grow were eaten by the birds, which seem to lack sufficient other food this year. Our peaches will also ripen this month, although there will be very few this year for the stated reason. In general, peach trees, which bear fruit both early and late, produce them abundantly when they are hardly three or four years old. The old trees grow almost as big as a man; however, they only live for about 12 years; they get worms which destroy them. Our domestic vines are not doing too well, undoubtedly because we lack experience. That this is a vineland is indicated by the very many wild vines which produce an abundance of grapes. We also have ripe apples already. We do not have any pears and German plums here.

8) Because the Indians are planning to start war now, the common people want all of them destroyed so that they can live in peace; however, this is probably a sinful and not at all decent wish. Not to mention the fact that the Indians were the first and legitimate inhabitants and hence are the rightful owners of this land.[23] Therefore, the great benefits which the inhabitants of this and our neighboring colony, Carolina, derive from trading and from the fact that they serve us as a protection against the French Indians should be sufficient reason for the English to do everything possible, following General Oglethorpe's example, to satisfy and keep them. The reason is that, since their tribes live toward the west and north, between us and the French Indians, they help protect us and prevent them from coming closer to us and turn over their land to the French. However, the foremost benefit is our trade with them: because Georgia and Carolina alone (primarily the latter) sell them English goods worth several thousand of pounds a year, and, in return, many tons of deer and beaver skins are delivered to England, and that is of rather significant benefit to both trade and shipping. I wonder why no antlers are collected and shipped to Europe since there is such a great demand for them there for the manufacture of knives, pharmaceuticals, etc. If the English traders treated the Indians better, the Indians would behave better. In recognition of that, the Lord Trustees have drafted very good laws, but it would be highly desirable for them to be observed in a better way.

AUGUST

Monday, the 1st of August. The pious orphaned girl, whom a benefactress in Hanover had remembered with a particularly generous gift, was sick when I, while distributing the presents, read to the audience this unknown dear benefactress's very edifying letter, which I have already mentioned in my diary on the 19th of July. Since then she visited here twice to have me read the letter to her, as I did again today. The letter not only says at the beginning: "Here is Immanuel," but also at its end it says: "So at all times it is written 'here is Immanuel'," which I explained to the girl. I also sent to her pious mistress, the widow Zant, these comforting words, which apply to our dangerous time: "Make a decision, and nothing will come of it, because here is Immanuel"; and therefore she and her children must not be afraid on their lonely plantation. Since the letter had admonished the orphan girl to love our Lord Jesus Christ with all her heart, I gave her the following well-known beautiful words to take home, "Love Jesus, and Him alone, otherwise you will not be saved."[1] Her pious mistress is sending this verse to thank the dear benefactress: "The works of the Lord are great, sought out of all them that have pleasure therein." But the orphan has asked me to tell her dear benefactors that she will include them in her prayers, and she has sent them the verse 1 John 5:3.

Tuesday, the 2nd of August. Last night, after finishing the important material about open and subtle idolatry, in accordance with the instructions in the Biblical story in 2 Chronicles 7:19-22, I began telling my dear audience something from our Fathers' and benefactors' beautiful letters which we received on the 9th day of last month; and I will do so again today. I could talk about the great blessing our merciful God has given us through them for His glory, our edification, and the enhancement of the good, as well as for our heartfelt intercession for them, if only I did not have to be brief in this diary.

The two short letters from our great and dearest Field Marshall Count von Seckendorf and our esteemed Senior Urlsperger were the first through which our gracious God gave us His great blessing and me new courage and religious joy. Almost all lines in their letters indicate that our dear benefactors are willing to assist us with advice and deeds in our continuing difficult tribulations, if God gives them the means to do so. I keep telling my listeners to look only to God in their misery and not to believe that the Lord Trustees and other well-to-do benefactors are able to help, provided they have the desire do so. As long as God says: "My hour has not yet come," they cannot help, even if they get together by the thousands. It is also an error for the common people to assume that, if the wealthy and generous benefactors wished to help us, they could aid all the poor. They forget that wealthy people have large expenses. As one of the dear letters says at the end: Our comfort should be: God is alive!

Also of great comfort to my heart was what dear Senior Urlsperger wrote about his old servant, who had worked for him for 25 years, namely, that in a few years she would probably join the pious Salzburgers who have gone to eternal rest. I have recommended to my audience that, as requested and deserved, they intercede in their prayers for his only son,[2] who moved last fall to the University of Tübingen; and I have no doubt that anybody with only the slightest bit of good in him would neglect doing so. May God enable us to make this and other deserved intercessions through His spirit!

Wednesday, the 3rd of August. For quite a number of years our congregation has held our noble benefector, Field Marshall Count von Seckendorf, in great esteem. Since our dear God has given us a beautiful blessing with his edifying, though short, letter, I told them that I could show them an engraving of this German Gideon and great benefactor of Ebenezer if they would like to see his image here on earth, until we meet face-to-face before God in Heaven. A significant number of them came today to have me or, in my absence, my wife show them the picture. They came before and after lunch and hence did not lose any time from work.

Our townspeople and some men from the plantations are busy cutting down the vast expanse of dense and tall underbrush surrounding the town so that harmful animals and pests as well as Indians and other bad people cannot hide there to harm us. They are not working for nothing: rather, everybody is paid one pound of gunpowder for a day's work. Recently, somebody gave me a small barrel, which I will use, like everything else, to the best of our community.

Thursday, the 4th of August. A pious simple Salzburger[3] is feeling very uncomfortable and is experiencing physical discomfort because he turned down another man's request to be his child's godfather. The man handled the matter in a way that is common in many places for people in Christian congregations, that is, they do not choose and ask the godparents until after the child is born and about to be baptized. Our Salzburgers ask the godparents of an unborn child quite some time before its birth to pray for the mother and the child and to prepare themselves

for the religious ceremony in a Christian way. In the eyes of this
pious Salzburger, a holy baptism and selecting godparents are a
very important matter of which he considers himself unworthy,
especially if it happens in such a hurry and he does not know
how to read. I helped him to get rid of his fears and soothed his
despair. Our people follow the laudable custom of baptizing
their children as soon as possible after their birth. Which Christian would want to miss a single day, knowing from the Bible that
this bath of rebirth will save his child? Becoming a child of our
Heavenly Father, a bride of Jesus Christ, a temple of the Holy
Ghost, and an ally of our triune God is indeed an important matter. It surely is an unwarranted comfort some Christians cling to
in their carelessness, namely, that Christian children who die before baptism cannot be damned. Although the lack of baptism in
itself is no reason for condemnation, negligence on the part of
the parents is.

Friday, the 5th of August. Once again our dear God has been
very good to us by providing us with the time, strength, and
means to stop up a small river above the milldam by sinking
heavy posts, clay, and boards into the ground. As a result, not
only do we get more water on the lower run in times of a severe
drought, but the solid structure keeps the actual river from rus-
hing through this particular spot and permits it to follow its
usual course. This new structure is, of course, very costly; but
our future mill earnings will make up for the expenditures.
Some Frenchmen[4] from Purysburg think so highly of our mills,
especially the grinding mills, that they have offered to help us
block off the small river that carries a very large volume of water
so that they may benefit from the mill during most of the year.
However, we do not accept work from outsiders, since our gracious Lord has given us so much, both through the mills and
from Europe, that we are able to pay cash for these and other
expenditures.

It gives us great joy to see that people from the outside (this
week somebody from Port Royal in Carolina) are coming to our
mill and then need not wait for their grains to be ground. They
say that the people of Ebenezer do not know what they have in
their mill. I hope our Almighty God will gradually give us the

means to equip the mills in such a way that we can operate them throughout the year; it is quite possible that we can accomplish this by digging a long canal from the Savannah river to the mill river. The money they then could earn for the community, especially if we could operate the sawmill for the major part of the year! We trust in our Lord: He will help us.

Many people from Carolina are telling us that they expect a bad harvest in many places and that the price of grain will again be high this year because of the lack of rain. Our crops, including Indian corn, are growing better than in most of the past years. May we all recognize God's great loving kindness, and may it lead us to penitence. I fear that many of us continue to be like those elsewhere, including those in our German Fatherland, about whom the dear field marshal wrote,

> Many in our country pay no attention to God's love, and hence sinning is on the increase and it becomes much more difficult to administer punishment. The number of those who fill the breach is very small; may God save them for us.

I have strongly emphasized this remarkable quotation vis-a-vis my dear audience. We have every reason to do so since we have had such abundant proof of God's caring and comforting love during this long, dangerous, and difficult war.

Everything our great God does is wondrous, in particular His great kindness, patience, and forbearance (Romans 11:4), and He does uncountable good to even His worst enemies (Luke 6:35). Even the oft-repeated warnings in His words are a sign of His great kindness. The fact that He so often repeats His warnings to the hypocrits and godless not only shows how deeply corrupted the human heart is but it is also a sign of the never-ending grace and mercy with which He puts His just warnings into effect, so-to-speak *lento gradu ad vindictam* (Jeremiah 18:7,8).[5] However, the longer the clouds and storms gather, the more violently they will hit us afterwards. Spiritually and physically, God has demonstrated His great love in numerous ways here and far away, but he has also warned *verbaliter* and *realiter*[6] (through the example of the punished sinners in Scripture and in our times).

But some among us are like Jeremiah's listeners: they do not believe it and ignore it. However, thank God, there are also some like the men of Nineveh (Matthew 12:41): they did penance after Jonah's sermon.

Saturday, the 6th of August. We received the upsetting news from Savannah that, according to a rumor in Savannah, all women and children from Frederica had fled to Darien, a community on the mainland settled by the Scots, because they were afraid of the Spaniards. However, nobody will give any credence to this rumor until we have confirmation. News from the Indian nation tells us that nobody up there knows anything about a war with the Indians, but that, on the contray, the white people there are leading quite peaceful lives. Still, some Indians roaming the country have caused trouble by forcing their way into the plantation of one of the inhabitants. While ignoring all protestations, they removed several times over not only what two men could carry away, but what two horses could cart away. This made me ask the officer of our soldiers to post a guard in that area of our plantations because I know that the Indians are afraid of the soldiers' red coats.

Since I have again started keeping a diary for the Lord Trustees, I now have the opportunity to inform them of regrettable misfortunes and incidents like these and of what we have done about them, although they have not yet made any amends to our poor people for the damage the Indians inflicted upon them in past years, except for the medicines distributed to the entire congregation and, before that, a couple of millstones, oil, and paint for both churches, etc. Our Heavenly Father keeps imposing many different hardships and much physical suffering on our inhabitants, but we have to admit to His glory that He has never tried us beyond our endurance, but that He has shown us an early way out of all temptations, when we sometimes did not know what to do, so that we have been able to endure them well.

2. God's wisdom has always seen to it that, in times of great suffering and temptation, our hearts were filled with God's strong comfort either from His living word or the letters from our pious Fathers and friends. This is happening again at our regular meetings through their dear letters, which put our lack

of belief to shame and evoke and strengthen our true belief. I would like to add some comforting words from a letter from two God-fearing benefactors and friends that was read yesterday and will be read again today so that we will remember them in the future:

> The outflow of charities from that region to the East and West Indies may have to cease in most instances, something I regret wholeheartedly: However, God can see to it that new sources will open up in other places which result in even richer flows to those nearby and far away. Undoubtedly our Heavenly Father will see to it that His children, whose needs He knows well, do not want for anything but that they will continue to have an abundance of all good things in the future.
>
> May you, together with your beloved congregation, who believe in God's mercy, strongly believe in this. God be praised for everything He does for His people of Ebenezer. May He bless these dear people, and may He hold His hand over them, to give them His lasting grace and Fatherly protection! May He continue to bestow on them even more good. Yet the sum of His small deeds will add up to more than what the whole world can do without Him. And even if you do not see any sign in the future, believe Him.
>
> It was our Savior himself who expressly forbade his disciples to worry or to wonder where this or that would come from, even if they failed to see before their eyes any ways and means of how they could help themselves, but that they, like the fowls of the air and the lilies of the field, should trust in their Father to graciously take care of them. Rather, since we see, through His blessings, something before our eyes and in our hands, we must not disgrace our Heavenly Father by not believing that, in His time, He will show us ways and means to ensure that what we need from time to time is available. He surely will see to that. Whatever decision our Lord, in His grace, has made for the people of Ebenezer, He will surely carry it out. Although we may face many kinds of difficult trials, and although our eyes may be much too dark to see through them, the end will be glorious. Now, oh Lord, we trust in Thy name; help us, and we will be helped. Amen!

Monday, the 8th of August. This morning, before daybreak, I traveled to Savannah to ask the president and members of the Council for a verbal response to several important issues because

I have been unable to get it in writing. On the way there, we had several very strong rainshowers which, however, had no ill effect on my health or that of my co-travelers. At dinner time, the German population came together to listen to God's word, which this time was about the first part of Chapter 10 of the First Epistle to the Corinthians, and for which our dear Lord had given me much joy and strength. My honest prayer is often this: "When I speak as a minister, give my words the strength and effect without letting me feel any misgivings." Ever since the Lord Trustees transferred Mr. Zuberbüller to Savannah to serve the English and Germans as their minister, I have not insisted on preaching God's word during my stays in Savannah; yet I have done so whenever people asked me to preach, and that occurred very frequently.[7]

I received the good news that the Spaniards at the St. Wans or St. Johns River (the border between St. Augustine and the territory of this colony) retreated when the Col. and Capt. Heron advanced with his troops from Frederica.[8] Therefore we are not worried about a large-scale Spanish attack on this colony. Rumors that all Frederica women and children fled to Darien to be safe proved to be unfounded. A vessel loaded with Spaniards had very daringly arrived at the Savannah river, and they pirated and took to St. Augustine a fully laden ship from Carolina that had attempted to sail in secret to either Frederica or, under a pretext, to St. Augustine. Peace with the Indians was restored when they fought an internal struggle among themselves.[9] Thus it seems that our good Lord did not seek to ravage us with the rod of war or the sword; He seems to have other ways of punishing sinners, since wickedness is gaining the upper hand everywhere.

Wednesday, the 10th of August. On my way back I heard in Purysburg that Gebhart's eldest son (whose father died two years ago near Palachocolas, and the mother and youngest brother some time ago in our community) died there and was buried today.[10] For some time he lived here with his two married sisters and diligently attended our preparations for the Holy Sacrament, and he had grown in knowledge. Because he was physically sick (for which he himself, like many children, was

probably responsible),[11] his eldest sister had taken him to Purysburg to cure him through the baths there; however, eventually
he died. I remember the father of these children with sadness.
He and his wife did not recognize that it was God's will and a
great blessing that, as a result of General Oglethorpe's assistance, three of his children—all female—had come to our
community to work, be educated, supervised, and raised. He
hated me and my late colleague for no reason at all and often
cursed in such as terrible way that we were afraid he was cursing
himself and everything he had.

Thursday, the 11th of August. On Monday, the wife of our cat-
tlepen worker went to gather some wood in the forest not far
from her home, and on the way there she got so lost that they
could not find until the following day in the late afternoon.
Many men from our community went searching for her, but she
did not hear their shooting nor their calls because she was so
scared and tired that she was no longer in control of her senses.
Without God's blessing for this search, she would have perished.
Perhaps our wondrous God is using this disciplinary measure to
truly convert her: while she always had good intentions, she
never actually got down to doing something about them. Her
hands and feet are in bad shape because, when she was lost, she
had to make her way through much thorny undergrowth. During their mother's two-day absence, her four small children got
hardly any food and care.

Saturday, the 13th of August. It has been announced not only
in this, but also our neighboring colony, that a number of beautiful books have arrived from Germany; and many people we
know and we do not know are holding out their hands for them.
They are particularly interested in bibles, hymn books, Arndt's
Books of True Christianity,[12] and sermon books. But, because we
know from experience that some people treat these uplifting
books not the way these gifts would require it, we will be more
circumspect and distribute these great books only to people we
know, hoping that they will put them to good use.

Sunday, the 14th of August. On this 10th Sunday after Trinity, seventy people in our community took the Holy Sacrament, including four Germans of the Lutheran confession from the Purysburg area. Many illnesses and fevers are making the rounds in our congregation, but our merciful God has spared us two leaders of the congregation and given us steady health and full mental strength. May He make us deeply grateful for this grace and let us use all our strength to serve only Him! Each year we read on this Sunday the story of the destruction of the city of Jerusalem and the Jewish country; and I wish we had as many books about this story as we have households in our congregation so that every family could have one for use at home and in church.

Monday, the 15th of August. Bartholomäus Rieser, the old widower, became sick on Friday; and yesterday evening I was informed of his death. Because his illness and death were so sudden, I could not to talk with him at the end, but I heard from his eldest son that he had prepared himself well for a blessed death in the Christian faith and that he did not doubt that he would join at the place of eternal joy his pious wife who passed away in the Lord some years ago. He never could forget his former wife and and was unable to think of her without tears. For quite some time he lived with his son on Thomas Bacher's plantation. And, because he had seen that the old Bacher's serious and sudden illness would have made it impossible for him to prepare himself for a blessed death unless he had started early, this made a great impression on him and awakened him to the seriousness of Christianity. He loved God's word greatly and read and listened to it diligently. The late Schaitberger's *Sendbriefe* were, with God's blessing, of very great spiritual benefit to him.[13] When I heard of his illness on Saturday before Confession, I had the pithy saying read for him, "For God so loved the world," etc. etc. His eldest son told me that he believed in it and benefitted from it. This afternoon he was buried in town, and our good Lord gave us much comfort with beautiful songs and the funeral sermon.

Wednesday, the 17th of August. I noticed that old Rieser's unexpected death had a healing effect on our sawmiller Kogler. At the funeral we used the beautiful and inspiring example of shoemaker Gerlach from Naumburg as well as the first part of his own thoughts on his funeral text from Psalm 16:5-7. God willing, I am planning to continue with it at the next funeral. This rather uplifting treatise, together with a short excerpt from Chief Pastor Schamelto's funeral sermon in Leipzig, appended at the end, was printed by Mr. Walter; and it was one of the books we received from Hanover. In his sermon, the Chief Pastor said of the pious shoemaker, "In him we had a man who can serve others as example of an active Christian and good citizen: somebody who combined knowledge with practice, the listening to sermons with actions, and his inner with his outward heartfelt prayer: somebody who had supreme trust in God, raised his children well, and had an edifying intercourse with God's servants," etc.

Friday, the 19th of August. The Lord be praised for permitting us to harvest our Indian corn and squash once again in peace! They turned out so well in our community that we could not have wished them to be any better; and the mill is close-by so that our inhabitants can make good use of their crop at an early date and utilize it in any way they like. Because of the harmful starlings, woodpeckers, and crows, some of the Indian corn dropped too early; and, as a result, the grains of many ears are mealy and not very ripe. The many squirrels force some people who have very fertile land to cut the corn they grow near oak forests before it has dried at the stems.

On some plantations, deer inflict very great damage on squash and beans (and probably potatoes as well),[14] and some people harvest no beans at all and only a few squash. For that reason, some of the people do not plant any because they know from experience that they cannot protect anything from the deer (which come at night). Since they work very hard during the day, they do not have the strength to guard the fields at night as well. If they had farmhands and if the farmers did not have to do all the work themselves, a lot could be saved despite these destructive animals. With fall approaching, we hope the many snakes in our and other areas are going to disappear gradually. I have often heard that both old and young people were dangerously close to being bitten by them but that God protected them in His miraculous and self-evident way. Although people do not usually spare snakes they happen to see and since many are therefore killed each summer, some continue to live near homes, in stables and gardens, and many in the fields and woods.

It is typical for this country, in Georgia as well as in Carolina, that whenever a garden or field has not been cultivated for a year, tall shrubs and bushes such as fennel grow into dense thickets in which humans can easily hide. On land that has not been cultivated for several years (we have such areas around town because their owners have moved to their plantations) a large number of bushes have started to grow in addition to the afore-mentioned tall and thick weeds, and over time they have developed into young oak, walnut, and chestnut trees as well as into useless shrubs that make good breeding grounds for pests. We are short of people and therefore unable to cultivate this beautiful, well-located land. The grass in the woods is tall, and all kinds of bushes grow there. Nevertheless, people often have to go there because they lack the farmhands and means to guard their cattle and, without God's protection, they are easily bitten by snakes. It really is true here: *Latet anguis in herba*.[15]

Saturday, the 20th of August. B. Bacher seems to be a *Candidatus aeternitatis*.[16] He became ill soon after his wife's blessed and edifying death. He later married the late Peter Reuter's hard-working and pious widow, with whom he also had a very Christian and good marriage. Some time ago he became, through God's grace, a completely different man; and his first wife's good example and her memorable words and prayers keep touching his heart every day and in a blessed way. Last night, in particular, he all of a sudden fell again so weak that he seemed to be near death. In his fever and phantasies he talked about the beautiful town described in Revelations 21. He accepts all suffering from God's hand, humbles himself under it, and is patient with all his heart. He has very little pain, but his limbs are so weak that he can hardly talk.

Monday, the 22nd of August. When the dog days and the summer come to an end, a number of people in our community suffer from cold fever; but now it does not seem as bad as during the first years. From the beginning, fever has been the most

wide-spread illness among us, and it may be the cause of other
dangerous afflictions from which many physically sick men and
women suffer.[17] It is almost impossible for them to work in the
summer heat, and if they cool down too fast after they have been
too much exposed to the heat, or if they drink a lot of cold spring
water, they ruin their health completely. May God help us and
may He apply the suggestions we have received, which benefit
us, according to His wisdom and grace! With Him, nothing is
impossible. It is particularly harmful to the health of our
women, whether married or unmarried, to work alongside their
husbands or relatives in the fields. It would be better if their men
would plant so much flax that the women could spin it in the
shade or weave some household linen or material out of cotton.
However, most of them do not have spinning wheels, and in this
country none are available for less than 15 shillings Sterling; also
they do not have the money for it. This long-lasting war makes
everything expensive and difficult.

Wednesday, the 24th of August. The day after tomorrow, my
dear colleague Lemke will travel to Savannah to preach the word
of our living God to the Germans there and to administer the
Holy Sacrament to our Lutheran brethren. Through him, I am
writing a friendly, but serious, letter to the Council president informing him of the concern he is causing me because the masters and mistresses do not permit their German servants, especially young people of both sexes who are so much in need of
instruction, to attend our public church services, particularly
since God, our Lord, has not only given holidays to the masters
and mistresses, but also to their servants to strengthen their
souls and rest their bodies.

The president and the most prominent councilman have two
adult German girls on their plantations, who are both fatherless
and motherless orphans and have been especially recommended to me by their kinsmen. Although I had asked some
time ago that the girls be permitted to come to church so that I
can talk with them to enhance their spiritual and physical welfare, nothing came off it. My letter may not be pleasant, although I wrote it in very humble terms. I cannot keep God's
truth from anybody. I am just amazed at people who claim that

they bring in Negroes in order to turn them into Christians but do not allow their Christian servants to observe the means of grace and the Sunday once every two months. May God not allow me to fall into the temptation of wanting Negroes or of making the slighest contribution to bringing them here!

Thursday, the 25th of August. A certain incident in the story from 1 Kings 9, which we are currently reading in our weekly sermons and evening prayers, has made me warn my listeners seriously against the bad habit of many Christians, namely, of preferring to read the writings of human beings instead of the book of all books, the Holy Scriptures, and of enjoying the former more than the latter. It is appropriate to read other spiritual writings our dear God has given us as a great blessing, but under no circumstances must they be preferred over the Holy Scripture, since the latter is read and used primarily as a way to salvation: otherwise, reading other (in other respects very useful) books is of little benefit. This is because our Holy God cannot condone bad habits, and even the subtle contempt for His dear word. Since some of them had a guilty conscience, they were unhappy with my 1 new admonition and also sinned by using bad words.

In order to put them to shame and to reprimand those who are secretly talking against me, I expressed myself even more explicitly during the subsequent meeting when I not only referred them to the short instruction (at the beginning of our small Bibles) with the recommendation that they read the Holy Scripture for their true inspiration, but also read to them the following words by Luther, God's blessed man, about John 4:39-42,

> Oh, if only God would make disappear all my interpretations and those of all ministers, and if only every Christian would read the Holy Scripture for himself and nothing but God's word! Those, who could do so without explanations and interpretations would not need my interpretations or those of other people and they would even view them as obstacles. Therefore, dear Christians, get with it, get with it! And let my interpretations and those of other ministers merely be a scaffolding for the right building, so that we

ourselves comprehend, taste, and stay with God's blessed
true word, because only in them does God live in Zion.

To strengthen my own belief in the truth, I also read to my
audience something on the same subject from the late Dr.
Spener's beautiful letter to a blind pious linen-weaver in
Fraustadt, which is in the third part of his theological contempla-
tions on page 829.[18] It also contains concise and thorough instructions to him to read the Holy Scripture for his own benefit.
In addition, I referred them to Prof. Dr. Francke's very percep-
tive and instructive introduction to his folio German Bible
printed in a special edition under this title and which is to stimulate and provide instruction on how to read the Holy Scripture,
etc., daily, thoroughly, and consistently. This small book is in the
hands of some of our audience and we are also lending it out to
them. May God bless these testimonies of the truth as He has
done with me in His great grace; so that they prefer God's dear
word to all, even the best, writings by men and make good use of
it, as instructed, as a blessed means to salvation for their salvation!

> After writing this, another word by Luther happens to come to
> mind, By reading in, and listening diligently to, the Bible, one will
> realize that nowhere else can one find comfort in patience. That is,
> whenever one needs it for one's conscience and in times of death.
> There is no other book in Heaven and on earth that teaches and
> tells us how God's son has triumphed for us over sin, death, and the
> Devil. And even golden books, golden wisdom, and golden minis-
> ters are nothing compared to the comfort this book provides, with-
> out which there cannot even be any patience.

Saturday, the 27th of August. A planter and merchant in the
Purysburg area has written and informed me that several plan-
ters in his region would like to bring their European and local
grains to our mill. However, they believe that the way via Purysburg is too far, and they have decided to build a bridge across
an unpassable spot to the Savannah River, about six English
miles or 1½ hours from us, and they have asked for our carpenter Kogler and some men from our community to help them. As
much as I would like to improve communication between us and

Purysburg and the areas there, it is beyond my ability. We have few good workers in Ebenezer; and, since they are without help, they are so busy on their plantations and houses, particularly at haymaking and harvesting time, that one cannot get anybody to do the necessary work.

The orphanage is in urgent need of repair, the Jerusalem Church should be repaired and painted; and, above and below the mill, the millrace must be cleared of fallen trees; yet we have to postpone it time and again. We are very glad that a certain, very urgent construction to improve and reinforce our mills, which I wanted to do for several years, was finally completed last week. Although it cost much money, namely, 27 pounds 11 shillings 6 d Sterling (in addition to the days of free work contributed by our inhabitants), we do not regret these expenditures because the construction is very important, necessary, and useful and has turned out well with God's help.

Monday, the 29th of August. Yesterday, on the 12th Sunday after Trinity, it rained all day and I was surprised at the large number of people who came from the plantations to attend the sermon. I am afraid my dear colleague in Savannah had only a small audience. On Saturday, it also rained a lot, as it did today, so that he probably will not be able to leave Savannah. It seems to be the usual steady rain. At night, we had several heavy rainstorms which, however, were not accompanied by thunder. About this time of the year, thunderstorms tend to become less and less frequent. Over the last couple of months, we had much (although not too much) rain in and near our town; on the plantations, above and below the mill, we had less; and we had least in the area of our cowpen (three hours from here toward the south-southwest), so that our cattle suffered a great deal for lack of water. However, for the first time, we had so much rain last Friday and Saturday that we have water again in the watering places or lower areas. Yesterday and today, they must have had much rain there.

Tuesday, the 30th of August. My dear colleague returned this morning, happy and healthy. Because of the rain he had few listeners and communicants from the plantations near Savannah. Among other things, he brought the good news that, for all practical purposes, the Great Allies and France have made peace.[19] The news was published in the Charleston newspapers and presumably had been brought here by some merchant vessels which, together with a war ship, had entered Charleston. We had promised our merciful God for a long time that we in our congregation would praise Him with a thanksgiving service for this peace for which we have asked and prayed, and we are going to do so, with His help, with willing and joyful hearts as soon as we get the confirmation that peace has been concluded.

The pious widow Bacher has sent me a message informing me of her illness and asking me to come and talk with her. I visited her this morning before school and the morning sermon. She is poor in spirit but rich in God and His grace. The hymn *Hallelujah immer weiter,* etc., has been blessed on her.

Wednesday, the 31st of August. Our blacksmith Leitner has a very well-situated plantation on the Savannah River, with one of the best landings in our entire region. However, he has a great deal of trouble with, and suffers great damage from, the Negroes and other boat-people who, because of their trade with the Indians, travel up and down the river. They not only beg him for all sorts of things, but they also steal in his fields at night and play all sorts of pranks on him; and he has complained to me about that. They have also burnt many hundred, or rather several thousand, barrel staves, partly wilfully and partly by being careless; and the spreading fire would have enveloped homes and fences, if the owner and his neighbor—contrary to habit—had not stayed home from the morning sermon that Sunday and extinguished the fire. Yesterday, I wrote to the master of the Negroes who caused a lot of damage last week; and I will also talk to the President about it in order to prevent further damage. It would require much complicated effort for us to receive restitution for the damage we have suffered. We have not yet been compensated for what the Indians stole or shot. God is holding His hand over us; otherwise we would have more damage and discomfort.

SEPTEMBER

Thursday, the 1st of September. During these past late-summer months, even throughout the summer, our merciful God has been indescribably good to our souls and bodies, to our adults and children, ministers and listeners from near and far. Hence we felt obligated to praise and thank His holy name in songs and prayers during yesterday evening's prayer hour; and I heard afterwards that this Christian exercise had been blessed. Before our prayer, I mentioned some good deeds, including the invaluable period of grace and the great goodness, patience, and forbearance God has shown us during that period; the continued tranquility in times of war; the means of salvation, and the desired opportunities for edification; good weather, and a rich crop, the mills and their strengthening and improvement; and now the good news which reached us again yesterday that there is peace with France. Although the long and costly war has made commercial goods expensive and this time to be a difficult one, the troubles in our community have not really been so bad as we have heard from the experiences and tales of people who came to the mill from other places.

Our wise and merciful God has protected, fed, and provided for us so wonderfully throughout this difficult period, although we were undeserving and unworthy of it: why should we not trust Him to do likewise after He gave us peace? May He give us faith and strengthen it! In the prayer hour in my house today God strengthened me with His wonderful promise in Joel 3:26. The Lord will live in Zion, which is also promised in Psalm 132, and there it also says: "I will abundantly bless their provision and satisfy her poor with bread." Neither will they lack the clothing they need, which is part of our daily bread and specifically mentioned in Deuteronomy 10:18 and Matthew 6:31-33. Previous pious intercessions for us by God's servants and children have always been a great blessing to us: may the Lord reward them for this good deed and permit us to keep enjoying it!

Friday, the 2nd of September. Our two best carpenters[1] traveled with me and two other experienced men to the Uchee land

beyond the Ebenezer River in order to look over the quality of
the land there and a small river that might be suitable for the
construction of a mill; especially since we hope to receive the entire district after peace has been concluded (as is likely to be
done with Spain in due time), so that our brethren who come
after us will eventually settle there and, with God's word, make a
living in its solitude. The location of the land is very good, high,
and hence healthy, and it is superior to ours in every respect,
except that it is farther up the Savannah River and its owners
cannot get to Ebenezer except by boat. Before reaching the good
land, about four or five miles English miles up the Ebenezer
Creek, there is a very large cypress swamp or low area which gets
flooded in times of high water. For that reason it is impossible to
build a bridge there. Whatever cattle or other things one would
want to take on land from there to our community would have to
be taken via Old Ebenezer, and a sturdy bridge would have to be
constructed across the river. This is how far the plantations
would probably extend over time. However, water traffic is the
most convenient and effective way of transportation here since
boats can carry large cargoes.

It seems to me that I have never seen such a fertile, level, airy,
and pleasant region, with plenty of water, as this one. There is
also some kind of stone here that lends itself to building and lim-
ing. We particularly investigated whether it is really true what
local people and strangers have repeatedly told us, namely, that
they have here a beautiful, although small river, with plenty of
water, where a profitable grist mill could be built for the benefit
of new settlers. This no doubt is the case and it would cost little
to construct such a useful installation, which would be a great
blessing to our new population.

Sunday, the 4th of September. Sometimes, in His eagerness to
save humans, our wonderful God wills for strangers from other
places to come to us for business reasons, as it happened yesterday. And since we in our community talk every day after work in
public about God's word, sing and pray, those people who know
German join us in our assemblies; and then it happens that His
word moves their hearts and helps them reflect on it and take
care of their immortal souls. This time I heard it from a woman

stranger, whose heart was so greatly moved by what we discussed about the non-salvation of false Christians, and the salvation of true ones, that she praised God for His gracious guidance. I also lent her, to take home, our dear Count Henkel's *Last Hours*,[2] since we enjoy not only giving, but also lending, good books to other communities, in hopes that this will establish the Kingdom of God in our region.

Monday, the 5th of September. We have had much rain for two weeks, every day and sometimes at night; and at the moment our weather is quite like so-called April weather. However, we did not get too much rain in our community, although rain did keep some people from haymaking. We now have several sick people in our community, and this may be due to the changing weather: still, there is a high and hidden hand which directs everything; oh, may we center our hearts and eyes on this in all things, even the most insignificant ones, and recognize that nothing happens by chance or stems from natural causes! With this in mind, the fourth chapter of the Prophet Amos proved very beneficial to me in today's prayer hour and evoked in me very necessary and comforting memories, also with respect to natural occurrences and incidents.

Last week, I met at our mill three Jews from Savannah, who brought wheat and Indian corn for grinding. One of them tends to ridicule things, and last summer he bad-mouthed the Indian corn meal we had brought to Savannah for sale, by scoffing at it and putting it down (claiming that, after two weeks, it would not be worth a pipe of tobacco); and he probably made other similar remarks (because he was envious and resentful of us); now they would be happy if they could get our flour for their basic needs, and they traveled far in order to buy a few bushels. They told us that they had never before been so badly off in Savannah, and our people would easily find buyers if they could bring corn and flour down to them. But now they do not have the time to do so.

Thursday, the 8th of September. Carpenter Balthasar Bacher was quite close to death about two weeks ago. He was unconscious for several days and his screaming and violent behavior showed that he was suffering great pain. He finally regained conciousness and thanked God from the bottom of his heart for

granting him a reprieve. Although he is in control of all his physical capabilities, he continues to be weak and miserable; and it is
likely that he will have a sudden death. He is still a young man;
but it seems that, like other young people, he had neglected his
health in earlier years when he was a journeyman carpenter and
that, in time, his life became too hectic. He often complains
about his journeyman travels, and how evilly he lived then.

We have very few carpenters. The few we have are not very
good, except for Kogler and Rottenberger; they are very slow in
their work and are so busy with farming and their household
affairs that they have very little time to work as carpenters. Even
the two aforementioned well-trained men are spending too
much time on farming and raising cattle. Hence they are unable
to help our community as carpenters when we need them. I
would have liked to have the orphanage repaired and a room
equipped for teaching during the winter, yet I cannot get anybody to do it. If there are any people in Germany who would like
to come here in peacetime and increase our congregation, it
would be good to have among them some skilled and industrious carpenters and a good cabinet-maker and turner. They
would find enough work and income here, particularly if they
wanted to manufacture houses from the timber and boards near
the mill for the West Indies and do a variety of carpenter and
turner jobs for them.

We often think that we are in urgent need of loyal servants. No
doubt our Lord Trustees would show themselves as gracious and
benevolent toward those who decided to come here, as they did
vis-a-vis other servants from Germany, in that they would not
only give them 50 acres of land free, which they could pick out
for themselves, but also provide each family at the end of their
service time with a cow and a calf, a pig for breeding, and
various tools and farming implements, including cooking utensils. Perhaps they would also supply them with some food during the first year after completion of their service time. At the
very least, every master among us would give his loyal and satisfactory servant enough food, of what God gives him, so that he
could make a new start on his own land.

If only the servants were loyal, industrious, and honest and if only they really helped and eased the work of our worn-out people, we would gladly try to assist them with setting up their first household. Not only would I help them get a good 50-acre plantation for farming, in addition to the communal, very desirable cattle pasture, on the recently mentioned, very fertile land in our neighborhood (that land is to be set aside for the exclusive use of our hopefully loyal servants),[3] but I also hope to persuade our Lord Trustees to build a grist mill on that land before they have completed their service years; in view of the excellent water conditions, that would not cost much. Over time, a sawmill could be added here; and the earnings could be used to benefit Ebenezer and its new inhabitants because we would always consider ourselves a community and prepare ourselves for blessed eternity by the same means of salvation and seek to enhance our common spiritual and physical best. People who are dissatisfied for no reason, useless opinionated people, and religious troublemakers do not fit in here since we live here as in 1 Corinthians 11:16 and Romans 14:13.

I would also like loyal servants to enjoy, on both their healthy and sick days, all possible spiritual and physical assistance from us ministers, our doctor and surgeon, and the upright members of our congregation. And, in addition, at the completion of their service, I would like to give each servant who wants to start his own household on the new land or at Ebenezer and its district, from our mill, 500 feet of the best boards and 20 bad, but still usable, boards (that may add up to about 300 feet), and they could only be picked up by such a man by water or by land. Also, for one year they should be free to use the mill or would not have to pay any mill money. This is a benefit which only our widows and orphans enjoy.

I cannot say much about other kinds of freedom: we already have more freedom than is good for some people. We have no communal work or forced labor here; neither do we have assessments, excise duties, tariffs, billeting, or other hardships: everybody enjoys freedom of conscience and other freedoms, for which we must be grateful to God. In a sense, our dear inhabitants have broken the ice; and, as the first to come, they endured very great hardships so that those after them would not suffer and bear one-tenth of them, and the willing and intelligent ones would do nothing in vain. They would learn from the mistakes of our people and receive from them good advice on how to make good use of this good, though strange, country and stay healthy, start their farming and cattle-raising, etc. Either we did not get such advice from anybody or we ourselves did not want to be, or could not be, convinced by it, since in the early days we had here many envious people, who did not like us us and were obvious enemies of the Lord Trustees, our benevolent authority.

Since our present inhabitants endured so much and want to be the tools of God's gracious providence by giving other German fellow-countrymen every possible assistance in getting started on land that is more fertile and better situated than ours, there is probably nobody who would consider it unreasonable for those people to serve our worn-out inhabitants for about four years, while getting used to the land, the environment, and our way of life, and learning how to plant and do other work. In return, they would receive a small wage to buy their clothes and pay for their ship passage. No German finds such a good thing and comfort in any other colony in America; that is why it is a shame that so many poor people are moving to Pennsylvania each year, letting mean-spirited people in Holland and England malign our fertile, healthy country, which offers so much to people willing to work. God willing, I do not want to live and die in any other country and want to share the good things our gracious God has given me and others in this quiet corner with other dear people, particularly those in Europe suffering from moral constraints because of their religion and unable to make a living.

Nobody should be talked into moving here, and everybody must think of God's will and his own strength, health, and age before undertaking such a long journey. It is easy for everybody to understand that this uncultivated land requires hard work. Because it is on the best land that the biggest oak trees, walnut trees, beech trees and other known and unknown deciduous trees grow; and, although free timber is available close-by, the building of houses, stables, and threshing floors requires much effort. Also, we have to fence in not only our yards, but also our fields as well, because otherwise our horses, cattle, and pigs, which are permitted to roam freely in the woods, would damage the crops.[4] Our main routes are the big Savannah River (on which Ebenezer is situated and where the above-mentioned fertile land for those who come after us is) and several other easy-to-navigate rivers, which permit us to transport bigger loads in a cypress-tree barge or boat (which almost everybody can construct himself and for which we have here an abundance of cypress-trees) than in a cart, as they must do in Pennsylvania.

But there is one more thing I have to report. I remember only too well the story of the stubborn old Israelites in the desert, for which I also know many examples of our time here in this country: I am therefore afraid of dealing in wordly matters with people who want to come here either as free men or as servants. There are many mean-spirited, ungrateful, and disobedient Germans in this country, who, although they have received so much good, are envious of us and hate and malign us. They try to turn the new colonists who were sent here against us ministers so that we would fail in our teachings or could accomplish little; and that means everything to us. For these and other reasons, which I cannot mention now, a Christian, wise, and modest police commissary should accompany them and have plenipotentiary power to advise these people in legal matters and to serve as justiciar and administrator.

Well-to-do people who want to come here, pay for their own passage across the ocean, and settle here, would be well advised to bring their own servants, just as the Salzburgers did in Prussia. However, their servants in England would commit themselves contractually to work a certain number of years at a specific wage and resist any attempts by evil-spirited fellow-countrymen to change their minds, because, here, people who used to be serfs and led miserable lives in Germany want to play the role of masters and gentlemen very quickly.[5] They are very disloyal in their work, annoy their masters and landlords, and incite others to do likewise. I believe many who were rebellious during their years of service have taken their weakness with them to their own land and household, and some have perished miserably or are not nearly as well off as during their service years with their Christian masters or the Lord Trustees and their authorized representatives in this country. Our loyal servants, on the other hand, tend to use the plow soon and, hence, do very useful work.

I am thinking of another plan that would very much help our inhabitants and their dedicated servants and could greatly enhance the utility of those among our well-situated areas that are a long distance from the Spaniards, French, Indians, and Negroes: but I am almost tired of making suggestions. This is because it is considered a great loss unless this colony is settled with Negroes instead of industrious German people of the Protestant faith. My idea now is this: experience has convinced not only the Lord Trustees, but all of us, that the production of silk is easy and very profitable work, which only takes six weeks of work and does not impinge on other major tasks. In good soil here white and Spanish mulberry trees grow well, fast, and very tall and broad.

Now, if, instead of paying for other useless expenses (because they do not know any better as a result of their absence), our Lord Trustees advanced a certain amount of money, e.g., in the beginning 12 or 14 pounds Sterling, for establishing a six-acre mulberry farm in a convenient and fertile area of our community, we could grow there at least 1,000 rather tall mulberry trees in three or four years. The costs of setting up such a garden would be largest during the first year because we would have to chop down the trees, destroy the underbrush, put up a high fence, and plant the trees. However, in our community, these expenses would not amount to much more than 12 pounds Sterling; in subsequent years we could plant corn and gourds among the young trees that would help them grow until, after four years, the trees themselves would be tall enough to produce silk. As long as the trees are small, much effort must be made, partly by plowing and partly by raking, to keep them free from fast-growing, very destructive (although as hay and fodder very useful) crabgrass; but this is no longer necessary once the tree roots and trunks have grown thick.

Also, at the proper time the Lord Trustees would have to contribute to the garden some heads of cattle for fertilizer at the proper time around the trees. For three years these mature mulberry trees could then be left, subject to some supervision, to the care of servants who completed their service, until such time as they themselves plant such trees on their new land. In this way making silk would provide them with some good help every year and it would be easier for them to set up a good household. It would also encourage the servants if they were told in advance that they may expect many kinds of help for getting started and honest payment for their loyalty.

These and similar incentives would be a more effective way of keeping people from leaving and moving to other colonies than giving them supplies, money, cattle, etc., which nearly exhausted the Lord Trustees' resources and accomplished very little. During the first year, the proposed six-acre, 1,000 mulberry-tree garden would cost the Lord Trustees about 12 or 14 pounds Sterling in wages; in the following three years about 4 pounds a year; and after four years very little because the servants, who would get the leaves for silkmaking, would also have to maintain the fence around the garden. That would not take much trouble, since a so-called English fence lasts 10 years and requires little repair.

If the 1,000 grown trees were distributed among 50 servants, each of them would get 20 trees, with which he could easily produce at least 40 pounds of silk and, at its current price, expect 4 pounds sterling in earnings. What a nice help that would be for starting a household, and this would continue for three to four years until the trees on their own land are fully grown! After completing their service years, other loyal servants would then enjoy these and other good deeds. Carrying out this simple-minded, but well-meant idea and achieving its goal would require the following measures.

1) Somebody who enjoys these things and who genuinely looks out for the welfare of these people, as the Lord Trustees so laudably intended it, and who therefore would spare no efforts, should become these people's legal counsel and superior. If they

pay such a man well, he would take care of designing, maintaining, and properly utilizing the tree garden, in addition to the other things that are part and parcel of management and good order. They would have to try to keep such a man who has these qualities and who has proven himself loyal in his office, since frequent changes of superiors in this country have caused very great damage. I will not get involved in such a complicated undertaking, neither will my colleague; and nobody can hold that against us. However, we would be willing to advise and assist such a man as much as possible because we would like nothing better for us all than to have good housing and better food.

2) The current price of silk would have to remain unchanged and must not decline as a result of increased production, as it very well may do if we produce several thousand pounds in one spring. Apparently, as a rule, the price of goods that are grown or produced in large quantities gradually falls. If the people realize that, before being fully established, they may soon be discouraged. They have already been repeatedly discouraged by people in this land who told them that the Lord Trustees will not govern for more than twenty-one years and that this period will soon come to an end, and that then the production of silk and everything else will come to an end. If the people had enough trees nearby, if they were fully established, and if they were very skilled in manufacturing silk, a slight drop in the price of silk would not be so bad.

3) The silk must be made in buildings that are not only clean, but, depending on the type of weather, will also provide air and warmth for the worms. Manufacturing 2,000 to 3,000 pounds of silk, which 1,000 mulberry trees could produce, will require several buildings or large sheds, which, however, poor servants cannot afford in the beginning. They also would not need them since they would move to their own land and use these trees and the silk-producing facility for only a few years, and others would take their place. For that reason, it might be desirable for the Lord Trustees to divert some money or some heads of cattle from their Old Ebenezer cowpen or cattle ranch (which costs them 200 pounds Sterling a year) to the construction, near the large mulberry-tree garden, of some houses that could be used

for many years. These houses could easily be equipped for silk spinning.

4) For such a large supply of silk, many silk-spinning women would be needed who could soon be found here, if they were rewarded for their efforts. A reliable man would have to be appointed unter the supervision of the legal advisor and superior to receive the silk from the people, to weigh it, and to take care of early payment. Since the people do not have to pay for the trees and leaves, we would insist that they sell only well-spun silk in hard balls and keep the bad silk for themselves.

5) Some money would also be needed during the first year to purchase young trees. We would plant only two-year-old trees, 6, 8 to 10 feet apart, and each would cost twopence; that would come to somewhat more than 8 pounds Sterling for 1,000 trees. Subsequently, enough young trees would be grown in the garden to be used by servants on their own land. They themselves could also easily do so on their master's plantation during their service years, and they would do so if they saw that this is profitable. Although, in the beginning, this silk-producing plant would cost the Lord Trustees considerable money, it would not be lost like many other expenditures because, in my humble view, they would achieve their objective of settling the land earlier than otherwise. The money would stay in the community and the worn-out masters would have the opportunity to earn some additional money with their servants. That money could then be used for farminmg, cattle raising, and silk production on their own plantations. Certainly, help must come in time by this or other ways. Lord, may Thou bless Zion and build the walls of Jerusalem!

Saturday, the 10th of September. Some years ago, a young man, the son of a Reformed knitter who died in Purysburg, lived in our community.[6] He could not be persuaded to lead an orderly life. While he had no serious vices and was not an idler, he was so thick-headed that he did many things in his work in his own way, in his trade, in moving about, etc., and he did not let anybody advise him. There was no way we could get him to study the catechism and Bible verses we emphasize on Sundays

and the holy days and to attend instructions for the Holy Sacrament, although he goes to our public sermons and outwardly
seems to be completely absorbed by them. He is the only one of
this loose type of people in our community; otherwise, the country is full of fellows like him, who do, or do not do, whatever
pleases them. No good can come of this. It is now my hope that
this man will acquire more orderly habits, since he has signed a
three-year contract with our blacksmith, according to English
law, to learn the trade and is strong enough for such work. Now
he will also be encouraged to attend our church services and
practice hours on a regular basis. If he obeys and displays more
discipline, I will give him a present.

Monday, the 12th of September. A pious widow was very glad
that during her recent illness our dear Savior gave her the good
sense to spend the rest of her short life quietly to His glory and
in the service of her neighbors; and she inquired whether I
would help her ask God to be steadfast in this and other good
deeds. May God give us precious and important material for a
blessed and enlightening conversation, which I hope He will also
bless in her daughter, who has been reminded in friendly words
not only of her earlier promise and vow, but also of her re-
belliousness.

I have urged our sick Balthasar Bacher in serious and friendly
words to spend his short period of grace with prayers and God's
word so that he may experience in his lifetime the benefits of
conversion, the forgiveness of sins, or the state of grace. Some
people are satisfied with acting seriously in accordance with the
means of salvation, hoping that this will take them to Heaven,
and they do not pray from the bottom of their hearts that God's
grace may be with them in their true conversion and renewal.
The former belong to the "Oh Lord, oh Lord" sayers, and the
latter are among those who do the will of our Heavenly Father
and go to Heaven.

Tuesday, the 13th of September. Now our carpenter Rottenberger has lost all his children. His youngest, four years old, was
buried today, and the two eldest children also died this year, one
after the other. All three died because they had eaten raw Indian
corn, beans, and other unnatural things, and they could not be

stopped from doing so.[7] He himself has also been sick for quite a while and does not take enough care of himself. I hope these tragedies will help him prepare for blessed eternity.

Monday, the 19th of September. A week ago God struck me with a painful illness, but in His mercy, which I do not deserve, he has already started to deliver me from it. I am humbly and deeply grateful for His eternal loyalty and goodness, and I have resolved to praise Him for the rest of my life for His grace. In this illness He has shown my soul once again His indescribable mercy through the Law and the Gospel and, with the assistance of the Holy Ghost, He has helped me resolve to make good and to do everything in my Christianity and office that I neglected in the past, often—unfortunately—under the pretext of well-sounding excuses. Oh, how our sins of omission can torment us on our sickbed! Praised be my Savior for not letting me violate the Law in my feelings of misery and with my troubled conscience, but always to permit me, unworthy one, to cling, with the help of the gospel to His forgiveness and grace like a tender child holding on to his mother's breast. That did my aching and frail poor body much good.

Yesterday was the 15th Sunday after Trinity, and the possibility was strong that our congregation might not hear a sermon about the instructive, comforting, and so greatly needed gospel according to Matthew 6. The reason was that my dear and very industrious colleague also fell sick on Friday evening and was weak from vomiting and fever attacks on Saturday. However, our gracious Father in Heaven who can, and does, do beyond all bounds whatever we ask Him for or understand, made him recover quickly and become strong enough to preach in the morning and to teach the cathechism in the afternoon. Oh, if we would only recognize how good our Lord was when he gave us two ministers so that we never had to be without a public church service and instruction on Sundays or holidays. Neither did we ever miss a weekly sermon and prayer hour, nor school or other necessary official business when one of us was taken ill.

Tuesday, the 20th of September. a Several sources brought us today the following sad news from Savannah:

1) that a yellow contagious fever is raging in Charleston, suddenly striking about 17 people a day. It makes them turn yellow, hemorrhage very violently, and die, and then they turn black like a moor. Mr. Harris and his wife had just arrived in Charleston from London, when she was stricken by the fever. However, she was quickly taken to a plantation between Charleston and Port Royal and treated. This is why he has not yet arrived in Savannah.

2) We were surprised that he did not have a letter for us from London. My consolation is that no evil can happen to our people, goods, and letters without our Heavenly Father's will and permission. By these and other trials, our will is subordinated to His, the only good will.

3) In Savannah, they desperately waited for wheat flour and salt; although Mr. Habersham brought both from Charleston, it was only in small quantities, and it is very expensive, namely, 100 lbs. of flour cost 20 silver shillings and one bushel of salt costs 8 silver shillings, and each inhabitant may only have a few pounds to cover his most urgent needs. Oh, may these sad things cause the inhabitants of this land to show true penitence; yet most of them do not have the slightest inclination to do so: instead Jeremiah 5:3 occurs. We, too, are short of salt but, thank God, not flour and other healthy food; hence we have every reason to praise God for His goodness.

4) Mr. Habersham has asked me to come down to Savannah because he has much to tell me. Colonel Heron, who moved from Frederica to Savannah, has sent me his regards. Thus I would have had to discuss business matters with both him and Mr. Habersham. However, I did not dare make a trip to Savannah because of my present weak physical condition. So I put the necessary information on paper and sent the letter to the two gentlemen on our large boat, which left this afternoon to pick up the salt and some of the cauldrons Mr. Harris brought over with him.

Thursday, the 22nd of September. Last evening, a trading boat stopped here on its way to Savannah Town and brought us the news that another ship from England recently arrived off the coast of Charleston and that its captain confirmed that the sovereign rulers, who were waging that costly and bloody war, had made peace. May God see to it that we soon get a confirmation of this! It was reported that there was widespread smallpox on the incoming ship, that this was the reason why it was prohibited from landing in Charleston, and that it probably would not have wanted to do so anyway because of the extremely contagious fever that had claimed the lives of so many people in Charleston. Oh, sin is such an evil, and yet it is heeded so little! In our readings from the Holy Scripture we should emphatically point out the evils of sin and punishment.

Friday, the 23rd of September. Last evening our boat, which carried a big barrel of salt and nine distillation kettles or brandy-stills for our community, brought me a very friendly letter from Col. Heron, which is new proof of his truly favorable attitude towards me and our inhabitants. He is paying me the money for housing his soldiers, to which the Council in Savannah is unwilling to contribute and which I would otherwise lose; and he is purchasing more than 300 pieces of low-grade boards from our mill, although he does not really need them. He is giving our people all the old iron they find in the magazine there.[8] He is concerned with getting new iron from Philadelphia so that our blacksmith and locksmith will not lack any, as they have done so far to the harm of their trade. He plans to visit us next winter and, in the meantime, offers all types of services. Since the soldiers who are here for our protection will be relieved shortly, the gentleman is taking care that they will be replaced by other good, quiet, and well-behaved soldiers.

Sunday, the 25th of September. On this 16th Sunday after Trinity, after recovering from my illness, I was able to resume my official duties by preaching and administering the Holy Sacrament (thank God for that!); our dear Savior has given me remarkable strength to accomplish this. A week ago, my dear colleague, who is not well either at the moment, was responsible for all official matters, and that continued throughout the week, because the doctor told me not to resume work prematurely until I had regained my strength.

Today we had much and very cold rain from the northeast; and, since the entire congregation had to assemble at Jerusalem

Church in town for the Holy Sacrament because the service could not be held outdoors at the Zion Church, it must have been very difficult for women, children, and other frail people to come to church. Surely our dear Savior has rewarded them for their efforts with a blessing from the beautiful gospel and Holy Sacrament as He tends to do with people who come here with an eager heart. We also had three Evangelical-Lutheran people from Carolina here, who joined the congregation at the Lord's table. This time we had altogether 62 communicants; some people were discouraged by the bad weather and some were sick. The sick will have the service at home, if they ask for it. I am glad that I can go back to the congregation and visit their sickly members.

Monday, the 26th of September. The lame orphan girl in my home[9] had the great desire to attend public communion with the congregation. However, since she is now lame in both her legs and therefore unable to walk, she was blessed with this great good deed this morning. I familiarized her in her physical condition, which God has imposed on her without anybody's fault, with the two verses in Luke 14:13,21. They made it clear to her that our gracious Savior also takes cripples and lame people like herself to His heart, that He takes care of them, and that He does not spurn them at His Sacrament; and that has awakened in her the feeling of trust, love, and obedience towards such a charitable Lord. She dearly loves Jesus Christ, His word, and Sacrament, and she is well satisfied with his guidance. She gets everything in our house she needs, and she has the time and opportunity to prepare herself for blessed eternity. Both inwardly and outwardly, Mr. Thilo and Mr. Mayer tried their best, but her condition became worse, rather than better.

Wednesday, the 25th[10] of September. Balthasar Bacher has been sick for a long time; although he has no pain, he is unable to leave his bed. The widow /Gertraut/ Reuter, who married him when he was already sick, has taken on a considerable burden.[11] May God graciously help her after this has served His purpose for her! As a widow, she did well with her household, better than before her marriage. However, since her remarriage she has

lived in poverty and debt. I did not find him today like somebody who is preparing himself for the important change of time
and eternity; hence I gave him serious encouragement from
God's word and showed him the way to save his soul.

After three consecutive days and nights of heavy rain, the Savannah River has risen very high and fast and is now expanding
onto the low banks. Our inhabitants have planted much rice on
the low-lying areas of the mill river, and they will have to cut and
bring it home fast before it is covered by water. Mature rice is
almost less sensitive to wetness than any other crop. The mills
are already flooded because the mill river underneath the mills
is full of water from the small tributaries flowing into it and because there is not enough time for the water to run off. Reportedly, in some places, the pine forests are reported to have more
water than our people have ever seen. Also, we do not know
whether the Savannah river has ever risen so high in such a short
time.

The unexpected and sudden flooding is likely to kill a large
number of cattle in the lowlands along the Savannah river in
Carolina and in our colony, where cattle tend to graze wild all
year round. The flood and flooding are the result of the rain in
our vicinity. The water that has accumulated from the rain north
of Savannah Town and in the mountains will not reach us down
here until seven or eight days. In view of this problem and new
danger for our mills, my heart says: In times of distress, think of
His mercy. It is due to the Lord's goodness that we are not lost;
His mercy is boundless, it is new every morning.

Friday, the 30th of September. Yesterday afternoon we had a
short visit from Dr. Graham and two officers from Frederica
who inspected our mills, our plantations, and our facilities. After a few hours they returned to Abercorn. I got from them two
letters—one from Monsieur Martyn, secretary to the Lord
Trustees, and one from Monsieur Verelst—, which provide ample evidence of the Lord Trustees' favorable disposition toward
me and our congregation.[12] They also indicate that our letters of
January of this year arrived properly, and we are very glad about
that. The Lord Trustees have now given Mr. Mayer the authority, written on parchment, to act as *Conservator Pacis*[13] at

Ebenezer, and the Salzburger Bichler has been appointed constable, for which he will be paid 5 pounds Sterling annually, compared to Mr. Mayer's 20 pounds. They liked the silk we sent through Monsieur Harris, and each of the two young spinner-women will be paid 5 pounds Sterling a year. I hope they will like even better the 24 pounds of silk we sent the Lord Trustees in two small boxes. We hope we will get restitution for the lost boxes, notably from Halle. We plan to start trading barrel staves, shingles, etc. The wild and very harmful cattle in the large swamp near our cowpen are to be destroyed, and the Lord Trustees will try to send over servants from Germany.

DECEMBER[1]

Thursday, the 1st of December. In Savannah, they are very happy because they received a letter from Capt. Thomson in London which raises hopes that the Lord Trustees, at the request of our Council and Maj. Horton, will, under certain conditions, permit Negroes or Negro slaves in this colony. Even the poorest and lowest people are happy about this prospect and want it to happen soon. Time will tell whether the poor in this country will benefit as much from the import of Negroes as they believe.[2]

Friday, the 2nd of December. Since the 29th of November we have had very violent weather. At that time we heard far-away thunder; and this morning we had a big thunderstorm with lightning and much rain, which prevented us from holding our weekly sermon at the Zion Church as we usually do on Tuesdays and Fridays. Thank God, I returned to Ebenezer before this very wet and miserable weather started. The pestilential yellow fever is said to continue raging in Charleston.

Saturday, the 3rd of December. Yesterday's thunderstorm and heavy rain were followed by rather cold weather. During the night we had strong gusty winds that moved in a westerly direction. Some time ago we had a lot of rain which prevented people from plowing and tilling the land. The soil here is very loose and light; it gets saturated easily, but dries up just as fast.

Balthasar Bacher continues to be so weak from his long illness that he cannot work. Hence I gave him some money from our dear God's blessing so that he can hire some workers, and I also promised him to pay for part of his medical expenses if he continues to take effectice medication. Although he needed medicines in the past, he discontinued taking them for fear that he might get into debt.

I bought for our young schoolboys some colorful cotton caps in Savannah which they enjoyed very much. Several girls, whose parents are poor, will get some linen for shirts and scarfs. Praised be our Lord for once again giving us funds from Augsburg and Halle to share with the poor in our community! In addition, the good Lord bestowed on me the great grace of enabling me to pay off all debts I incurred for our community and facilities. It is wonderful what our devoted God and Father has done for us through dear Mr. von N. with regard to a very large debt we had to assume three years ago while we were building the mills.[3] At the present time I do not dare put it down on paper until several people have given me permission to do so. Oh, how good our Lord is to us, now that we have lived through the war! I often think of our text for Thanksgiving on the 7th of November of this year, Jeremiah 32:38, etc. Everything is going to come true: no sigh of petition from our pious Fathers and friends can or will go unanswered.

Sunday, the 4th of December. We in our congregation have used the good news from the East Indies in dear Mr. Albinus's letter to inspire one another to praise God and humbly intercede in our prayers for the important and blessed work of the missionaries at Trankebar, Cudulur, and Madras and for their expensive tools, and to draw inspiration from the example of the new converts whose number has now risen to about 100 souls in six months.[4] Although the news we received about the Protestants in U.[5] is sad indeed, it helps us to sincerely feel with them and pray for them and to gratefully acknowledge the precious freedom of conscience and religion we enjoy here so amply.

Monday, the 5th of December. A Reformed young man has served an 18-month apprenticeship with our shoemaker; today he moved away before completing his two-year apprenticeship, taking with him his stubborn and obstinate mind.[6] He used to hear God's word frequently on Sundays and during prayer meetings, and now he will have no excuse on that day.[7] I have made a great effort to help both his spirit and body in all possible ways; still he continues to suspect that we do not like him as much as others because of his religion. To fill his stomach, he used to live in various places for a long time among ill-mannered people; and people like him almost never come to pursue an orderly life. In our place he had, to be sure, to stay within the bounds of respectability.

I very much enjoyed my visit today with the widow Granewetter. She had many examples to tell me of God's concern for herself and her minor children, and she and her family praise the Lord for the many good things He lets her enjoy in our community. And others do likewise: this is not only indicates their simple Christian needs, but also reinforces my belief that God will continue to be among us with His grace and give us His blessing for our spiritual and physical welfare.

Wednesday, the 7th of December. In one of our most recent letters, our dear Mr. Albinus provided us with a short and penetrating explanation of Jesus Christ's important words, John 12:20-33, including the main points of Court Chaplain Ziegenhagen's last Good Friday sermon. We are now using it in our evening prayer meetings; and, to God's glory, I can say that He has blessed it not only with my better understanding of this important discourse of Christ, but also with the edification of Christianity, as a pious woman in our congregation also told me yesterday.

Thursday, the 8th of December. Some time ago, Mr. Mayer took in a serving boy, who had been in the service of a Salzburger and, at that time, behaved so well at church, school, and work and who, before his confirmation, had given such good evidence of his Christian thinking that we hoped that, through the consistent use of the means of salvation, he would grow in his goodness and be able to help Mr. Mayer and his sickly wife. He is also sensible, skilful, and quite industrious. However, since then his spirit has deteriorated so much that he is now a big cross for these two dear people. We are urging him patiently to listen to

God's word, to pray, and to do all good exercises; he sees only good examples at home and outside, and I, too, am making every effort to encourage and chastize him; yet he is completely unresponsive and uses desperate language like somebody who faces the most difficult spiritual temptations. He does not accept any good advice that could help his soul; instead he is thoughtless and talks to his mistress in a rude and defiant manner. I believe the poor lad has been ruined by his bad mother and stepfather in Vernonburg, who let him come to their house some time ago and do not like him to live in our community.[8]

Friday, the 9th of December. All week, during our evening prayer hours, we have enjoyed dear Court Chaplain Ziegenhagen's excellent, sincere, and inspiring thoughts on Jesus's important talk, John 12:20-33, for which we must humbly worship and glorify the great name of our great, beloved Immanuel. I variously read in the East Indian reports[9] about the blessing the missionaries have derived from their relationship with, as well as sermons and instruction from this experienced and trustworthy servant of Christ, and I wish they had mentioned some details about it in their diary in order to inspire in particular all *Studiosi Theologiae,*[10] and preachers.

Pastor Muhlenberg, during his visit with us,[11] and my current dear colleague told me some things from these collected instructive and comforting morsels. Should the planned meditation and its actual execution in his Good Friday sermons be printed (I wholeheartedly wish they would), God's church would greatly benefit from it. Our dear God has aroused in my heart new admiration for His holy word, and particularly for the words of His son, our greatest prophet; and it has given me strength and pleasure to impress on my dear audience the Gospel's truth. May He bless and support this chosen servant of His, and may He keep him for many years for the benefit of His church, our small group, and the blessed work of the missionaries! We also pray for this in our public and private prayers!

Saturday, the 10th of December. Last evening I had the pleasure of receiving some very nice letters from Europe, such as from Monsieur Verelst, Mr. Albinus, Prof. Francke, Mr. von Münch, and Councillor Waldbaum, which are full of praise of

God and our dear friends. Glory to God and the Father of Jesus Christ, who again and again fills us unworthy people with joy; nearby through His holy word, sacrament, and concern for our welfare, and from afar through inspiring letters, news, and books! May He give us the wisdom and unchanging devotion to put everything to good use!

Sunday, the 11th of December. This evening, after our public Sunday prayer meeting, we had a violent thunderstorm and lightning, followed by very heavy rains that lasted way into the night. This winter, we have had more rain and warm weather than ever before; hence the soil, which by nature is loose and light, has become so soft and waterlogged that in some usually dry places, e.g., the soil in the pine forest, our horses sink deep into the ground, and frequently water collects two or three feet deep when we dig a hole. The consistency of our land, especially in the pine forest, is such that the soil is light or sometimes sandy on top, and that three or four feet down, there is nothing but clay so that it is difficult for the rain to penetrate. Digging wells is easy here, but it is impossible to keep our cellars dry, and those that were dug earlier must be filled again. Unless our dear God's grace prevents it, our European seeds, including wheat and rye, will be damaged by the heavy rain which, in some fields, keeps the seed under water for one or two days. It is a consolation to us today that God, our Lord, is called Israel's comfort and helper in case of need.

Monday, the 12th of December. Three days ago I got a letter from Savannah reporting the arrival from Frederica of a big boat that had come to get the Indian corn flour our people had been asked to bring down there as fast as possible. I am surprised they sent a boat to get flour since I reported earlier this month from Savannah that the water level of the river had risen fast and that I was afraid we would have to stop the mills, as we have had to do since. If we had the means, we could have arranged for one mill to keep operating in water as high as the current level. However, usually the high water does not last very long: either it rises so high that everything along the mill river in the lowlands is flooded, or it soon falls. Even if we were able to make changes in the mills, we would not have enough workers, since we hardly can get anybody for the most urgent work.

After the great concern Mr. Mayer's serving boy had caused us with his desperate talk and rowdy behavior, our merciful God is once again beginning to give us joy.[12] During our Friday evening prayer meeting He started to bless His holy word on him; and yesterday, Sunday, He started to convince him graciously that sinners must not despair, that everybody can be helped through Christ and His mercy, unless the person becomes wilfully stubborn and rejects the mercy offered to him. This morning Mrs. Mayer received private communion (because her illness and pain do not allow her to take communion with the congregation), when both she and he were informed of their boy's marked improvement.

Tuesday, the 13th of December. The warm rainy weather continues; hence we have much water everywhere. May our merciful God let this rain be not a punishment, but a good deed or a Fatherly chastisement! The roads are so washed out that the English preacher in Savannah, who some time ago went to Augusta on business, was unable to return by land, but passed by our community by boat yesterday just as I was giving my weekly sermon at Zion Church. As yet no ways or country roads have been made in this colony; and what the first Salzburgers built between Abercorn and Old Ebenezer has long since disappeared. The servants of our Trustees in Old Ebenezer have done nothing to maintain any construction.

Thursday, the 15th of December. Yesterday, in the late afternoon, we had strong gusty winds from the west; they chased away the rain clouds and now we have once again dry, although cold weather.

During yesterday's evening prayer hour we talked about two short letters from our dear benefactors, with which they sent some alms to dear Prof. Francke for our Salzburger congregation. We very much enjoyed reading and hearing them and they encouraged us to thank God to intercede for our benefactors who are suffering so many trials and to appreciate our still-bearable situation as well as to fear God. One letter said, "If they remain in fear of our Lord, the Salzburgers will not want for anything. I am sending them Psalm 67. May God bless us and may all the world fear Him. Oh, Jesus Christ, spread Thy Kingdom in ever greater splendor throughout the world, and let us hear much more of the welcome news that great harm has been inflicted on Satan and that Thy Kingdom is growing. Amen."

Friday, the 16th of December. We have made several attempts to send to one of our noble benefactors in Germany some seeds as well as other plants and things. However, we heard in the past, and are now hearing again, that this was very costly to our dear benefactor and that he derived no benefit from them since the things in the box had gone bad by the time they arrived; which we regret very much. Last summer and fall we collected a large variety of flowers, herbs, and insects; but because we live 150 miles from Charleston, where the ships land and from where they set sail, it is difficult to send such things. I am afraid of the high expenses for shipping and postage; and if the herbs get ruined on the way over and the jars with the insects break, we will cause our benefactors needless expenses. Usually the ship captains store boxes like these in the humid and inaccessible places of the ship, while they and the passengers keep their things and amenities in the cabin.

As for sending seeds, again there is not much we can do. In most instances they arrive here in a spoiled condition, and this is probably how they will arrive over there. I was told that, unless they are kept way up in the ship during the voyage in an airy but not humid spot and now and then exposed to fresh air, they will suffocate on their trip across the ocean. If we could only get to the point where we develop some trade in Savannah and ships leave from there for London, it would be easier for us to serve our friends and benefactors with some curios and products of nature. However, it would less difficult to send a *Herbarium vivum*.[13] It is easy to collect herbs and flowers.

Saturday, the 17th of December. Some days ago a young man asked me to visit him on the plantation he had just moved to, and I did so today. I found him and his wife working hard in the fields: they now want to have better housing than before and produce their own food. Some time ago I lent him some money to get started, which encouraged both him and his wife. I told her at our most recent prayer-hour that, if they continued to fear God, they would not want for anything good, and I referred her to the 67th, and him to the first, Psalm.

One of the German servants has asked my permission for himself and his wife to settle in our community. His reason is that, although he and some fellow-countrymen will get a plantation on the new land near our cowpen, that land has not yet been subdivided into plantations. The time for preparing the soil and for planting is almost over and he must not miss it because he is so poor. He has a countryman here who is willing to let him start on his plantation. I have referred him to the Savannah authorities because he would have to ask them for approval. For that purpose, I wrote a letter to the Council president informing him of the man's request and of his stated reasons. He is going to take the letter down there personally. I am sorry for people who are like sheep without shepherds, and it is held against us that we take care of them. Wherever the Negro mind prevails, the poor are held in low esteem; however, some people do not recognize it and consider the importation of Negroes a beneficial, or at least innocent and harmless matter. My comfort is with the poor people: Thou art the Lord of this earth, the hope of the poor; Thou wilt not abandon Thy people in their sorrow and distress.

This evening I read to my dear audience some important and precious words from Mr. N.'s recent letter in which he, first, informs us confidentially of some worrisome matters concerning this country and then closes for our information and comfort with the following words, "We are looking to our Lord, the true Father of our house, who will advise and help us in His time. We are quiet. We are praying: Oh Lord, help Thy people. We are filled with hope. He will make everything right. May they carry this with them and put it before God in their prayers and be comforted by hope. Nothing can happen to us unless God has planned it and it is to our benefit."

Monday, the 19th of December. Our soldiers keep asking me
to put in a good word for them with their officers so that they
may stay in our community. They love our place and its inhabitants and very much want to start planting so that they can have
a better life with their wives and children on their soldiers' pay.
Our people speak highly of them, and whenever we need them
as day workers, they do their work well. Their wives behave so
orderly that they are not a burden on anybody: they like to work
and attend our church sermons with their husbands although
they do not understand the language, which they are gradually
learning, however. I have lent them some inspiring English
books, including Arndt's *True Christianity* and the *Little Garden of
Paradise;*[14] and the corporal, who knows well how to read and
otherwise is a skilful and honest man, will read to them from the
books.

Some time ago we had an hour of edification twice a week on
the plantations at Ebenezer Creek. But after the people there
died, moved away, or took over other plantations in our district,
we discontinued these meetings, thinking that the remaining
three families would attend our regular prayer hours in town.
However, because of their many evening chores, the inclement
weather, and the long way, the men were rarely able to come, and
their wives and children not at all; and this, they admitted, is
causing them great spiritual harm. When I became aware of
their great longing for edification, offered to resume, in God's
name, early next year these twice-a-week hours of instruction
and inspiration, and to read to them from God's word the same
material I covered at the Jerusalem Church and, farther out, the
Zion Church. May God give us His blessing for this undertaking!

I wrote today to dear Pastor Brunnholz in Philadelphia and
gave him the good news that dear Mr. von N. from A.,[15] our
great benefactor, donated 5 pounds Sterling to the Evangelical
people there to build the Germantown church, and I will send
the money to him through a merchant in Savannah. May God
bless our generous patron a thousand times for this and the
many other good things he has contributed to the construction
of Zion!

Tuesday, the 20th of December. A young man committed some sin against our dear God. Therefore he will not be admitted to the Holy Sacrament until he shows that he is truly sorry. He visited me today and told me about his troubled soul and willingly let me instruct and guide him in God's ways and holy order, which is the only way to attain the forgiveness of sins and to achieve eternal salvation for Christ's sake. I keep warning against the big misunderstanding, since some people consider the diligent use of the means of salvation to be the order of salvation itself and probably get lost in the process. They tend to believe that the diligent use of the means of salvation is part of their justification, which hence makes it hard for them to be converted.[16]

Thursday, the 22nd of December. This morning at 4 o'clock, Anna Kurz, a truly pious widow, passed away in my home, blessed in the Lord.[17] Her death came earlier than expected. Four days ago she still felt well, but she was taken ill during our evening repetition hour. Once she lay down, she never got up again, and the medicines we gave her did her no good. She has left behind two pious step-daughters of minor age who are now in my house. Her own daughter died about two years ago in my house, content and blessed. The mother took the girl's strange talk and her edifying end so much to heart that she began to prepare in earnest for death and Heaven and became very upright. Also to remind herself even more of her mortality and to evoke in herself a joy of death, she frequently went out to the graveyard, and this strengthened significantly her love for her Savior and her longing to soon be with Him and her pious daughter.

While she was frail in body and soul, she did her work very loyally, honestly, and willingly, so that our life together was pleasant. She served as an irreproachable and inspiring example to all people who came and left our house and displayed great love and gentleness towards our and other children. She said that among the best things our merciful God had done for her was that He saved her from the papacy and that she was led to Ebenezer where God was very good to her, her late husband, and her three children in both spiritual and physical terms. For that reason she very much wanted the members of her family she left behind in the Netherlands to come here as well.[18] The word of God and praying meant everything to her, and she used them in her outside work and with God's creatures.

Friday, the 23rd of December. The men in our congregation met yesterday in my house, and today in the Church of Zion on the plantations. Mr. Mayer and I told them of dear Mr. von N.'s wise and quite practicable proposals,[19] and we explained and recommended them highly for implementation. As it is proper and customary among us, each meeting started out by asking God for His blessing, and closed with a prayer, intercession, and thanksgiving. I mentioned at the beginning what this generous benefactor (and others whose names are on God's list) had done for us in the past, what he was doing now, and what he was willing to do in the future. This greatly reinforced my faith, and I now have reason to believe that our gracious God wants to help our congregation in our physical needs as well. He does so through supplies and intermediaries. However, He also wants us to do our share while we trust Him, and to adapt ourselves to the given order; because otherwise we would tempt Him. We then read the points our highly esteemed benefactor made in the recent letter on how our condition could be improved; and in each case we reminded them of, and underlined, the necessary details. They deal with:

1) starting and continuing the small volume of trade between here and Savannah, possibly expanding it soon to Frederica and Charleston as well, which so far have been of considerable benefit.

2) setting up a community treasury, to which the congregation members contribute, each at his own discretion, to thank God after the harvest has been brought in, when a blessing from God is sold, contracts are signed, distributions made, or after other signs of God's blessing, etc.; we would also contribute to it from the benefactions we receive from Europe. Some of this money would be used for the poor to help them start or help them support their households, for paying some expenses for maintaining church and school buildings, and for starting a small trade

to benefit the entire community; and profits from it would always be paid into the treasury.

3) laying out meadows, notably on our large and very fertile island. Those who want to band together and prepare them for planting fruit and growing meadows were assured of all possible assistance, as much as God will give us.

4) managing the wood in the forest. Nobody is permitted to cut firewood or building timber on other people's plantations (although nobody may be living on them now). Rather, emphasis should be on planting young trees in cleared spaces.[20] The congregation has asked us to put in a word for them with the Lord Trustees to get them some free wood or larger plantations, and we find this request quite reasonable. The area near town, where free or communal wood is available, is so small that everything would have been used up years ago if we had not taken wood from adjacent gardens and plantations, although nobody ever gave us the necessary permission to do so. From the very beginning, people have not been very careful with wood. Because here wood rots so much faster than in Germany, more building must be done (we have no stones, and they would be too expensive for us beginners anyway), and that requires wood.

On both sides of the town, there is only a 60 foot-wide lane left; and then the gardens start, for which everybody has two acres of land. The plantations start behind the gardens. There is no communal wood at all on the plantations. And since the landholders at the mill river have most of their land on the large island, and least on the high-lying lands where they live, and since trees in the pine forest grow not nearly as dense as in Germany, they use up their timber fast. The wood on the island is not very well suited for building because it comes mostly from oak, sweet gum, cypress, and walnut trees, and there are no pine trees.

5) continuing and improving our community cowpen. Three knowledgeable and gentle overseers have now been elected by a majority of votes to take charge of it and work for the best of the cowpen and the entire community, and they will consult with us frequently. They will also take care of upcoming business matters both as agents and middlemen. I am glad that most votes went to Kalcher, Leimberger, and Mr. Flerl, three pious and very

intelligent men. They will hold that office for a period of six months.

6) making use of the opportunity we have close to town, to build, at little cost, a small mill which would profit our townspeople and out-of-towners greatly. It would also provide useful services whenever the other mills cannot operate because of either too much or too little water, except when we have a long-lasting drought. For a long time the people living in and around town have offered to help, without pay, with the milldam, provided I bear the other expenses for building the mill and for the carpenters, which I will gladly do in God's name if it is really helps to further the welfare of our town, as we hope it will. As far as I know, there was not a single man of our community who did not attend this and yesterday's meetings. It was held with much joy and I expect great benefit from it.

Saturday, the 25th of December. The locksmith Schrempff and Bischoff,[21] who moved to Carolina some time ago, came to see us today to attend our church services over the holidays and to take the Holy Sacrament. They are planning to take land here again and eventually move here. Since they left, they have suffered more harm than benefit with regard to their physical well-being: Schrempff had made room for our locksmith Brückner, who then took up his trade and, with God's blessing, prospered and did well in his household affairs. He is a decent man who is devoted to serving his God and neighbors well.

Sunday, the 25th of December. We heard God's word abundantly during these holidays and had good weather and very welcome peace outside. God graced our congregation with seriousness and loyal attendance of our sermons, catechization, repetition and prayer meetings. To us ministers he gave enough strength and pleasure to preach His word. On the second holiday we held the Holy Sacrament with 67 persons attending, among them four persons from Carolina and one from Abercorn. The young man used to live in our community some years ago, and later he was like a lost sheep; also, for no reason, he held a big grudge against me and our congregation. But for some time now he has permitted himself to be found again; and I have now heard that he is doing well. Our Lord will also grant new mercy to Mr. Mayer's boy.[22] On the first holiday, he asked me to examine him about God's word to see whether he deserved to participate in the Holy Sacrament. When he learned from our verse of preparation in the First Book of Moses 3:15 and from the sermon we held on the first holiday that he was one of the penitent and eager-for-mercy souls, he attended in Christ's name.

Our soldiers wished to celebrate their Christmas, or Bacchus feast, in their own wordly way, but they were easily kept from doing so when the innkeeper refused to serve them rum, brandy, or other strong brews. Before the festival, Kohleisen, who likes to drink too much, misbehaved and had to stay away from the Sacrament.

Tuesday, the 27th of December. I received from Savannah a small treatise in English, printed and published this year in Venice by David Aboab, a Venice-born Jewish convert to Christianity, under the title *Grace and Truth, or a Short Account of God's Guidance of David Aboab*[23] and it is very nice to read. In the first part of the treatise he talks, to God's praise, about God's wondrous guidance and his acceptance of the Protestant Christian religion. In the second part he seriously tries to convince the Jews, his blood brethren, that 1) the one Divine Being consists of three persons; 2) the Messiah has already come, as promised by God through the prophets, and that they are waiting in vain for another; 3) the Jewish Talmud is full of untruths and superstitions, and this is one of the main reasons why they are blind and superstitious. If God grants him a long enough life, he plans to show them clearly the wrong teachings, superstitions, slanders against God, and the Talmud's ridiculous fables. It seems to me that this treatise demonstrates very clearly that this man, who may have great natural gifts, has not accepted the Christian religion with false intentions, but through the effect of the Holy Ghost, and through His word, and that he is a true convert to his Savior, for whose glory he works hard and will continue doing so.

I also read in a recent letter from our dear friend and benefactor, Mr. L., to Mr. Mayer a very nice story and information about an educated Jewish convert to Christianity; we hope to get some additional edifying details about it. Perhaps our wondrous and Almighty God will choose some capable tools from among their own midst to enlighten and convert His blind people of Israel. The persons he selects will no doubt be more successful with them than ministers of Christian blood, against whom they hold so much prejudice. How easy it is for our Lord, for whom nothing is impossible, to call on another Paul of the Jewish people at a time when that is least expected, and to endow him with talents to do the very important work of converting the stubborn and—because of the many problems with Christians— hardened Jews!

Wednesday, the 28th of December. When Schrempff and Bischoff said good-bye to me before returning to their families in Carolina, I read to them an important passage from dear Senior Urlsperger's letter that applies to them because it deals with the harm people who move away from Ebenezer inflict on themselves. On the second holiday they also heard much about this in the introductory verse to the Acts of the Apostles 20:28 and in words about the great joy of being an Evangelical minister, which most people do not fully recognize and appreciate.

They say here that poor people in Carolina with perhaps one or two Negroes are anxiously awaiting permission to import Negroes; then they want to move in droves to this colony, so that this land will soon be full of people, mostly Negroes, like Virginia and Carolina.[24]

Yesterday an Englishman came to me saying that he had made the long way down from Savannah Town with his wife, children, and household belongings to move to new land on the Ogeechy River. He asked me to baptize his six-month-old child. But, since he is going to proceed to Ogeechy by water, I referred him with his child to the preacher in Savannah.

Thursday, the 29th of December. After the Christmas holidays we repeat in our prayer hours and weekly sermon the precious Evangelical truths that we publicly considered during the holidays. Repetition is very much needed by us and beneficial to us. Although it is primarily meant for the children to be catechized, the adults, as they themselves admit, also derive great benefit from these exercises. Since children are a very important part, even the core, of a Christian congregation, I like to gear my words not only to the adults, but also to the children. And, from the word of God, I frequently show the parents and masters their duty towards these lambs of Christ, whom He loves so dearly and whom He wants to see raised in the fear of the Lord, and there is plenty of opportunity for that. This church year my dear colleague will catechize from Luther's beautiful catechism on Sunday afternoons; and he then will have a very good opportunity to introduce the adults and children to God's way to eternity.

Friday, the 30th of December. Monsieur Habersham has given me 24 arias, or songs, in English, with extremely good and easy discants and general bass, which he got not too long ago from London, where they were printed in 1746 in large quarto, with the notes neatly engraved in copperplate. Maybe the famous Mr. Händel is the author of the composition. It is entitled *Songs for the Great Holidays, and Other Occasions.*[25] It would be very easy to parody these lovely and moving melodies which can be sung or played on an instrument.[26] My mentioning it here may help our friends. Also, I hope God will give me some pleasure in my fear of Him. With such beautiful, well-composed songs, our dear God has filled us and our children with inspiration and pleasure, as He did during the recent holy days. Glory to Him alone and at all times!

Appendix

HYMNS SUNG BY
THE SALZBURGERS
IN 1748

Hymns followed by F-T and volume and song (not page!) number are reproduced in Albert Friedrich Fischer—W. Tumpel, *Das deutsche evangelische Kirchenlied des 17. Jahrhunderts* (Gutersloh, 1916, reprinted Hildesheim 1964). Authors of all identified hymns are listed in (AF) Albert Friedrich Fischer, *Kirchenlieder-Lexikon* (Gotha, 1878, reprint Hildesheim 1967).

Alle Menschen müssen sterben . . . (All men must die), by Johann Georg Albinus. p. 54

Der lieben Sonnen Licht und Pracht . . . (The dear Sun's Light and Splendor), by Christian Scriver. p. 60.

Hallelujah, immer weiter . . . (Halleluiah, ever onward), unidentified. p. 83.

Hoffnung macht doch nicht zu Schanden . . . (Hope does not bring disgrace), by Heinrich Ernst, Graf zu Stolberg-Wernigerode. pp. 16, 17.

Immanuel, des Güte nicht zu zählen . . . (Immanuel, whose kindnesses can not be counted), by Henriette Catharine von Gersdorf. p. 25.

Meinen Jesum lass ich nicht . . . (I shall not desert my Jesus), by Christan Keymann. p. 54.

Sey Lob und Ehr dem höchsten Gut . . . (Praise and glory be to the highest Good), by Johann Jacob Schutz. p. 59.

So bin ich nun nicht mehr ein fremder Gast . . . (So I am no longer a stranger), by Johann Eusebius Schmidt. p. 59.

Wenn ich in Nöthen beth und sing . . . (When I pray and sing in my need), unidentified. April, note 5.

Wunderbar ist Gottes Schicken . . . (Marvelous is God's Providence), unidentified.

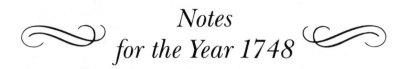

Notes
for the Year 1748

JANUARY

1. This appears to have been Johann Adam Treutlen, the later governor of Georgia. See entries for 8 & 12 Dec.

2. Pica, or clay-eating, is caused by a dietary deficiency, perhaps of iron. Eighteenth-century doctors mistook the symptoms for the cause and put the blame on the victims' gratifying his uncontrolable appetite for inedible substances. See entries for 7 & 11 Jan., 16 & 22 March, 10, 11, & 16 April and 16 July.

3. Matthias Zettler, of the 2nd Salzburger transport.

4. See note 2, above.

5. Johann Tobler of New Windsor in South Carolina, former governor of Appenzell.

6. Dr. Joachim Lange, *Evangelische Lehre der allgemeinen Gnade*.

7. Heinrich Schubart, *Predigten über die Evangelien und Episteln*.

8. See note 6, above. The reports from East India were published as *Der Königlichen Dänischen Missionarien aus Ost-Indien eingesandte Ausführliche Berichte*, Halle 1735.

9. Heinrich Melchior Muhlenberg, later the patriarch of the Pennsylvania Germans, had stopped off at Ebenezer in 1742 on his way from Halle to Philadelphia.

10. The evangelist George Whitefield had collected money for Ebenezer in Europe and the northern colonies.

11. The snow in the area drained by the Savannah River being negligible, the high water resulted from rainfall.

12. This was obviously Augsburg, see entry for 22 Jan.

13. These were for feeding silk worms. The Trustees wished to advance silk culture in Georgia to keep from sending good English money abroad.

14. From the Ogeechee to the Ebenezer mill would have been an arduous voyage of many days via the inland waterway.

15. The SPCK had given the Salzburgers a still for making peach brandy.

MARCH

1. It is to be noted that Urlsperger failed to publish the report for February, as he also did October and November.

2. Normally, the flood tide reached Purysburg just below Ebenezer; but unusually high river water would flow downstream despite the flood, thus making it difficult to row upstream. Some relief could be had by turning into Abercorn Creek, which was relatively sluggish even when the Savannah was high.

3. Zoar, one of the cities of refuge that were not destroyed.

4. The reader must remember that, although Luther led the Reformation, the word "Reformed" referred to the church of Calvin or to that of Zwingli.

5. The local magistracy in Georgia was the Council, consisting of a President and five Assistants.

6. In Pietistic parlance the word *Anfechtung*, usually meaning "temptation," connoted "temptation to doubt that Christ, through His merits, can save even the worst sinner if he is truly penitent." People who harbored such doubts were legalists, believing more in the law of the Old Testament than the grace of the New.

7. Senior Urlsperger. Samuel Urlsperger was the Senior of the Lutheran Ministry in Augsburg.

8. *Positiv*, a kind of an organ.

9. Allusion to a hymn. This is typical of Boltzius' frequently expressed theodicy.

10. See Jan., note 2.

11. "The incidence and nature."

12. Johann Junker, professor of medicine at Halle.

13. The word "Father," when capitalized, refers to the three "Reverend Fathers" of the Georgia Salzburgers: Samuel Urlsperger, the Senior of the Lutheran ministry at Augsburg; August Hermann Francke, the professor at Halle; and Friedrich Michael Ziegenhagen, the court chaplain in London.

14. See note 6, above.

15. "What is to be believed and that what is to be done."

16. See Jan. note 2.

17. It is surprising that there were so many Negroes in view of the fact that slavery was still illegal.

18. This was the Carolina parrakeet, then numerous but now extinct.

APRIL

1. The Leinebacher children had come in 1746 on the *Judith* with a large party of Germans who had sailed for Pennsylvania but had been captured by Spanish corsairs and detained at Bilbao before being ransomed by the British.

2. Karl Heinrich Bogatzky, *Güldenes Schatz-Kästlein der Kinder Gottes*. Halle, many printings.

3. By "ignorant" (*unwissend*), Boltzius meant uninformed about Pietist dogma.

4. Although Salzburg was in the Holy Roman Empire, anyone leaving there was said to be going "into the Empire." See entry for 7 April.

5. *Wenn ich in Nöthen beth und sing, so wird mein Herz recht guter Ding.*

6. See note 1, above.

7. Because the arable land around Ebenezer was limited, most of the Salzburgers removed to plantations along Abercorn Creek, where the soil was enriched every winter when flooded by the Savannah. Since the plantations were too far away for the children to walk to town, they needed their own school and church.

8. See Jan., note 6.

9. Although he was Reformed, Tobler could not accept the *decretum abso-*

lutum, or principle of predestination, preferring to think that any sinner can be saved by Christ's merits if he truly believes.

10. See Jan., note 7.

11. Unfortunately, the son soon followed his father.

12. Because most pregnant women in Colonial Georgia had malarial fever, many children were brain damaged.

13. See Jan., note 2.

14. Pastor Albinus, a chaplain at the English Chapel, was gradually taking over Court Chaplain Friedrich Michael Ziegenhagen's heavy load.

15. Archpriest Schumann maintained communications between the Georgia Salzburgers and their kinsmen and co-religionists in East Prussia.

16. Whereas this was a folk belief, it is true that electric storms do fixate nitrogen and thus improve the soil.

17. Joseph Ottolenghe, the manager of the filature in Savannah, wished the Salzburgers to send all their cocoons to Savannah to be spun off. This meant that the major profit would be made there, not in Ebenezer.

18. Grains like wheat, rye, barley, and oats.

19. In other words, Ebenezer had both Jerusalem Church and Zion Church, while the people in Savannah had no church at all.

20. Boltzius was right. Through his Indian wife, Bosomworth did try to incite the Indians against the Trustees. His correspondence with the Trustees runs into hundreds of bitter pages.

21. His daughters were Apollonia and Maria.

22. See March, note 7.

23. The War of the Austrian Succession.

24. The physician Christian Ernst Thilo, who had no salary, was then giving Greek and Latin lessons to Boltzius' two sons.

M A Y

1. *Tumblerinn.* A member of a religious sect.

2. In the War of the Spanish Succession, England was fighting against France and Spain.

3. Pieta Clara, the widow of Paul Häfner and the mother of his six children, had married Adam Straube.

4. Ruprecht Zittrauer, a Salzburger from Gross-Orel, married Anna Leihoffer in 1736. She was probably the widow in question. Zittrauer was one of the few true Salzburgers to leave Ebenezer.

5. Dürrenberg (Tirnberg) was a principality adjacent to Salzburg, from which all Protestants were also expelled. Most of them, including the recently mentioned Kurtz family, went to Cadzand in Holland.

6. Boltzius is contrasting the legalism of the Old Testament with the grace of the New Testament. See the following note.

7. Boltzius is still contrasting the grace of Christ with the law of Moses. See the preceding note and April, note 9.

8. Josef Schaitberger was a Protestant from Salzburg who had been expelled before the great expulsion of 1731. He settled in Nuernberg as a wood carver and wrote tractates, such as the *Sendschreiben*, back to his co-religionists at home. He was also the author of the "Exiles' Song" (*Exulantenlied*).

9. See April, note 18.

10. Boltzius called raccoons *Wildkatzen*.

11. A trading station in South Carolina not far from Augusta, not to be confused with the city of Savannah.

12. This was certainly true of William Norris and Thomas Bosomworth.

13. (Johann) Ulrich Driessler, a minister from Wurttemberg, was greatly esteemed during his short ministry at Frederica from 1743 to 1746.

JULY

1. The new woman in charge of the filature in Savannah followed the policy of her predecessor, Mary Camuse (Maria Camuso), in belittling the silk spun in Ebenezer so as to keep a monopoly of the more remunerative work of processing the cocoons.

2. While this diary has been lost, it probably included the same material as found in Boltzius' extensive correspondence with the Trustees, which is found in the Colonial Office Papers of the Public Record Office, mostly from CO 5 634 to CO 5 665.

3. See Jan., note 2.

4. The chapter number is illegible in my photographic copy.

5. Karl Heinrich Bogatzky, *Armenbüchlein*.

6. See March, note 6.

7. The Calvinistic dogma of predestination. See April, note 9.

8. Johann Arndt's *True Christianity (Vier Bücher vom wahrem Christenthum)* was the favorite reading of most German families in America, being reprinted in Philadelphia. The English translations were also popular. Arndt's *Paradies-Gärtlein* was also very popular.

9. Knowing nothing of germs and viruses, eighteenth-century people, including the best doctors, attributed most fevers to changes in the weather.

10. Lady W. in Stuttgart, who was the wife of an Imperial Knight (*Reichsritter*). See next note.

11. He was an Imperial Knight (*Reichsritter*) and therefore had no territorial lord between himself and the emperor.

12. He was from Purysburg. See entries for 23 June, 10 Sept., and 5 Dec.

13. Johann Anastasius Freylinghausen, *Geistreiches Gesang-Buch*. Halle 1704 ff.

14. "He who is absent may do without."

15. A town in eastern Germany where Boltzius and Gronau were ordained on their way from Halle to Georgia.

16. *Die Lehre von der Busse und Vergebung der Sünden, in kurze Sätze gefasst.*

17. Col. Heron's memory may go back to some fine linen sent, quite unsolicited, by a merchant of St. Gall named Schlatter. Since it was too fine for the Salzburgers, the storekeeper Causton sold it; but he failed to pay for it and Boltzius had to write numerous letters before the Trustees did so.

18. "with deliberation."

19. Locally, these gourds are called calabash.

20. For some reason this seems to be Boltzius' first mention of ducks and geese, birds dear to European peasants. Perhaps they were taken for granted in the word "poultry" (*Federvieh*). Although all hawks in Georgia are called

"chicken hawks," most of them, particularly soaring hawks like redtailed, red-shouldered, and marsh hawks, are beneficial to the farmers, since they eat far more rats and mice than they do chickens.

21. Boltzius may be distinguishing between the large fox squirrels of the pine groves and the small grey cat squirrels of the oak groves.

22. Although Boltzius seldom complained of the royal government, he was well aware how much Georgia's progress was harmed by Britain's mercantilistic policies.

23. Here Boltzius is expressing Oglethorpe's views more than his own.

AUGUST

1. *Jesum liebe, und allein, sonst kannst du nicht selig sein.* Apparently from a hymn.

2. Johann August Urlsperger.

3. For the Pietists, a good Christian should be simple (*einfältig*) and trusting.

4. Along the Savannah River the word "Frenchman" usually designated the French Swiss of Purysburg, language being more important than nationality. Neuchatel, from whence they had come, was the private property of the King of Prussia.

5. "To punishment by slow steps." The quotation from Jeremiah refers to God's warning, not to the slow steps.

6. "By word and deed."

7. Finding no living for a Reformed minister in Georgia or South Carolina, Zouberbuhler tried to get a military commission. Failing in that, he had himself ordained in London in the Anglican Church. When he returned to Georgia, the Reformed avoided him even though he spoke their language.

8. It is not clear why Boltzius calls Heron *Herr Oberste und Capitain.*

9. Boltzius means that, when the alliance between the Creeks and the Cherokees broke down and they fought each other, the English enjoyed peace.

10. Philip Gebhart and his family had come to Georgia with Capt. William Thomson in 1738. Boltzius arranged for the three girls, Elisabetha, Eva, and Magdalena, to come to Ebenezer, where they all married. Magdalena married Simon Reiter. There were two sons when the family arrived, Hans Georg and Philip. A third must have been born if the oldest died in Purysburg and the youngest died in Ebenezer, leaving Hans Georg to receive a grant in 1752.

11. See Jan., note 2.

12. See July, note 8.

13. See May, note 8.

14. The word *Potatoes* always designated sweet potatoes or yams. Irish potatoes, which were not grown at Ebenezer, would have been *Erd-Aepfel*, from French *pommes de terre.*

15. "A serpent lieth in the grass."

16. "A candidate for eternity."

17. Boltzius was right in thinking that malaria, although not a killer itself, weakened people for more fatal diseases.

18. *im dritten Theile seiner theologischen Bedenken.* Jacob Spener is often considered the father of German Pietism.

19. Treaty of Aix-la-Chapelle.

SEPTEMBER

1. Georg Kogler and Stephan Rottenberger. See entry for 8 September.
2. Graf Erdmann Heinrich Henckel von Donnersmart, *Die letzten Stunden einiger der evangelischen Lehre zugethanen, selig in dem Herrn entschlafenen Personen*, etc., etc. Halle 1720–1733.
3. The Salzburgers received servants just a year later, but not all were loyal.
4. Georgia had the open range, or fencing-out, policy common on our western frontier.
5. Boltzius is arguing that they should be indentured servants with a fixed contract, rather than redemptioners free to redeem themselves or seek out the most liberal bidder.
6. Jacob Mohr, the stranger from Purysburg. See entries for 2 Jan., 23 June, and 10 Dec.
7. See Jan., note 2.
8. Boltzius must mean the iron stored at Old Ebenezer, the scene of the destroyed sawmill.
9. This girl is never identified.
10. The wrong date was probably the error of the typesetters in Halle, mostly children from the Orphanage.
11. Gertraut Schoppacher married first Simon Steiner, then Peter Reiter, and then Balthasar Bacher.
12. There is no explanation of why Boltzius called these two Englishmen "Monsieur" instead of "Mr."
13. Justice of the peace.

DECEMBER

1. Note that Urlsperger has deleted both October and November.
2. Boltzius' skepticism was later justified by the plight of the "po' whites" in both the Antebellum and Postbellum South.
3. This was surely Chretien von Münch, a banker in Augsburg and a benefactor of the Georgia Salzburgers.
4. See Jan., note 8.
5. Surely Hungary (*Ungarn*).
6. Jacob Mohr again. See entries for 23 June and 10 Dec.
7. On the Day of Judgment.
8. Johann Adam Treutlen. See Jan., note 1. The records do not show whom his widowed mother, Maria Clara Treutlen, married; and therefore she disappears from view.
9. See Jan, note 8.
10. "Theology students."
11. Heinrich Melchior Muhlenberg had stopped at Ebenezer in 1742 on his way from Halle to Philadelphia. Boltzius' current colleague was Hermann Heinrich Lemke.
12. Johann Adam Treutlen again, see Jan., note 1.
13. An herb garden.
14. See July, note 8.

15. Again, Chretien von Münch. See note 3, above.

16. Boltzius reiterates that justification must come from faith alone, not from good works. See May, notes 6 & 7.

17. Anna and her husband Matthias were the last Salzburgers to arrive in Ebenezer, having come with Muhlenberg in 1742. Anna lost her husband in 1743 and a daughter in 1747 and left two daughters, Eleanora and Gertraut.

18. Like other Dürrenberger exiles, the Kurtz family had been at Cadzand in Holland before going to England.

19. See note 15, above.

20. This is an exceedingly early case of reforestation, since most Americans exploited the forest with no thought of its future. Credit for introducing reforestration in America is usually given to nineteenth-century Germans such as Carl Schurz and the Weyerhausers.

21. Henry Bishop, son of a green-grocer in London, was sent to Georgia to be Boltzius' servant and totally assimilated with the Salzburgers, learning German and marrying a German girl, Friedrica Unselt.

22. Treutlen. See Jan., note 1.

23. *Gnade und Wahrheit, oder eine kurze erzählung der Führungen Gottes mit David Aboab.*

24. Boltzius' prediction soon became reality in coastal Georgia.

25. *Lieder auf die grossen Feste, und andere Gelegenheiten.*

26. By *Parodien machen* Boltzius means to make contrafacts. He wished to discourage his parishioners from singing secular songs.

Index
for the Year 1748

Aug., note 14; watermelons 66; wheat, eaten by worms 17, damaged by mildew 44; Sicilian wheat 44, good crop 50

Cudulur, city in India, Lutheran missions at 102

Currency, see Coins.

Darien, Scots village, mentioned 72

Deaths: Mrs. Balthasar Bacher 9, Thomas Bacher 39, Schweiger's boy 2, Georg Adam Leinebacher 30, Mrs. Glaner 42, Bartholomäus Rieser 76, Rottenberger's child 95, Anna Kurtz 101

Deer. mentioned 3, 64, 77

Doctrine of Atonement, religious treatise, 62

Driesler (Driessler), Johann Ulrich, minister at Frederica, respected 51; May, note 13

Dürrenberg, province adjacent to Salzburg, mentioned 47; May, note 5

Dysentary, in Savannah, 53

East India, missionary reports from, 6, 102, 104: Jan., note 8

East Prussia, see Prussia.

Ebenezer, Salzburger settlement near Savannah *passim*

Ebenezer Creek, unnavigable waterway from Old to New Ebenezer 85, 109

Eischperger, Ruprecht, Salz, his son epileptic 27

Ernst, Heinrich, hymnist 117

European crops (wheat, rye, barley, oats), 36, 49, 50. See Crops.

Evangelische Lehre, by Joachim Lange 5.

"Fathers," Salzburger patrons, 34, 68. See G.A.Francke, Urlsperger, Ziegenhagen.

Fences 11

Fever (malaria), 78

Flax, for weaving 79

Flerl, Hans, Salz, elected overseer 112

Flerl, Anna Maria, née Höpflinger, w Hans, serious Christian 47

Francke, August Hermann, founder of Francke Foundation in Halle, author 6, 81

Francke, Gotthilf August, s A. G. Francke, letter from 104, collects money 106

Frederica, British outpost near Florida 8, 51, 72

Freylinghausen, Johann Anastasius, professor at Halle, author of *Geistreiches Gesangbuch* and *Compendium Theologicum* 117

Freylinghausen Hymnbook (*Geistreiches Gesangbuch*), favorite hymnal at Ebenezer, printed at Halle in many editions 60, 117; July, note 13

Fruit, grapes, wild 66; peaches 66, for brandy 15

Gebhart, Philip, Palatine: Aug., note 10

Gebhart boy, dies 74

Geistreiches Gesangbuch, see Freylinghausen.

Gerlach, shoemaker in Naumburg, mentioned 77

German crops, see wheat, rye, oats, barley.

Germans in Savannah, 15, 30, 37, 74, 79

Germantown, German settlement near Philadelphia, mentioned 45, 109

Gersdorf, Henriette Catharina, hymnist 117

Glaner, Gertraut, Salz, née Lemmenhoffer, w Georg, weak 3, 4, 19, 31, 36, dies 42

Goldeck, district in Salzburg 49

Graham, Dr., practices around Savannah, 54, 100

Graniwetter, Anna Catharina, nee Sturmer, Salz, wid Caspar, has paroxisms 23, recovers 28, 39, visited by Boltzius 103

Grapes, wild 66